THE SCARECROW AUTHOR BIBLIOGRAPHIES

1. John Steinbeck (Tetsumaro Hayashi). 1973.
   See also no. 64.
2. Joseph Conrad (Theodore G. Ehrsam). 1969.
3. Arthur Miller (Tetsumaro Hayashi). 2nd ed., 1976.
4. Katherine Anne Porter (Waldrip & Bauer). 1969.
5. Philip Freneau (Philip M. Marsh). 1970.
6. Robert Greene (Tetsumaro Hayashi). 1971.
7. Benjamin Disraeli (R.W. Stewart). 1972.
8. John Berryman (Richard W. Kelly). 1972.
9. William Dean Howells (Vito J. Brenni). 1973.
10. Jean Anouilh (Kathleen W. Kelly). 1973.
11. E.M. Forster (Alfred Borrello). 1973.
12. The Marquis de Sade (E. Pierre Chanover). 1973.
13. Alain Robbe-Grillet (Dale W. Frazier). 1973.
14. Northrop Frye (Robert D. Denham). 1974.
15. Federico Garcia Lorca (Laurenti & Siracusa). 1974.
16. Ben Jonson (Brock & Welsh). 1974.
17. Four French Dramatists: Eugène Brieux, François de Curel, Emile Fabre, Paul Hervieu (Edmund F. Santa Vicca). 1974.
18. Ralph Waldo Ellison (Jacqueline Covo). 1974.
19. Philip Roth (Bernard F. Rodgers, Jr.). 2nd ed., 1984.
20. Norman Mailer (Laura Adams). 1974.
21. Sir John Betjeman (Margaret Stapleton). 1974.
22. Elie Wiesel (Molly Abramowitz). 1974.
23. Paul Laurence Dunbar (Eugene W. Metcalf, Jr.). 1975.
24. Henry James (Beatrice Ricks). 1975.
25. Robert Frost (Lentricchia & Lentricchia). 1976.
26. Sherwood Anderson (Douglas G. Rogers). 1976.
27. Iris Murdoch and Muriel Spark (Tominaga & Schneidermeyer). 1976.
28. John Ruskin (Kirk H. Beetz). 1976.
29. Georges Simenon (Trudee Young). 1976.
30. George Gordon, Lord Byron (Oscar José Santucho). 1977.
31. John Barth (Richard Vine). 1977.
32. John Hawkes (Carol A. Hryciw). 1977.
33. William Everson (Bartlett & Campo). 1977.
34. May Sarton (Lenora Blouin). 1978.
35. Wilkie Collins (Kirk H. Beetz). 1978.
36. Sylvia Plath (Lane & Stevens). 1978.
37. E.B. White (A.J. Anderson). 1978.
38. Henry Miller (Lawrence J. Shifreen). 1979.

39. Ralph Waldo Emerson (Jeanetta Boswell). 1979.
40. James Dickey (Jim Elledge). 1979.
41. Henry Fielding (H. George Hahn). 1979.
42. Paul Goodman (Tom Nicely). 1979.
43. Christopher Marlowe (Kenneth Friedenreich). 1979.
44. Leo Tolstoy (Egan & Egan). 1979.
45. T.S. Eliot (Beatrice Ricks). 1980.
46. Allen Ginsberg (Michelle P. Kraus). 1980.
47. Anthony Burgess (Jeutonne P. Brewer). 1980.
48. Tennessee Williams (Drewey Wayne Gunn). 1980.
49. William Faulkner (Beatrice Ricks). 1981.
50. Lillian Hellman (Mary Marguerite Riordan). 1980.
51. Walt Whitman (Jeanetta Boswell). 1980.
52. Jack Kerouac (Robert J. Milewski). 1981.
53. Herman Melville (Jeanetta Boswell). 1981.
54. Horatio Alger, Jr. (Scharnhorst & Bales). 1981.
55. Graham Greene (A.F. Cassis). 1981.
56. Henry David Thoreau (Boswell & Crouch). 1981.
57. Nathaniel Hawthorne (Jeanetta Boswell). 1982.
58. Jean Genet (R.C. Webb). 1982.
59. August Derleth (Alison Morley Wilson). 1983.
60. John Milton (Michael A. Mikolajczak). 1983.
61. Algernon Charles Swinburne (Kirk H. Beetz). 1982.
62. George Washington Cable (William H. Roberson). 1982.
63. Christine de Pisan (Edith Yenal). 1982.
64. John Steinbeck (Tetsumaro Hayashi). 1983.
    See also no. 1.
65. John G. Neihardt (John Thomas Richards). 1983.
66. Yvor Winters (Grosvenor Powell). 1983.
67. Sean O'Casey (E.H. Mikhail). 1985.
68. Tennyson (Kirk H. Beetz). 1984.
69. Floyd Dell (Judith Nierman). 1984.
70. R.C. Hutchinson (Robert Green). 1985.
71. Charlotte Perkins Gilman (Gary Scharnhorst). 1985.
72. Maxwell Anderson (Alfred S. Shivers). 1985.
73. Theodore Dreiser (Jeanetta Boswell). 1986.
74. Ezra Pound (Beatrice Ricks). 1986.
75. Robert Bly (William H. Roberson). 1986.
76. Edward Albee (Richard Tyce). 1986.
77. Robinson Jeffers (Jeanetta Boswell). 1986.
78. Edward Bellamy (Nancy Snell Griffith). 1986.

EDWARD ALBEE:
a bibliography

by
Richard Tyce

Scarecrow Author Bibliographies, No. 76

The Scarecrow Press, Inc.
Metuchen, N.J., & London
1986

Library of Congress Cataloging-in-Publication Data

Tyce, Richard, 1947–
    Edward Albee, a bibliography.

    (Scarecrow author bibliographies ; no. 76)
    Includes index.
    1. Albee, Edward, 1928–   --Bibliography.
I. Title. II. Series.
Z8021.17.T93 1986 [PS3551.L25] 016.812'54 86-25969
ISBN 0-8108-1915-5

PS
3551
L25
Z894
1986

CONTENTS

Introduction   v

1. Chronology of Initial Productions of the Plays   1
2. Initial Publications of the Plays (excluding acting editions)   3
3. Early Writings by Albee   5
4. Other Writings by Albee   7
5. General Works About Albee   11
6. Theses and Dissertations on Albee   50
7. Criticism and Reviews of Individual Works   63

Index   195

INTRODUCTION

Edward Albee is best known by the public for the success of Who's Afraid of Virginia Woolf? Yet he is also known for his other plays and his outspoken views on the theater and criticism. Unsuccessful Broadway openings are highly publicized and his uncompromising posture continually attracts controversy.

Scholarly interest in Albee remains high; there are over 150 theses and dissertations on his works listed here. There have also been a number of earlier checklists and bibliographies covering specific time periods or restricted to specific types of materials. The latest separately published bibliography, a 1980 publication (item 286) of Charles Lee Green's 1978 master's thesis (item 652), covers the period from 1968 to 1977. Additional recent bibliographic contributions include those of Bigsby (item 138), King (item 342), Reed and Evans (item 460), and Wilson (item 572). This compiler has gone beyond these efforts to provide a bibliography as broad as possible dealing with Albee and his works that will be useful to scholars and researchers. This is the most detailed bibliography to date and much of this material has neither been listed nor cited anywhere before.

All of the listed items have been physically examined by the compiler either in the original or photocopy or microform, with a few exceptions to be noted. This has enabled proper classifying and indexing and has also ensured accuracy. A 1969 Albee checklist erroneously listed an article by Elemér Hankiss (item 2174) as being in the "New Hampshire Quarterly" instead of the New Hungarian Quarterly and this error has been repeated as recently as in a 1982 bibliography on American playwrights. One area in which the compiler did not always examine the material itself is dissertations and theses, in cases for which the bibliographical information could be

v

verified and the title or abstract were deemed sufficient to classify and index the item.

The compiler has gone beyond traditional indexes and reference sources to identify much of the Albee material listed here. The impressive scrapbook and clipping files at the Performing Arts Research Center of the New York Public Library were examined. This has enabled the inclusion of many New York reviews in sources previously elusive. A variety of British newspapers were checked for reviews of London openings to provide sources in addition to the oft-cited Times. Since a number of Albee plays have been first produced outside of New York, efforts were made to locate as many reviews of these and other regional productions as possible. Reviews in newspapers have sometimes posed difficulties in bibliographies; incomplete citations or erroneous information due to different editions have been frequent. To ensure accuracy, the compiler has verified the information for newspaper reviews and articles on the standard microfilm editions. Regardless of how the information was first obtained, it was not listed if it could not be verified either on microfilm or by direct communication with the newspaper itself. One exception is the references that will be found to reviews in the New York Morning Telegraph, for which neither microfilm nor complete files could be located; these references were located through the clipping files at the Performing Arts Research Center and the researcher is referred there for the originals.

Albee has spoken out frequently on the state of the theater today, theater criticism, and the tastes of the theater-going public. In references to items in which he is quoted extensively or significantly, the notation "INTERVIEW" has been made and also indexed. This has been done even when the item was not precisely an interview. The critical reception of his works is a major topic of scholarly interest. The compiler has attempted to identify as broad a range of reviews as possible, including a limited number from the college student press and small city newspapers.

The scope of the items listed is also intentionally broad so as to satisfy as wide a spectrum of research interests as possible. A poem (item 1803) dealing with Tiny Alice is included, as is a Mad magazine parody (item 2441) of the film version of Who's Afraid of Virginia Woolf? The film versions of both A Delicate Balance and Virginia Woolf have been of particular interest to some scholars; the compiler has indicated "FILM" after appropriate citations in the sections dealing with those two works and they are also separately indicated in the index. Efforts have also been made to include material from the trade press of the motion picture industry.

The censorship difficulties encountered by Who's Afraid of Virginia Woolf? have already been the subject of some study. The compiler has focused on a few specific cases and identified articles from the local press on the censorship battles over the play in Boston and South Africa and over the film version in Nashville, Tennessee, and Dubuque, Iowa. Censorship cases as well as reviews of Albee plays themselves frequently have elicited letters to the editor from the public; letters are designated as such in the appropriate citations. For those who believe the issue of public outrage has passed, the compiler has included a reference (item 2449) to a 1982 letter to the editor which proves that it most definitely is not over.

A chronology of initial productions of the plays is included as an aid to the researcher. The plays themselves have been widely translated and reprinted in anthologies and textbooks. They are widely available in various editions, especially with the collection issued as The Plays by Atheneum in 1981-82 (4 vols., vol. 1 published by Coward, McCann & Geoghegan). Only a list of initial publications of the plays, excluding acting editions, is included. The best effort to date toward a descriptive bibliography of Albee writings is that of Wilson (item 572). The compiler has included sections on the early writings as well as writings other than the plays. Unpublished works have not been included.

A number of efforts have been made to enhance the usefulness of this bibliography to researchers and scholars. The compiler has tried to indicate reprintings of any items in other works; if the reprinting was made with changes, this is noted. Attempts were made to identify full names of authors and reviewers if they appeared in abbreviated form or not at all; bracketed information concerning names was supplied only if conclusive verification could be obtained. Some abbreviated names remain, however, especially for reviews in Variety, whose editorial offices could not always supply complete names for former reviewers.

vii

The compiler has attempted to be as complete as possible for material published through 1984, given the self-
imposed restraint of requiring physical examination. Some
1985 material is included, in particular to include reviews of
Albee's play segment Envy in The Show of the Seven Deadly
Sins. References are made in the index under the title of a
specific play to material listed in other sections. However,
this has been done only for material discussing no more than
three individual works. Items discussing more than three
works or studies of Albee's entire output are listed in the
Part 5: General Works without cross-references. Descriptive
notes have been included only in cases where the title may be
misleading or uninformative and especially when the item deals
with aspects of Albee's career outside of the theater. Material in a number of foreign languages will be found. However,
non-English reviews of individual plays have been excluded;
many of these have been verified, but the compiler has elected
to exclude them since they would not be of primary interest
to most researchers and since this work had to be kept to a
manageable length.

The compiler hopes that this bibliography will be found
useful. Any errors or omissions are the compiler's own; he
would be grateful to have them brought to his attention.

1. CHRONOLOGY OF INITIAL PRODUCTIONS OF THE PLAYS

1959: The Zoo Story in German at the Schiller Theater Werkstatt, Berlin

1960: The Zoo Story at the Provincetown Playhouse, New York
The Sandbox at the Jazz Gallery, New York
The Death of Bessie Smith in German at the Schlosspark Theater, Berlin
Fam and Yam at the White Barn Theatre, Westport, Connecticut

1961: The American Dream and Bartleby at the York Playhouse, New York
The Death of Bessie Smith at the York Playhouse, New York (replaced Bartleby on the double bill)

1962: Who's Afraid of Virginia Woolf? at the Billy Rose Theatre, New York

1963: The Ballad of the Sad Café at the Martin Beck Theatre, New York

1964: Tiny Alice at the Martin Beck Theatre, New York

1966: Malcolm at the Shubert Theatre, New York
A Delicate Balance at the Martin Beck Theatre, New York

1967: Everything in the Garden at the Plymouth Theatre, New York

1968: Box and Quotations from Chairman Mao Tse-tung at the Studio Arena Theatre, Buffalo, N.Y., and subsequently at the Billy Rose Theatre, New York

1971: All Over at the Martin Beck Theatre, New York

1974: Seascape in German at the Akademietheater, Vienna

1975: Seascape at the Shubert Theatre, New York

1976: Listening broadcast by the BBC, London
Counting the Ways at the National Theatre of Great Britain, London

1977: Counting the Ways and Listening at the Hartford Stage Com-
       pany, Hartford, Connecticut

1980: The Lady from Dubuque at the Lyceum Theatre, New York

1981: Lolita at the Brooks Atkinson Theatre, New York

1982: The Man Who Had Three Arms at the Coconut Grove Playhouse,
       Miami

2. INITIAL PUBLICATIONS OF THE PLAYS
   (excluding acting editions)

1. All Over; a Play. New York: Atheneum, 1971.

2. The American Dream; a Play. New York: Coward-McCann, 1961.

3. Box and Quotations from Chairman Mao Tse-tung; Two Inter-Related Plays. New York: Atheneum, 1969.

4. Counting the Ways and Listening: Two Plays. New York: Atheneum, 1977.

5. A Delicate Balance; a Play. New York: Atheneum, 1966.

6. Everything in the Garden; a Play. From the play by Giles Cooper. New York: Atheneum, 1968.

7. The Lady from Dubuque; a Play. New York: Atheneum, 1980.

8. Lolita; a Play. Adapted from the novel by Vladimir Nabokov. New York: Dramatists Play Service, 1984. (acting edition; the only publication as of this writing)

9. Malcolm. From the novel by James Purdy. New York: Atheneum, 1966.

10. The Man Who Had Three Arms. New York: Atheneum, 1986. (not yet issued as of this writing)

11. The Play, The Ballad of the Sad Café. Carson McCullers' novella adapted to the stage. Boston/New York: Houghton Mifflin/Atheneum, 1963.

12. The Sandbox, The Death of Bessie Smith, (with Fam and Yam). New York: New American Library, 1963.

13. Seascape; a Play. New York: Atheneum, 1975.

14. Tiny Alice; a Play. New York: Atheneum, 1965.

15. Who's Afraid of Virginia Woolf? A Play. New York: Atheneum, 1962.

16. The Zoo Story; The Death of Bessie Smith; The Sandbox; Three Plays. New York: Coward-McCann, 1960.

3. EARLY WRITINGS BY ALBEE

17. "L'Après-midi d'un faun." [Short story] Choate Literary Magazine, v. 31 no. 1 (November 1944), 43-44.

18. "Associations." [Poem] Choate Literary Magazine, v. 31 no. 3 (May 1945), 15-16.

19. "Birthday Poem." [Poem] Trinity Review (Trinity College, Hartford, Conn.), v. 2 no. 2 (March 1948), 37.

20. "Caucer: The Legend of Phyllis." [Translation] Choate Literary Magazine, v. 32 no. 1 (November 1945), 59-63.

21. "Chopin." [Poem] Choate Literary Magazine, v. 32 no. 1 (November 1945), 11.
    Reprinted in Kaleidograph (Dallas), v. 18 no. 5 (September 1946), 12.
    Reprinted in item 353.

22. "Eighteen." [Poem] Kaleidograph (Dallas), v. 17 no. 5 (September 1945), 15.
    Reprinted in item 353.

23. "Empty Tea." [Short story] Choate Literary Magazine, v. 31 no. 3 (May 1945), 53-59.

24. "Frustration." [Poem] Choate Literary Magazine, v. 31 no. 3 May 1945), 60.

25. "Interlude." [Poem] Choate Literary Magazine, v. 32 no. 2 February 1946), 29.

26. "Lady with an Umbrella." [Short story] Choate Literary Magazine, v. 32 no. 3 (May 1946), 5-10.

27. "Monologue--The Atheist." [Poem] Choate Literary Magazine, v. 32 no. 1 (November 1945), 10.

28. "Nihilist." [Poem] Choate Literary Magazine, v. 32 no. 3 (May 1946), 22.

29. "Old Laughter." [Poem] Choate Literary Magazine, v. 31 no. 1 (November 1944), 37-38.

30. "A Place on the Water." [Short story] Choate Literary Maga-
     zine, v. 32 no. 2 (February 1946), 15-18.

31. "Question." [Poem] Choate Literary Magazine, v. 31 no. 3
     (May 1945), 81.

32. "Reunion." [Poem] Choate Literary Magazine, v. 32 no. 1 (No-
     vember 1945), 71-72.

33. "Richard Strauss." [Non-fiction] Choate Literary Magazine, v.
     31 no. 3 (May 1945), 87-93.

34. "Schism." [Play]. Choate Literary Magazine, v. 32 no. 3 (May
     1946), 87-110.

35. "Sonnet." [Poem] Choate Literary Magazine, v. 31 no. 3 (May
     1945), 60.

36. "Sonnet." [Poem] Choate Literary Magazine, v. 32 no. 1 (No-
     vember 1945), 10.

37. "Sort of a Test." [Short story] Choate Literary Magazine, v.
     32 no. 1 (November 1945), 45-47.

38. "To a Gold Chain Philosopher at Luncheon." [Poem] Choate Lit-
     erary Magazine, v. 31 no. 2 (February 1945), 34.

39. "To a Maniac." [Poem] Choate Literary Magazine, v. 32 no. 2
     (February 1946), 71.

40. "To Whom It May Concern." [Poem] Choate Literary Magazine,
     v. 31 no. 2 (February 1945), 61.

41. "Well, It's Like This." [Short story] Choate Literary Magazine,
     v. 32 no. 1 (November 1945), 31-34.

4. OTHER WRITINGS BY ALBEE

42. [Advertisement signed by Albee and placed upon the closing of Malcolm] New York Times, 13 January 1966, p. 48.

43. "Albee on Censorship." [Letter] Newsweek, 62 (30 September 1963), 4.

44. "Albee Says 'No Thanks'--To John Simon." [Letter] New York Times, 10 September 1967, Sec. 2, pp. 1, 8.

45. "Albeit!" In The Off-Broadway Experience, ed. by Howard Greenberger, pp. 52-62. Englewood Cliffs, N.J.: Prentice-Hall, 1971.

46. "The Author of Virginia Talks with the Author of Bessie." San Francisco Examiner & Chronicle, Date Book section, 27 December 1964, p. 7.

47. "Carson McCullers--The Case of the Curious Magician." Harper's Bazaar, 96 (January 1963), 98.

48. "Critics Are Downgrading Audience's Taste and Have Obfuscated Simple Tiny Alice." Dramatists Guild Quarterly, 2 (Spring 1965), 9-14.
    Reprinted partially in The Best Plays of 1964-1965, ed. by Otis L. Guernsey, p. 252. New York: Dodd, Mead, 1965.
    Reprinted partially in Playwrights, Lyricists, Composers on Theater, ed. by Otis L. Guernsey, pp. 357-362. New York: Dodd, Mead, 1974.

49. "A Czech Playwright Who Should Be Freed." [Letter signed by Albee and others urging the release of imprisoned Vaclav Havel] New York Times, 10 July 1981, p. A22.

50. "The Decade of Engagement." Saturday Review, 53 (24 January 1970), 19-20.

51. "Edward Albee, 1979." [Photograph of Albee and comments written to the photographer] In A Portrait of the Theatre, by Frederic Ohringer, pp. 106-107. New York: Crown, c1979.

52. "Foreword." In Dream Palaces; Three Novels, by James Purdy, pp. [vii]-ix. New York: Viking, c1980.

53. "The Freedom Fighter." [Letter signed by Albee and others protesting. Vladimir Bukovsky's continued imprisonment in the USSR] New York Times, 15 January 1975, p. 42.

54. "The Future Belongs to Youth." New York Times, 26 November 1967, Sec. 2, pp. 1, 7.

55. "Introduction." In Material Matters; Seven Young Contemporary Artists, pp. [3-5]. West Palm Beach, Fla.: Norton Gallery of Art, 1980.

56. "Introduction" to "Here Is a Resume of the Guild's Proposed Off-Broadway Contract." Dramatists Guild Quarterly, 8 (Winter 1972), 12-13.

57. "Judy Garland." In Double Exposure, ed. by Roddy McDowall, pp. 198-199. New York: Delacorte, 1966.

58. "The Lady of Tearful Regret." [Poem printed on the record sleeve of the phonograph recording "Blithe Lady of Tearful Regret"] New York: Composers Recording, Inc., [1963]. (CRI-163)

59. "Louise Nevelson: The Sum and the Parts." Introduction to Louise Nevelson: Atmospheres and Environments, pp. 12-30. New York: C. N. Potter; published in conjunction with the Whitney Museum of American Art, c1980.
    Reprinted as "Edward Albee on Louise Nevelson: 'The World Is Beginning to Resemble Her Art'" in Art News, 79 (May 1980), 99-101.

60. "The New Work of Mia Westerlund Roosen." Arts Magazine, 56 (March 1982), 120-121.

61. "New York! New York!" Introduction to New York in Photographs, photography by Reinhart Wolf, text by Sabina Lietzmann, pp. [1-3]. New York: Vendome, 1980.

62. "Notes for Noel About Coward." Introduction to Three Plays by Noel Coward: Blithe Spirit, Hay Fever, Private Lives, pp. 3-6. New York: Dell, 1965. (Reprinted 1979 by Grove Press, New York)

63. "Notes on an Anniversary." [Booklet accompanying the original cast recording of Who's Afraid of Virginia Woolf?] New York: Columbia Records, [1963]. (DOL 287 and DOS 687)

64. "A Novel Beginning." Esquire, 55 (July 1963), 59-60.

65. "On Making Authors Happy." Cinebill (American Film Theatre), 1 (October 1973), program accompanying the AFT production of A Delicate Balance.

66. "The Peaceable Kingdom, France (La Vieille Eglise--Gard)."
    [Poem] New Yorker, 51 (29 December 1975), 34.

67. "Program Notes on Box--Mao--Box." Studio Arena Theatre (Buf-
    falo, N.Y.) program, March 1968, pp. [6-7].
        Reprinted with minor changes as "Albee's Thoughts on His
    Box--Mao--Box" in Buffalo Evening News, 2 March 1968, Sec.
    B, p. 7.

68. [Review of Vertical and Horizontal, by Lillian Ross] Village
    Voice, 11 July 1963, pp. 7, 10.

69. [Self-portrait drawing and comments signed by Albee] In Self-
    Portrait: Book People Picture Themselves, by Burt Britton,
    p. 76. New York: Random House, c1976.

70. "Some First Plays Only Seem German." New York Herald Trib-
    une, 15 May 1960, Sec. 4, pp. 1, 3.

71. "Some Notes on Nonconformity." Harper's Bazaar, 95 (August
    1962), 104.

72. [Testimony concerning federal funding of the arts] In United
    States. Congress. House of Representatives. Committee on
    Education and Labor. National Foundation on the Arts and the
    Humanities Act Amendments: Hearings before the Select Sub-
    committee on Education on H.R. 3926 and H.R. 4288, Part 2,
    93d Congress, 1st session, March 1973, pp. 31-49. Washington,
    D.C.: U.S. G.P.O., 1973. (Supt. of Docs. classification num-
    ber: Y4.Ed8/11:N21f/2/973/pt.2)

73. "Theatre: Icarus's Mother." Village Voice, 25 November 1965,
    p. 19.
        Review of the play by Sam Shepard.

74. "Two Dramatists View ... Apartheid in the Theater." New York
    Times, 30 July 1967, Sec. 2, pp. 1, 6.

75. [Untitled essay on the work of artist Ellen Phelan] In MATRIX
    48 "artistsheet," pp. [2-3]. Hartford, Conn.: Wadsworth
    Atheneum, c1979.

76. [Untitled introduction] In Antoni Tàpies; Paintings, Collages,
    and Works on Paper, 1966-1968. New York: Martha Jackson
    Gallery, 1968.

77. [Untitled introduction to Box] In This Is My Best in the Third
    Quarter of the Century, ed. by Whit Burnett, p. 954. Garden
    City, N.Y.: Doubleday, 1970.

78. "Wants to Know Why: A Playwright Discusses the Excessive

Importance Attached to Broadway." New York Times, 7 October 1962, Sec. 2, pp. 1, 3.

79. "'What's It About?'--A Playwright Tries to Tell." New York Herald Tribune, 22 January 1961, Sec. 4, p. 5.

80. "Which Theatre Is the Absurd One?" New York Times Magazine, 25 February 1962, pp. 30-31, 64, 66.
Reprinted in American Playwrights on Drama, ed. by Horst Frenz, pp. 168-174. New York: Hill and Wang, 1965.
Reprinted in Directions in Modern Theatre and Drama, ed. by John Gassner, pp. 329-336. New York: Holt, Rinehart and Winston, 1965.
Reprinted in Discussions of Modern American Drama, ed. by Walter J. Meserve, pp. 145-150. Boston: Heath, 1966.
Reprinted in The Modern American Theater; a Collection of Critical Essays, ed. by Alvin B. Kernan, pp. 170-175. Englewood Cliffs, N.J.: Prentice-Hall, 1967.
Reprinted in Contexts of the Drama, ed. by Richard Goldstone, pp. 770-775. New York: McGraw-Hill, 1968.

81. "Who Is James Purdy? Edward Albee Tells." New York Times, 9 January 1966, Sec. 2, pp. 1, 3.

82. "Who's Afraid of the Truth?" New York Times, 18 August 1963, Sec. 2, p. 1.

83. "William Flanagan." American Composers Alliance Bulletin, 9 (1961), 12-13.

84. The Wounding: An Essay on Education. Charleston, W. Va.: Mountain State Press, c1981.
University of Charleston commencement address, May 10, 1981.

85. "The Writer as Independent Spirit: 6. Creativity and Commitment." Saturday Review, 49 (4 June 1966), 26.

5. GENERAL WORKS ABOUT ALBEE

86. Adams, Herbert R. "Albee, the Absurdists and High School English?" English Journal, 55 (November 1966), 1045-1048.

87. Adler, Thomas P. "Art or Craft: Language in the Plays of Albee's Second Decade." In Edward Albee: Planned Wilderness; Interview, Essays, and Bibliography, ed. by Patricia De La Fuente, pp. 45-57. Edinburg, Tex.: School of Humanities, Pan American University, 1980. (Living Author Series; no. 3)

88. "Admire Playwright Albee But Not His Scripts." Variety, 21 December 1960, p. 57.

89. "Albee and Barr Are Signed." New York Times, 10 March 1972, p. 47.

90. "Albee and Barr Dissect Plays, Playwrights, Critics." New York Herald Tribune, 3 October 1965, magazine, pp. 10-11.

91. "Albee at a Peak of Controversy." Washington Post, 25 April 1971, Sec. E, pp. 1, 9.

92. "Albee Directs Albee." Horizon, 22 (June 1979), 14.

93. "'Albee Directs Albee': A Powerful Personal Statement." A.C.T. Magazine (American Conservatory Theatre, San Francisco), 2 (November 1978), 12-13.

94. "'Albee Directs Albee' Coming to Columbia." New York Times, 10 January 1979, p. C21.

95. "Albee, Edward Franklin." In The Oxford Companion to the Theatre, 4th ed., ed. by Phyllis Hartnoll, pp. 15-16. Oxford: Oxford University Press, 1983.

96. "Albee, Film Studio Sign." Buffalo Courier-Express, 8 March 1968, p. 1.

97. "Albee: 'I Write to Unclutter My Mind.'" New York Times, 26 January 1975, Sec. 2, pp. 1, 7. (INTERVIEW)

98. "Albee Is Honored by Outer Circle." New York Times, 1 May 1963, p. 34.

99.   "Albee Method." Critical Digest, 18 (3 October 1966), p. [3].

100. "Albee Receives ANTA Award." Christian Science Monitor, 8 March 1963, p. 4.

101. "Albee to Continue Battle with Critics." New York Post, 8 August 1965, p. 47.

102. "Albee to Do Libretto for Flanagan." New York Times, 28 August 1963, p. 38.

103. "Albee to Teach." Variety, 30 January 1974, p. 57.

104. "Albee Wins a Pulitzer Prize." Times (London), 2 May 1967, p. 1.

105. "Albee Wins University Grant." New York Times, 3 May 1962, p. 19.

106. "Albee-Barr to Film for Universal but Not New Box-Mao-Box Property." Variety, 13 March 1968, p. 17.

107. Allen, Morse. "Plays of Worth." Hartford (Conn.) Courant, 20 August 1961, magazine, p. 15.

108. Amacher, Richard E. Edward Albee. New York: Twayne, 1969. (Twayne's United States Authors Series; TUSAS 141)
      Reviewed by Walter Meserve in American Literary Scholarship (1969), 302.
      Reviewed by James E. White in American Literature, 42 (November 1970), 419-420.
      Reviewed by Anthony Hilfer in Journal of Modern Literature, 1 (1971), 714-716.
      Reviewed by William Willeford in Modern Drama, 13 (February 1971), 450-452.
      Reviewed by Margaret W. Rule in Southern Humanities Review, 4 (Spring 1970), 191-193.
      Reviewed by Brian Lee in The Year's Work in English Studies, 50 (1969), 424.

109. _____. Edward Albee. Rev. ed. Boston: Twayne, 1982. (Twayne's United States Authors Series; TUSAS 141)
      Reviewed by John B. Vickery in The Year's Work in English Studies, 62 (1981), 446-447.

110. _____, and Margaret Rule. Edward Albee at Home and Abroad; a Bibliography. New York: AMS Press, 1973.

111. Amaya, Mario. "Edward Albee Interviewed." Plays and Players, 9 (December 1961), 5, 24. (INTERVIEW)

112. "American Actors Criticized." Times (London), 2 January 1965, p. 6.

113. Amory, Cleveland. "What's It All About, Albee?" Chicago Sun-Times, 26 March 1976, p. 84. (INTERVIEW)

114. Anastas'ev, N. "Profili amerikanskogo teatra" [Profile of American theater] Voprosy Literatury (Moscow), No. 6 (June 1969), 139-159.

115. "And Now, Heeere's Eddie...." New York, 8 (10 February 1975), 51.

116. Anderson, Mary Castiglie. Review of The Plays, v. 1-2. World Literature Today, 56 (Summer 1982), 516-517.

117. Andreucci, Costanza. "Chi ha paura di Edward Albee?" Il Dramma (Turin), 43 (June/July 1967), 83-92.

118. Armstrong, Madeleine. "Edward Albee and the American Dream." Quadrant, 9 (March/April 1965), 62-67.

119. Arnold, Christine. "Albee Plays Professor's Role." Miami Herald, 11 April 1980, p. 11D. (INTERVIEW)

120. Arnould, E. R. "Who's Afraid of Dietrich Bonhoffer? A Comparison of Bonhoffer and Albee." Journal of Religious Thought, 29 (Spring/Summer 1972), 57-75.

121. Arpe, Verner. "Edward Albee." In his Knaurs Schauspeil-führer: eine Geschichte des Dramas, rev. ed. pp. 384-386. Munich: Droemer-Knaur, 1977, c1976.

122. Ashley, Leonard R. N. "The Names of the Games and the Games of the Names: The Onomasticon of Edward Albee's Plays." Names, 30 (September 1982), 143-170.

123. Atkinson, Brooks. Broadway, pp. 441-443. New York: Macmillan, 1970. Rev. ed., pp. 452-455. New York: Macmillan, 1974.

124. "Aus New York." Theater heute, 9 (March 1968), 39.

125. Barr, Richard. "On Albee." [Letter] New York Times, 9 May 1971, Sec. 2, pp. 6, 30.

126. _____. "The Problem of the Producer." In The American Theater Today, ed. by Alan S. Downer, pp. 101-110. New York: Basic, 1967.

127. Bauzyte, Galina. "Iliuzijos ir tikroves konfliktas Edvardo

Olbio dramaturgijoje" [The conflict between illusion and reality in Edward Albee's plays] Literatura (Vilnius, USSR), 15 (1973), 79-94. (English summary, p. 94)

128. Baxandall, Lee. "The Theatre of Edward Albee." Tulane Drama Review, 9 (Summer 1965), 19-40.
       Reprinted in The Modern American Theater; a Collection of Critical Essays, ed. by Alvin B. Kernan, pp. 80-98. Englewood Cliffs, N.J.: Prentice-Hall, 1967.

129. Bennetts, Leslie. "Broadway Producers and Dramatists Lock Horns Over Antitrust Lawsuit." New York Times, 21 August 1982, p. 17.

130. Berger, Joseph. "Daily Closeup: Still an Angry Man." New York Post, 6 May 1975, p. 39. (INTERVIEW)

131. Berkvist, Robert. "Albee Returns to the Living Room Wars." New York Times, 27 January 1980, Sec. 2, pp. 1, 5. (INTERVIEW)

132. Bernard, Sidney. "Albee: Anger Between the Acts." Literary Times (Chicago), 3 (October 1964), 1, 11, 14. (INTERVIEW)

133. "Best Way to Boost American Theatre Is to Buy Off Critics: Edward Albee." Variety, 28 February 1968, pp. 1, 60.

134. Bigsby, C. W. E. Albee. Edinburgh: Oliver and Boyd, 1969. (Reprinted 1978 by Chip's Bookshop, New York)
       Reviewed in Times Literary Supplement, No. 3548 (26 February 1970), 221.

135. _____. "Edward Albee." In his Confrontation and Commitment: A Study of Contemporary American Drama 1959-66, pp. 71-92. Columbia: University of Missouri Press, 1968; London: MacGibbon & Kee, 1968.

136. _____. "Edward Albee." In his A Critical Introduction to Twentieth-Century American Drama, vol. 2, pp. 249-329. New York: Cambridge University Press, 1984.

137. _____, ed. Edward Albee: A Collection of Critical Essays. Englewood Cliffs, N.J.: Prentice-Hall, 1975.
       Reviewed by Jordan Y. Miller in American Literary Scholarship (1975), 405.
       Reviewed by Thomas P. Adler in Modern Drama, 19 (March 1976), 106-107.

138. _____. Edward Albee; Bibliography, Biography, Playography. London: TQ Publications, 1980. (Theatre Checklist; no. 22)

139. Bilbatua, Miguel. "Albee o la desnaturalización de la protesta."
     Informaciones (Madrid), 12 June 1969, "Informaciones de las
     artes y las letras" supplement, p. [8].

140. Billman, Carol. "Women and the Family in American Drama."
     Arizona Quarterly, 36 (Spring 1980), 35-48.

141. Binder, Wolfgang. Review of Stücke I [German translations by
     Pinkas Braun of The American Dream, The Ballad of the Sad
     Café, The Death of Bessie Smith, The Sandbox, Who's Afraid
     of Virginia Woolf?, and The Zoo Story]. Jahrbuch für
     Amerikastudien, 15 (1970), 315-317.

142. "Biographical Sketches of Those Selected by Jurors for Pulit-
     zer Prizes for 1975." New York Times, 6 May 1975, p. 34.

143. Björkstén, Ingmar. Dagar i New York; Anteckningar 1 maj--
     10 juli 1965, pp. 71-76. Stockholm: Gebers, 1966.

144. _____. "Den illusionsbekämpande Albee." In his Scenbild
     USA; en amerikansk teaterhistoria, pp. 112-119. Stockholm:
     Sveriges Radios, 1967.

145. Blake, Jeanie. "Tulane Speakers Write for Selves." Times-
     Picayune (New Orleans), 20 March 1977, Sec. 1, p. 25.
     (INTERVIEW)

146. Bo[ck], H[edwig]. "Albee." In Literaturlexicon 20.Jahr-
     hundert, ed. by Helmut Olles, pp. 19-21. Reinbek bei Ham-
     burg: Rowohlt, 1971.

147. Bogard, Travis; Richard Moody; and Walter J. Meserve.
     American Drama, pp. 290-292. London: Methuen; New York:
     Barnes & Noble, 1977. (The Revels History of Drama in
     English, v. 8)

148. Bolton, Whitney. "Theatre: Talented Albee Working on An-
     other; Wrote Zoo Story, American Dream." Morning Telegraph
     (New York), 13 February 1961, p. 2.

149. Booth, John E. "Albee and Schneider Observe: 'Something's
     Stirring.'" Theatre Arts, 45 (March 1961), 22-24, 78-79.
     (INTERVIEW)

150. Bosworth, Patricia. "Will They All Be Albees?" New York
     Times, 18 July 1971, Sec. 2, pp. 1, 3.

151. Bowers, Faubion. "Theatre of the Absurd: It Is Here to
     Stay." Theatre Arts, 46 (November 1962), 21, 23-24, 64-65.

152. Brackett, Samuel J. "Whose Fault?" [Letter] New York
     Times, 10 September 1967, Sec. 2, p. 13.

16   Edward Albee

153. Braem, Helmut M. Edward Albee. Velber: Friedrich, 1968.
     (Friedrichs Dramatiker des Welttheaters; Bd. 63)
     Reviewed by Kurt Tetzeli v[on] Rosador in Archiv für das
     Studien der neuren Sprachen und Literaturen, 208 (1971), 48-
     50.

154. Brede, Regine. "Forschungsbericht: Edward Albee."
     Literatur in Wissenschaft und Unterricht, 8 (1975), 30-46.

155. Brenner, Marie. "Tiny Montauk: On and Off the Beach."
     New York, 16 (22 August 1983), 13-15. (INTERVIEW)
     Albee as a resident of Montauk, Long Island.

156. "Bridgeport Students Seek to Aid Albee Productions." New
     York Times, 13 November 1964, p. 29.

157. "Broadway's Best." New York Times, 5 March 1985, p. C15.
     Albee is inducted into the Theater Hall of Fame.

158. Brockett, Oscar G., and Robert R. Findlay. Century of In-
     novation: A History of European and American Theatre and
     Drama since 1870, pp. 705-708. Englewood Cliffs, N.J.:
     Prentice-Hall, 1973.

159. Brown, Daniel R. "Albee's Targets." Satire Newsletter, 6
     (Spring 1969), 46-52.

160. Brown, Dennis. "Who's Afraid of the Albee Image? An
     Interview with Edward Albee." St. Louis Post-Dispatch, 7
     December 1976, pp. 2D, 6D. (INTERVIEW)

161. Brown, John Mason. "Epilogue: Albee, the Absurd and Af-
     firmation." In his Dramatis Personae; a Retrospective Show,
     pp. 535-542. New York: Viking, 1963.

162. Brüning, Eberhard. Amerikanische Literatur, pp. 36-37.
     Leipzig: VEB Bibliographisches Institut, 1967.

163. Brunkhorst, Martin. "Albees Frühwerk im Kontext des ab-
     surden Theaters: Etappen der Deutungsgeschichte."
     Literatur in Wissenschaft und Unterricht, 12 (December 1979),
     304-318.
     Reprinted in Maske und Kothurn, 27 (1981), 196-207.

164. Brustein, Robert. "The New American Playwrights." In
     Modern Occasions, ed. by Philip Rahv, pp. 123-138. New
     York: Farrar, Straus and Giroux, 1966.

165. Bucher, Bernadette. "Edward Albee ou la mort de Godot:
     vers une dramaturgie structuraliste." In La Mort de Godot;
     attente et évanescence au théâtre: Albee, Beckett, Betti,

Duras, Hazaz, Lorca, Tchékhov, ed. by Pierre Brunel, pp. 155-191. Paris: Minard, 1970.

166. Buck, Louise. "Hope for Albee." [Letter] New York Times, 11 December 1966, Sec. 2, p. 24.

167. Bunce, Alan. "Gloom and Hope in New York: Has Anyone Seen the Cultural Revolution?" Christian Science Monitor, 9 May 1969, pp. 1, 6.

168. Burns, Cherie. "Edward Albee Sets the Scene--and Lives in It." New York Times, 13 March 1980, pp. C1, C8. (INTERVIEW)
    Albee discusses his recently renovated Manhattan loft apartment.

169. C[ahill], K[athleen]. "Edward Albee's The Lady from Dubuque." On the Scene (Hartford Stage Co., Hartford, Conn.), v. 14, no. 6 (1980), 2-5. (INTERVIEW)

170. Calhoun, Charles. "Albee Returns in New Role: Curator of Art Exhibition." Palm Beach (Fla.) Post, 30 March 1980, Sec. C, pp. 1, 4. (INTERVIEW)

171. _____. "Albee's 'Material': Chilly, but not Impersonal." Palm Beach (Fla.) Post, 6 April 1980, Sec. G, pp. 1, 4.
    Review of "Material Matters" art exhibition curated by Albee.

172. Callow, James T., and Robert S. Reilly. "Edward Albee." In their Guide to American Literature from Emily Dickinson to the Present, pp. 159-160. New York: Barnes & Noble, 1977.

173. Calta, Louis. "Albee Leaving for Soviet to Join Steinbeck in Cultural Exchange." New York Times, 1 November 1963, p. 28.

174. _____. "Business Called Apathetic toward Arts." New York Times, 6 May 1969, p. 40.

175. _____. "Stage Prize Won by Edward Albee." New York Times, 6 June 1961, p. 41.

176. Capellán Gonzalo, Angel. "Albee: una década." Primer Acto, no. 116 (1970), 67-74.

177. Cappalletti, John. "Are You Afraid of Edward Albee?" Drama Critique, 6 (Spring 1963), 84-88.

178. Carey, Verna. "Edward Albee." USF (University of South Florida, Tampa), 22 (June 1980), 8. (INTERVIEW)

179. Carr, Jay. "Stage: Edward Albee Today: A Shrinking
      Violet in a One-Act Greenhouse." Detroit News, 2 April 1979,
      Sec. B, pp. 4, 6.

180. Carragher, Bernard. "An Interview with Edward Albee."
      Playbill (New York), (May 1976), 3-4, 6. (INTERVIEW)

181. Carver, Mabel MacDonald. "Another Award for Edward Albee."
      Villager (New York), 18 July 1963, p. 12.

182. Chabrowe, L. E. "The Pains of Being Demystified." Kenyon
      Review, 25 (Winter 1963), 142-149.

183. Chapin, Louis. "Albee, Copland, and Their Ideas--Playwright,
      Composer in Campus Talks." Christian Science Monitor, 17
      October 1962, p. 6.

184. Chapman, John. "How to Reject Critics Circle Prize: Albee
      Should Do It in Advance, If at All; He Bobbled the Pulitzer."
      Daily News (New York), 7 May 1967, Sec. 2, p. S3.

185. Cherrin, David. "Bright Future." [Letter] New York Times,
      10 September 1967, Sec. 2, pp. 9, 13.

186. Chodorov, Edward. "Not Literature?" [Letter] New York
      Times, 10 September 1967, Sec. 2, pp. 8-9.

187. Clarkson, Adrienne. "The Private World of Edward Albee."
      Montrealer, 41 (October 1967), 42-45, 47-49. (INTERVIEW)

188. Clay, Jack. "New Voice Speaks in Theater." Miami Daily
      News, 8 January 1961, Sec. 2, p. 6.

189. Cleaves, Henderson. "Plays and Players: 'A Healthy Ameri-
      can Boy'--Albee." New York World-Telegram and Sun, 2
      March 1961, p. 18.

190. Clurman, Harold. "Albee on Balance." New York Times, 13
      November 1966, Sec. 2, pp. 1, 3.

191. _____. "For the Young American Playwright." First Stage,
      1 (Winter 1961/62), 7-9.

192. Coe, Richard L. "Albee Directing Albee; In Steadfast Pursuit
      of the Abstract." Washington Post, 21 February 1979, Sec. B,
      pp. 1, 11.

193. Cohn, Ruby. "Albee." In Dramatists, ed. by James Vinson
      and D. L. Kirkpatrick, pp. 7-9. New York: St. Martin's,
      1979. (Great Writers of the English Language)

194. _____. "Camp, Cruelty, Colloquialism." In Comic Relief; Humor in Contemporary Literature, ed. by Sarah Blacher Cohen, pp. 281-303. Urbana: University of Illinois Press, 1978.

195. _____. Currents in Contemporary Drama. Bloomington: Indiana University Press, 1969.

196. _____. Edward Albee. Minneapolis: University of Minnesota Press, 1969. (University of Minnesota Pamphlets on American Writers, 77)
    Reprinted in American Writers; a Collection of Literary Biographies, ed. by Leonard Unger, vol. 1, pp. 71-96. New York: Scribner, 1974.
    Reviewed by Walter Meserve in American Literary Scholarship (1969), 302.
    Reviewed by A[rnold] P. Hinchliffe in Critical Quarterly, 12 (Spring 1970), 95.
    Reviewed by William Willeford in Modern Drama, 13 (February 1971), 450-452.
    Reviewed by Brian Lee in The Year's Work in English Studies, 50 (1969), 424.

197. _____. "The Verbal Murders of Edward Albee." In her Dialogue in American Drama, pp. 130-169. Bloomington: Indiana University Press, 1971.

198. "Columbia U. Does a 'Sarava' in No-Review Bid for 'Albee.'" Variety, 14 February 1979, p. 105.

199. Connolly, Patrick. "TV Isn't Spared Albee's Acidity." Chicago Sun-Times, 9 October 1978, p. 76. (INTERVIEW)

200. Contemporary Authors, ed. by Barbara Harte and Carolyn Riley, vol.s. 5-8 revised, pp. 18-21. Detroit: Gale Research, 1969.
    Reprinted in their 200 Contemporary Authors, pp. 17-20. Detroit: Gale Research, 1969.

201. Copeland, Roger. "Should Edward Albee Call It Quits?" Saturday Review, 8 (February 1981), 28-31.

202. Carona, Mario. "Edward Albee." Studi Americani, 10 (1964), 369-394.

203. Corrigan, Robert W. "The Soulscape of Contemporary American Drama." World Theatre, 11 (Winter 1962/63), 316-328.

204. Corry, John. "Broadway: Albee's New 'Perfectly Straightforward Play' to Open in January." New York Times, 19 October 1979, Sec. C, p. 2. (INTERVIEW)

205. Coy, Javier, and Juan José Coy. "Introducción a Edward
      Albee." In their Teatro norteamericano actual: Miller, Inge,
      Albee, pp. 243-278. Madrid: Editorial Prensa Española, 1967.

206. Coy, Juan José. "A la segunda fue la vencida; Edward Albee:
      el premio Pulitzer 1967." Sic (Caracas), 30 (September/Octo-
      ber 1967), 408-409.

207. _____. "Albee, el hombre que perdió un premio."
      Monteagudo (University of Murcia), No. 38 (1962), 4-27.

208. _____. "El teatro de Edward Albee." In La anarquía y el
      orden: una clave interpretativa de la literatura norteamerica-
      na, by Javier and Juan José Coy, pp. 91-187. Madrid: José
      Porrúa Turanzas, 1976.

209. Curley, Dorothy Nyren; Maurice Kramer; and Elaine Fialka
      Kramer, comps. Modern American Literature, Vol. 1, pp.
      22-26; Vol. 4 (Supplement), pp. 5-7. 4th ed. New York:
      Unger, 1969-76. (A Library of Literary Criticism)

210. Current Biography Yearbook, 1963, pp. 1-3. New York: H.
      W. Wilson, 1964, c1963.

211. Dalgard, Olav. "Amerikansk etterkrigsdrama: Tennessee
      Williams--Arthur Miller-Edward Albee." In his Teatret i det
      20. hundreåret, rev. ed., pp. 262-267. Oslo: Samlaget,
      1976. (Orion-bøkene; 192)

212. Dassylva, Martial. "Hargne et de vitriol Albee: un peu de."
      La Presse (Montreal), 16 October 1971, p. C11. (INTERVIEW)

213. De Jongh, Nicholas. "Edward Albee; a Casebook." Guardian
      (Manchester), 1 February 1972, p. 10.

214. Debusscher, Gilbert. Edward Albee: Tradition and Renewal.
      Translated by Anne D. Williams. Brussels: American Studies
      Center, 1967.
          Reviewed in Choice, 5 (March 1968), 74.
          Reviewed by Stephen Fender in Journal of American Studies,
      2 (1968), 145-147.
          Reviewed by Brian Lee in The Year's Work in English
      Studies, 50 (1969), 423-424.

215. Delatiner, Barbara. "The Lively Arts: Art Takes Shape at
      Albee 'Barn.'" New York Times, 30 May 1982, Sec. 21, p. 17.
      (INTERVIEW)
          Albee discussed the William Flanagan Memorial Creative Per-
      sons Center, Montauk, N.Y., funded by the Albee Foundation
      to provide living and working space for gifted young creative
      artists.

216. Dessau, Frederik. "Amerikansk dramatiker på vej; Edward Albee--hovedskikkelsen i det ny amerikanske drama." Berlingske Tidende (Copenhagen), 27 December 1961, pp. 12-13.

217. Dias, Earl J. "Full-Scale Albee." Drama Critique, 8 (Fall 1965), 107-112.

218. Diehl, Digby. "Edward Albee Interviewed." Transatlantic Review, No. 13 (Summer 1963), 57-72. (INTERVIEW)
    Reprinted in Behind the Scenes: Theater and Film Interviews from the Transatlantic Review, ed. by Joseph McCrindle, pp. 223-242. New York: Holt, Rinehart and Winston, 1971.

219. Dommergues, Pierre. "La conscience magique d'Edward Albee." Cahiers de la Compagnie Madeleine Renaud-Jean Barrault, No. 63 (October 1967), 18-22.
    Reprinted partially in Le Théâtre moderne, II: Depuis la deuxieme guerre mondiale, ed. by Jean Jacquot, pp. 187-189. Paris: Centre National de la Recherche Scientifique, 1967.

220. _____. "Entretien avec Edward Albee: La délicate balance entre le tolérable et l'intolérable." Le Monde (Paris), 22/23 October 1967, p. 23. (INTERVIEW)

221. _____. "Le nouveau théâtre américain entre deux aliéna-tions." Cahiers de la Compagnie Madeleine Renaud--Jean Louis Barrault, 63 (October 1967), 31-43.

222. _____. "Rencontre avec Edward Albee." In his Les U.S.A. à la recherche de leur identité; Rencontres avec 40 écrivains américains, pp. 362-376, Paris: Bernard Grasset, 1967. (INTERVIEW)

223. _____. "Le Théâtre américain de l'absurde." Les Lettres nouvelles, 13 (March/April 1965), 148-160.

224. Downer, Alan S. "An Interview with Edward Albee." In his The American Theater Today, pp. 111-123. New York: Basic, 1967. (INTERVIEW)

225. Drake, Sylvie. "Stage Review: 'Albee Directs Albee.'" Los Angeles Times, 18 October 1978, Sec. 4, p. 23.

226. Driver, Tom F. Romantic Quest and Modern Query; a History of the Modern Theatre, pp. 316-317. New York: Delacorte, 1970.

227. _____. "What's the Matter with Edward Albee?" Reporter, 30 (2 January 1964), 38-39.

Reprinted in American Drama and Its Critics; a Collection of Critical Essays, ed. by Alvin B. Kernan, pp. 240-244. Chicago: University of Chicago Press, 1965.
Reprinted in The Modern American Theater; a Collection of Critical Essays, ed. by Alvin B. Kernan, pp. 99-103. Englewood Cliffs, N.J.: Prentice-Hall, 1967.

228. Duplessis, Rachel Blau. "In the Bosom of the Family: Contradiction and Resolution in Edward Albee." Minnesota Review, N.S. no. 8 (Spring 1977), 133-145.

229. Duprey, Richard A. Just Off the Aisle; the Ramblings of a Catholic Critic, pp. 74-80. Westminster, Md.: Newman Press, 1962.

230. _____. "Today's Dramatists." In American Theatre, ed. by John R. Brown and Bernard Harris, pp. 209-224. New York: St. Martin's 1967. (Stratford-upon-Avon Studies; 10)

231. "Edward Albee: An Interview." In Edward Albee: Planned Wilderness; Interview, Essays, and Bibliography, ed. by Patricia De La Fuente, pp. 6-17. Edinburg, Tex.: School of Humanities, Pan American University, 1980. (Living Author Series; 3) (INTERVIEW)

232. "Edward Albee in Ithaca Sept.: Playwright to Direct Own Works." Post-Standard (Syracuse, N.Y.), 11 September 1978 (Cortland-Tompkins County edition), p. 6C. (INTERVIEW)

233. "Edward Albee Talks about the State of the American Theatre." New York Theatre Review, 2 (October 1978), 9. (INTERVIEW)

234. "Edward Albee Talks about: What Does a Playwright Do?; Playwrighting Is Not a Collaborative Process." New York Theatre Review, 2 (October 1978), 10, 13. (INTERVIEW)

235. "Edward Albee Turns to Films." Villager (New York), 15 August 1968, p. 2.

236. Edwards, Sydney. "Who's Afraid of the Talking Fish?" Evening Standard (London), 9 January 1970, p. 20. (INTERVIEW)

237. Eichelbaum, Stanley. "More Short Plays by Albee: They're Tantalizing Exercises." San Francisco Examiner, 30 October 1978, p. 28.

238. Elsom, John. Erotic Theatre, pp. 220-227. New York: Taplinger, 1974.

239. "Equity Assails Albee over Remark on Actors." New York Times, 1 January 1965, p. 10.

240. Esslin, Martin. The Theatre of the Absurd, pp. 225-227.
      Garden City, N.Y.: Doubleday, 1961. Rev. ed., pp. 266-
      270. Garden City, N.Y.: Doubleday, 1969. 3rd ed., pp.
      311-314. Harmondsworth, Eng.: Penguin, 1980.

241. _____. "The Theatre of the Absurd: Edward Albee."
      Excerpted from his The Theatre of the Absurd (see item 240)
      in Edward Albee: A Collection of Critical Essays, ed. by
      C. W. E. Bigsby, pp. 23-25. Englewood Cliffs, N.J.:
      Prentice-Hall, 1975.

242. Esterow, Milton. "2 Set to Produce Diamond Orchid; Theater
      Awards Scored." New York Times, 30 June 1961, p. 30.

243. _____. "Theater Figures Enliven Seminar; Albee and
      Whitehead Differ on What Ails Broadway." New York Times,
      21 April 1963, p. 86.

244. Falb, Lewis W. "New Playwrights of the Sixties: Edward
      Albee." In his American Drama in Paris, 1945-1970; a Study
      of Its Critical Reception, pp. 69-76. Chapel Hill: University
      of North Carolina Press, 1973.

245. Farrell, William E. "Yale Lauds Stage--With Restraint." New
      York Times, 7 November 1965, p. 76.
      Albee speaks at the Yale School of Drama.

246. Fields, Sidney. "A Long, Long Walk to the Typewriter."
      Daily Mirror (New York), 13 October 1960, p. 28.

247. Finkelstein, Sidney. "Cold War, Religious Revival and Family
      Alienation: William Styron, J. D. Salinger and Edward Albee."
      In his Existentialism and Alienation in American Literature,
      pp. 211-242. New York: International Publishers, 1965.

248. Fission, Pierre. "Edward Albee veut être le numéro un ... ou
      rien." Le Figaro littéraire, No. 1123 (23/29 October 1967),
      pp. 40-41. (INTERVIEW)

249. Flanagan, William. "Albee in the Village." New York Herald
      Tribune, 27 October 1963, magazine section, p. 27.

250. _____. "The Art of the Theater IV: Edward Albee, an
      Interview." Paris Review, 10 (Fall 1966), 92-121. (INTERVIEW)
      Reprinted in Writers at Work; the Paris Review Interviews,
      Third Series, pp. 321-346. New York: Viking, 1967.
      French translation by Claude Clergé: "William Flanagan
      interroge Edward Albee." Cahiers de la Compagnie Madeleine
      Renaud--Jean Louis Barrault, No. 63 (October 1967), 3-10.

251. _____. "Which Is the Victim?" [Letter] Village Voice, 20
      September 1962, p. 4.

252. Flatley, Guy. "Edward Albee Fights Back." New York Times, 18 April 1971, Sec. 2, pp. 1, 10.

253. Flynn, Betty. "Critic-Free Public Is All Albee Asks." Washington Post, 26 March 1967, pp. H1, H2.

254. Frankel, Haskel. "Interview: Albee Finds Hartford a Premiere Scene." New York Times, 6 February 1977, Sec. 23, p. 2. (INTERVIEW)

255. Frasconi, Antonio. "Agreement." [Letter] New York Times, 1 September 1963, Sec. 2, p. 3.

256. Freedman, Morris. The Moral Impulse: Modern Drama from Ibsen to the Present, pp. 122-124. Carbondale: Southern Illinois University Press, 1967.

257. _____. "Will Success Spoil the American Dramatist?" In his American Drama in Social Context, 73-93. Carbondale: Southern Illinois University Press, 1971.

258. Fruchter, Norm. "Albee's Broadway Break-Thru." Encore, 10 (January/February 1963), 44-48.

259. Funke, Lewis. "Off Broadway Uptown." New York Times, 1 October 1967, Sec. 2, p. 4.

260. Gabbard, Lucina P. "Unity in the Albee Vision." In Edward Albee: Planned Wilderness; Interview, Essays, and Bibliography, ed. by Patricia De La Fuente, pp. 18-32. Edinburg, Tex.: School of Humanities, Pan American University, 1980. (Living Author Series; 3)

261 Galey, Matthieu. "Albee sur le chemin de la gloire." Les Nouvelles littéraires, 11 February 1965, p. 13.

262. _____. "Un auteur modeste." L'Avant Scène, No. 334 (15 May 1965), 6.

263. Gardner, Paul. "News of the Rialto." New York Times, 2 September 1962, Sec. 2, p. 1.

264. _____. "TV: Albee Interviewed." New York Times, 16 October 1962, p. 79. (INTERVIEW)

265. Garfield, David. A Player's Place, the Story of the Actors Studio, pp. 141, 193-196, 212, 220-221. New York: Macmillan, 1980.
        Traces Albee's participation in the Actors Studio and its Playwrights Unit, the Studio's U.S. premieres of The Zoo Story

and The Death of Bessie Smith, and Albee's eventual resignation in 1964.

266. Garrity, Pat. "Playwright Albee Discusses Theatre." Springfield (Mass.) Daily News, 30 June 1980, p. 9. (INTERVIEW)

267. Gassner, John, and Bernard F. Dukore, eds. "Edward Albee." In their A Treasury of the Theatre, Vol. 2: From Henrik Ibsen to Robert Lowell, pp. 1196-1200. 4th ed. New York: Simon and Schuster, 1970.

268. Geisinger, Marion. "Edward Albee." In her Plays, Players, and Playwrights; an Illustrated History of the Theatre, pp. 601-603. New York: Hart, 1971. Rev. ed., pp. 601-603. New York: Hart, 1975.

269. Gelb, Arthur. "Dramatists Deny Nihilistic Trend." New York Times, 15 February 1960, p. 23.

270. Gelber, Benjamin. "Genius as Dramatist." [Letter] New York Times, 1 September 1963, Sec. 2, p. 3.

271. Gibson, Norman. "Theater: Albee's Plays Are a Lot of Fun." Ann Arbor (Mich.) News, 2 April 1979, p. B7.

272. Giger, Romeo. "'What a Sad and Shabby Time We Live in'; Notizen zur Werk des amerikanischen Dramatikers Edward Albee." Neue Zürcher Zeitung (Zurich), 4/5 February 1978, p. 69.

273. Gilroy, Harry. "Cast of The Front Page Covers First Assignment." New York Times, 9 April 1969, p. 54.

274. G[ingrich], A[rnold]. "Publisher's Page: A Lively Weekend at Princeton." Esquire, 60 (July 1963), 6, 112.
Albee participates in seminar on the arts.

275. Glover, William. "Albee: A Peep Within." Houston Post, 25 April 1971, Spotlight section, p. 21. (INTERVIEW)

276. _____. "Albee Not on a Soap Box, but...." Times-Picayune (New Orleans), 30 January 1977, Sect. 2, p. 11. (INTERVIEW)

277. Goetsch, Paul. "Edward Albees Zoogeschichten: Zur ein gelagerten Erzählung im moderne Drama." In Amerikanisches Drama und Theater im 20.Jahrhundert, ed. by Alfred Weber and Siegfried Neuweiler, pp. 289-318. Göttingen: Vandenhoeck & Ruprecht, 1975.

278. Goldstein, Richard. "Art Beat; the Politics of Culture: Kids

Do the Darndest Things." <u>Village Voice</u>, 24 September 1980, pp. 36-37. (INTERVIEW)

279. Golenpol'skii, T. G. "Edvard Olbi, ego geroi, ego p'esy." [Edward Albee, his heroes, his plays] <u>Voprosy yazyka i literatury</u> (Novosibirsk, USSR), 2 (1968), 63-74.

280. Goodman, Henry. "The New Dramatists: Edward Albee." <u>Drama Survey</u>, 2 (Spring 1962), 72-79.

281. Goodman, Randolph. "Playwatching with a Third Eye: Fun and Games with Albee, Ibsen, and Strindberg." <u>Columbia University Forum</u>, 10 (Spring 1967), 18-22.

282. Gottfried, Martin. [Letter] <u>New York Times</u>, 9 May 1971, p. 30.

283. _____ . <u>A Theater Divided; the Postwar American Stage</u>, pp. 264-274. Boston: Little, Brown, 1967.

284. Gough-Yates, Kevin. "Albee." In <u>Twentieth Century Writing; a Reader's Guide to Contemporary Literature</u>, ed. by Kenneth R. Richardson, p. 10. London: Newnes, 1969; Levittown, N.Y.: Transatlantic Arts, 1971.

285. Gould, Jean. <u>Modern American Playwrights</u>, pp. 273-286. New York: Dodd, Mead, 1966.
       Partially reprinted in French translation by Simone Benmussa as "Pauvre petit garçon riche" in <u>Cahiers de la Compagnie Madeleine Renaud--Jean Louis Barrault</u>, No. 63 (October 1967), 11-17.

286. Green, Charles Lee. <u>Edward Albee: An Annotated Bibliography, 1968-1977</u>. New York: AMS Press, c. 1980. (AMS Studies in Modern Literature; no. 6)

287. Greenfield, Thomas Allen. <u>Work and the Work Ethic in American Drama, 1920-1970</u>, pp. 154-160. Columbia: University of Missouri Press, 1982.

288. Guernsey, Otis L. "Edward Albee Confronts Broadway, 1966." <u>Diplomat Magazine</u>, 18 (October 1966), 60-63. (INTERVIEW)

289. Gussow, Mel. "Albee: Odd Man in on Broadway." <u>Newsweek</u>, 61 (4 February 1963), 49-52.

290. _____ . "Albee Stages Moss's Play on L.I." <u>New York Times</u>, 16 August 1972.
       Albee directs <u>The Palace at 4 A.M.</u> by Howard Moss.

291. Gysin, Fritz R. "Physician Needed." [Letter] <u>New York Times</u>, 1 September 1963, Sec. 2, p. 3.

292. Haas, Rudolf. "Wer hat Angst vor Edward Albee? Gedanken
      zum modernen amerikanischen Drama." Universitas, 25 (April
      1970), 347-362.
         Reprinted in Das amerikanische Drama von den Anfängen
      bis zur Gegenwart, ed. by Hans Itschert, pp. 420-435.
      Darmstadt: Wissenschaftliche Buchgesellschaft, 1972. (Ars
      Interpretandi, Bd. 5)

293. Haberman, Clyde. "Pulitzer Jr. Raps Salisbury Switch."
      New York Post, 2 May 1967, p. 5.

294. _____, and Krebs, Albin. "Notes on People: Albee on
      Choate at Choate." New York Times, 15 January 1979, p. C12.
      (INTERVIEW)

295. Hammel, Lisa. "Who's Afraid of Edward Albee's New House?"
      New York Times, 22 August 1966, p. 39.

296. Hardy, Hathaway. "Edward Albee." Architectural Digest,
      39 (March 1982), 150-155.
         Tour of Albee's Montauk, Long Island, home.

297. Harpprecht, Klaus. "US-Bühne im Rampenlicht: Organisierte
      Routine gegen freies Experiment." Die Weltwoche (Zurich),
      23 February 1977, pp. 53-55. (INTERVIEW)

298. Harris, Wendell V. "Morality, Absurdity, and Albee."
      Southwest Review, 49 (Summer 1964), 249-256.

299. Hassan, Ihab. "Edward Albee." In his Contemporary Ameri-
      can Literature 1945-1972, pp. 149-153. New York: Ungar,
      1973.

300. Hayes, Joseph. "Obtuse, Unjust?" [Letter] New York Times,
      8 September 1963, Sec. 2, p. 3.

301. Hayes, Richard. "At the Albee." Commonweal, 74 (25 August
      1961), 471-472.

302. Hayman, Ronald. "Albee and Shepard." In his Theatre and
      Anti-Theatre: New Movements Since Beckett, pp. 147-163.
      New York: Oxford University Press; London: Secker &
      Warburg, 1979.

303. _____. Edward Albee. London: Heinemann, 1971; New
      York: Ungar, 1973.

304. "He Can Try Anything." Newsweek, 69 (29 May 1967), 90,
      93.

305. Heilman, Robert B. "Edward Albee." In his The Iceman, the

Arsonist, and the Troubled Agent; Tragedy and Melodrama
on the Modern Stage, pp. 288-294. Seattle: University of
Washington Press, 1973.

306. Hensel, Georg. "Edward Albee: Gelächter in Hass und
Trauer." In his Theater der Zeitgenossen; Stücke und
Autoren, pp. 77-84. Frankfurt am Main: Propyläen, 1972.

307. Herridge, Frances. "Across the Footlights: Edward Albee
Turns to Producing." New York Post, 3 May 1963, p. 77.
(INTERVIEW)

308. _____. "Across the Footlights: Success Comes to Edward
Albee." New York Post, 5 February 1960, p. 56.

309. Hinchliffe, Arnold P. The Absurd, pp. 86-87. London:
Methuen; New York: Barnes & Noble, 1969; reprinted 1974.
(The Critical Idiom, 5)

310. Hirsch, Foster. Who's Afraid of Edward Albee? Berkeley,
Calif.: Creative Arts, 1978.
Reviewed in Choice, 16 (April 1979), 222.

311. Högel, Rolf K. "Edward Albee im Englischunterricht des
Sekundarbereichs II: Ein Unterrichtsversuch in einer gym-
nasialen 13. Klasse." Die Neueren Sprachen, 72 (N.S. 22)
(1973), 527-543.

312. Houghton, Norris. The Exploding Stage; an Introduction to
Twentieth Century Drama, pp. 186-198. New York: Wey-
bright and Talley, 1971.

313. Hughes, Catherine. "Edward Albee." In her American
Playwrights 1945-75, pp. 52-63. London: Pitman, 1976.

314. Hunter, Evan. "Hair-Pulling." [Letter] New York Times, 1
September 1963, Sec. 2, p. 1.

315. Hunter, Gregg. "Kerr at Shubert in Albee Seascape."
Glendale (Calif.) News-Press, 4 April 1975, Leisure Time sect.,
pp. A, E. (INTERVIEW)

316. "Institute of Arts Adds Members in 3 Departments." New
York Times, 26 January 1966, p. 14.

317. [Interview with Albee] Beverwyck (Siena College), (Winter
1965), 18-50. (INTERVIEW)
Reprinted in The Playwrights Speak, ed. by Walter Wager,
pp. 25-67. New York: Delacorte Press, 1967.

318. Jackson, Don D. "Play, Paradox, and People: To Be but Not

Albee." Medical Opinion and Review, 2 (December 1966), 136,
142-143, 146.

319. Jackson, Esther M. "American Theatre in the Sixties."
      Players Magazine, 48 (1973), 236-249.

320. Jamieson, Daniel J. "On Edward Albee." Teachers College
      Record, 68 (January 1967), 352-353.

321. "John Steinbeck Says: 'I Must Be Far More Guilty.'" Times
      (London), 15 November 1963, p. 14.

322. Johnson, Carolyn E. "In Defense of Albee." English Journal,
      57 (January 1968), 21-23, 29.

323. Johnson, Malcolm L. "Albee at 48: Writing, Directing,
      Traveling, Thinking." Hartford (Conn.) Courant, 23
      January 1977, p. 1F. (INTERVIEW)

324. _____. "Albee Undaunted by Death of Lady." Hartford
      (Conn.) Courant, 25 May 1980, pp. 1G, 4G. (INTERVIEW)

325. Johnston, Laurie. "Notes on People." New York Times, 2
      June 1976, p. 31.
          Albee receives honorary doctorate from Southampton College
      and makes commencement speech.

326. Julier, Laura. "Faces to the Dawn: Female Characters in
      Albee's Plays." In Edward Albee: Planned Wilderness;
      Interview, Essays, and Bibliography, ed. by Patricia De La
      Fuente, pp. 34-44. Edinburg, Tex.: School of Humanities,
      Pan American University, 1980. (Living Author Series; no. 3)

327. K., J. "Le dramaturge américain Edward Albee à Varsovie."
      Le Théâtre en Pologne, 6 (February 1964), 19. [English
      translation, p. 25]

328. Kakutani, Michiko. "The Famed Will Gather to Read the For-
      bidden." New York Times, 5 April 1982, p. C11.
          Albee to read from Solzhenitsyn as part of P.E.N.'s
      'American Right to Read' program.

329. Kane, Leslie. "Albee." In his The Language of Silence; On
      the Unspoken and the Unspeakable in Modern Drama, pp. 158-
      178. Rutherford, N.J.: Fairleigh Dickinson University Press,
      1984.

330. Kaul, R. K. "Albee and the Theatre of Cruelty." Indian
      Journal of American Studies, 10 (January 1980), 48-57.

331. Keating, John. "Action Speaks Louder...." New York Times,

20 October 1963, Sec. 2, p. 3.
Albee-Barr-Wilder Theater '64

332. Kelly, Kevin. "Edward Albee on Albee: The Superstar of
      Drama." Boston Globe, 14 March 1976, Sect. A, pp. 9, 14.
      (INTERVIEW)

333. Kerjan, Liliane. Edward Albee: Textes de Albee, points de
      vue critiques, témoignages, chronologie. Paris: Seghers,
      1971. (Théâtre de tous les temps, 14)

334. _____. Le théâtre d'Edward Albee. Paris: Klincksieck,
      1978.
      Reviewed in Bulletin critique du livre français, No. 399
      (March 1979), 383.

335. Kerr, Walter. "Making a Cult of Confusion." Horizon, 5
      (September 1962), 33-41.

336. _____. "Two Albees." In his Thirty Plays Hath November;
      Pain and Pleasure in the Contemporary Theater, pp. 203-206.
      New York: Simon and Schuster, 1969.

337. "Kerr, Albee on Judges' Panel for 1961-62 Voice 'Obies.'"
      Village Voice, 3 May 1962, p. 1.

338. Kidd, Robert. [Letter] New York Times, 9 May 1971, p. 30.

339. Kienzle, Siegfried. Modern World Theater; a Guide to Produc-
      tions in Europe and the United States since 1945, pp. 8-14.
      Translated from the German (Modernes Welttheater; ein Führer
      durch das internationale Schauspeil der Nachkriegszeit in 755
      Einzelinterpretationen; Stuttgart: Kröner, 1968) by Alexander
      and Elizabeth Henderson. New York: Ungar, 1970. (Revised
      German editions, 2d. [1973] and 3rd. [1978] published under
      the title Schauspielführer der Gegenwart)

340. Kilker, Marie J. "Children and Childishness in the Plays of
      Edward Albee." Players Magazine, 46 (August/September 1971),
      252-256.

341. Killinger, John. World in Collapse; the Vision of Absurd Drama,
      pp. 146-155. New York: Dell, 1971.

342. King, Kimball. "Edward Albee." In his Ten Modern American
      Playwrights, an Annotated Bibliography, pp. 1-108. New York:
      Garland, 1982.

343. "King of Off-Broadway." Newsweek, 57 (13 March 1961), 90.

344. Kingsley, Lawrence. "Reality and Illusion: Continuity of a

Theme in Albee." Educational Theatre Journal, 25 (March 1973), 71-79.

345. Kitchin, Laurence. "Albee." In his Drama in the Sixties: Form and Interpretation, pp. 196-198. London: Faber and Faber, 1966.

346. Kleiner, Dick. "Young-Old Albee Finds Success with Off-Broadway One-Acters." New York World-Telegram and Sun, 20 May 1961, magazine sec., p. 5.

347. Knepler, Henry. "Edward Albee: Conflict of Tradition." Modern Drama, 10 (December 1967), 274-279.
    Reprinted in Representative Men: Cult Heroes of Our Time, ed. by Theodore L. Gross, pp. 286-292. New York: Free Press, 1970.

348. Knickerbocker, Paine. "Edward Albee's View: 'The Theater Should Inflict Pleasure, Pain.'" San Francisco Chronicle, 20 May 1968, p. 43. (INTERVIEW)

349. Kohen, Helen L. "Playwright's Art Feeds the Mind." Miami Herald, 11 April 1980, p. 11D.
    "Material Matters" art exhibition curated by Albee.

350. Köhler, Klaus. "Drama als Allegorie." In Studien zum amerikanischen Drama nach dem zweiten Weltkrieg, ed. by Eberhard Brüning, pp. 110-133. Berlin: Rütten & Loening, 1977. (Neue Beiträge zur Literaturwissenschaft; Bd. 39)

351. Kolin, Philip C. "A Classified Edward Albee Checklist." Serif, 6 (September 1969), 16-32.

352. _____. "A Supplementary Edward Albee Checklist." Serif, 10 (Spring 1973), 28-39.

353. _____. "Two Early Poems by Edward Albee." Resources for American Literary Study, 5 (Spring 1975), 95-97.

354. Kosner, Edward. "Social Critics, Like Prophets, Are Often Honored from Afar; Closeup: Edward Albee, Playwright." New York Post, 31 March 1961, p. 38. (INTERVIEW)

355. Kostelanetz, Richard. "The Art of Total No." Contact, 4 (October/November 1963), 62-70.
    Reprinted partially in his On Contemporary Literature, pp. 225-231. New York: Avon, 1964.

356. _____. "The New American Theatre." In his The New American Arts, pp. 50-86. New York: Horizon, 1965.

357. Krebs, Albin. "Notes on People." New York Times, 30
      January 1974, p. 21.

358. Krohn, Charles S., and Julian N. Wasserman. "An Interview
      with Edward Albee, March 18, 1981." In Edward Albee; an
      Interview and Essays, pp. 1-27. Houston: University of St.
      Thomas, 1983. (INTERVIEW)

359. Kuner, M. C. [Letter] New York Times, 1 September 1963,
      Sec. 2, p. 1.

360. Kyria, Pierre. "Edward Albee ou le bourgeois 'antibourgeois.'"
      Combat (Paris), 2 March 1965, p. 8.

361. La Fontaine, Barbara. "Triple Threat On, Off and Off-Off
      Broadway." New York Times Magazine, 25 February 1968, pp.
      36-37, 39, 41-42, 44, 46.

362. Lahr, John. "Theater: A Question Long Overdue." Arts
      Magazine, 41 (May 1967), 21-23.

363. Landon, Bert. "Ad Absurdum." [Letter] New York Times
      Magazine, 18 March 1962, pp. 82, 84.

364. Lapole, Nick. "Edward Albee--Man or Myth?" New York
      Journal-American, 27 October 1963, p. 13S.

365. Lask, Thomas. "Dramatist in a Troubled World." New York
      Times, 22 January 1961, Sec. 2, pp. 1, 3. (INTERVIEW)

366. Lawson, Carol. "Broadway: Festival of One-Actors Reopens
      Newhouse Theater in March." New York Times, 23 January
      1981, p. C2.

367. Lee, A. Robert. "Illusion and Betrayal: Edward Albee's
      Theatre." Studies (Dublin), 59 (Spring 1970), 53-67.

368. Lerman, Leo. "Five Playwrights Talk About How They Got
      There." Mademoiselle, 56 (March 1963), 170-171, 215-219.

369. Lester, Elenore. "Albee: 'I'm Still in Process.'" New York
      Times, 18 September 1966, Sec. 2, pp. 1, 6. (INTERVIEW)

370. _____. "Where Have All the Playwrights Gone?" New York
      Times, 22 August 1976, Sec. 2, pp. 1, 6, 10.

371. Levy, Alan. "The A* B** B*** of Alan Schneider." New
      York Times Magazine, 20 October 1963, pp. 27, 30, 37, 39-40,
      44, 52.

372. Levy, Maurice. "Albee: un théâtre qui fait peur." Caliban

(University of Toulouse), No. 8 (1971), 151-164.

373. Lewis, Allan. "The Fun and Games of Edward Albee." Educational Theatre Journal, 16 (March 1964), 29-39.
     Reprinted in his American Plays and Playwrights of the Contemporary Theatre, pp. 81-98. New York: Crown, 1965. Updated in the rev. ed., pp. 81-98. New York: Crown, 1970.

374. Little, Stuart W. "The Importance of Being Edward Albee." In his Off-Broadway: The Prophetic Theater, pp. 216-228. New York: Coward, McCann & Geoghegan, 1972.

375. Loggem, M[anuel] van. "Een nieuwe dodendans." In his Drift en Drama, pp. 67-68. The Hague: NVSH, 1968, c1967.

376. Loney, Glenn M. "Theatre of the Absurd: It Is Only a Fad." Theatre Arts, 46 (November 1962), 20, 22, 24, 66-68.

377. Long, Mary. "Interview: Edward Albee: 'I Don't Write Reassuring Plays, No Opiates.'" Mademoiselle, 82 (August 1976), 230. (INTERVIEW)

378. Louson, Dzhon Govard [Lawson, John Howard]. "Souvremennaia dramaturgiia SShA" [Contemporary drama of the US] Inostrannaia Literatura (Moscow), No. 8 (August 1962), 186-196.

379. Lukas, Mary. "Who Isn't Afraid of Edward Albee?" Show, 3 (February 1963), 83, 112-114.

380. Lumley, Frederick. New Trends in 20th Century Drama: A Survey Since Ibsen and Shaw. 3rd. ed., pp. 319-324. New York: Oxford University Press, 1967. 4th ed., pp. 327-333. New York: Oxford University Press, 1972.

381. Luri [Lourie], S. "Griaz' na podmostakh' [Dirt on the stage] Izvestiia (Moscow), 31 May 1963, p. 2.

382. Lyons, Leonard. "The Lyons Den." New York Post, 27 January 1968, p. 27.

383. "M. Albee saisi par le succès." L'Express, No. 712 (8/14 February 1965), 51.

384. MacBeath, Innis. "Storm in U.S. over Pulitzer Prize." Times (London), 3 May 1967, p. 1.

385. MacPherson, Myra. "Congress, Funds and the Arts." Washington Post, 15 March 1973, Sec. D, pp. 1, 11.

386. "Man in the News: New Voices on Broadway: Edward Franklin
      Albee." New York Times, 15 October 1962, p. 33.

387. Marowitz, Charles. "Charles Marowitz: An Interview." Trans-
      atlantic Review, No. 16 (Summer 1964), 24-31.
      Reprinted in Behind the Scenes: Theater and Film Inter-
      views from the Transatlantic Review, ed. by Joseph McCrindle,
      pp. 182-190. New York: Holt, Rinehart and Winston, 1971.

388. Marshall, Thomas F. "Edward Albee and the Nowhere Genera-
      tion." Mexico Quarterly Review, 3, No. 1 (1968), 39-47.

389. Matlaw, Myron. Modern World Drama; an Encyclopedia, pp.
      16-17. New York: Dutton, 1972.

390. McCormick, John. "The Lady from Dubuque Lies and Lies."
      Telegraph Herald (Dubuque, Iowa), 28 May 1978, p. 32.
      (INTERVIEW)

391. McCullers, Carson. "The Dark Brilliance of Edward Albee."
      Harper's Bazaar, 96 (January 1963), 98.

392. McGinn, Larry. "Actors Carry Albee: Drama at Carrier
      Theater." Post-Standard (Syracuse, N.Y.), 5 May 1979, p.
      32.

393. Meehan, Thomas. "Not Good Taste, Not Bad Taste--It's
      Camp." New York Times Magazine, 21 March 1965, pp. 30-31,
      113-115.

394. Meserve, Walter J. "Edward Albee." In An Outline History
      of American Drama, p. 358. Totowa, N.J.: Littlefield,
      Adams, 1965.

395. Michaljević, M. "Suvremeni amerićki teatar: Lionel Abel,
      Edward Albee, Kenneth Brown, Jack Gelber, Arthur Kopit,
      Jack Richardson." Republika (Zagreb), 21 (1965), 400-403.

396. Mignon, Paul-Louis. "1960: Albee, Gelber...." In Le
      Théâtre contemporain, pp. 165-170. Paris: Hachette, 1969.

397. _____. "Les complexes américains à la croisée du réalisme
      et du symbolisme." In his Panorama du théâtre au XXe siècle,
      pp. 219-221. Paris: Gallimard, c1978.

398. _____. "Le Théâtre de A jusqu'à Z: Edward Albee."
      L'Avant Scène, No. 339 (August 1965), 8.

399. Miller, Terry. "Albee." In McGraw-Hill Encyclopedia of World
      Drama, 2nd ed., Vol. 1, pp. 38-43. New York: McGraw-Hill,
      1984.

400. Mohanty, H. P. "The Image of the Absurd: How Absurd Is
      Absurd Drama?" Literary Half-Yearly (Mysore), 15 (July
      1974), 88-94.

401. Molli, Jeanne. "Troupe in Paris to Stage Albee; English-
      Language Theater Association Opens June 6." New York
      Times, 25 May 1963, p. 12.

402. Morgan, Thomas B. "Angry Playwright in a Soft Spell."
      Life, 62 (26 May 1967), 90-90B, 93-94, 96-97, 99.

403. Morris, Penny W. "Albee." In Encyclopedia of World Liter-
      ature in the 20th Century, rev. ed., Vol. 1, pp. 39-41. New
      York: Ungar, 1981.

404. Morrison, Kristin. "Albee." In Crowell's Handbook of Con-
      temporary Drama, by Michael Anderson et al., pp. 5-9. New
      York: Crowell, 1971.

405. Moses, Robbie. "Edward Albee: A Voice in the Wasteland."
      Forum (Houston), 12 (Winter 1975), 35-40.

406. Moskow, Shirley. "Albee, Clurman, Kerr Draw Crowd."
      News-Tribune (Waltham, Mass.), 24 April 1979, p. 8.
      (INTERVIEW)

407. Mottram, Eric. "The New American Wave." Encore, 11
      (January/February 1964), 22-41.

408. Munk, Erika. "Cross Left: Albee or Not Albee." Village
      Voice, 19 February 1979, p. 82.

409. _____. "Cross Left: Tiny Albee." Village Voice, 29
      January 1979, p. 76. (INTERVIEW)

410. Mussoff, Lenore. "The Medium Is the Absurd." English
      Journal, 58 (April 1969), 566-570, 576.

411. Natale, Richard. "Edward Albee: 'I Think I'm Getting
      Better.'" Women's Wear Daily, 8 October 1973, pp. 1, 28.
      (INTERVIEW)

412. Nelson, Benjamin. "Avant-Garde Dramatists from Ibsen to
      Ionesco." Psychoanalytic Review, 55 (1968), 505-512.

413. Nelson, Gerald. "Edward Albee and His Well-Made Plays."
      Tri-Quarterly, No. 5 (1966), 182-188.

414. Nemy, Enid. "'Non-Social' Party Aids Playwrights Unit."
      New York Times, 29 March 1971, p. 29.
         Includes comments by Albee's mother.

36 Edward Albee

415. "New Outlook Urged for Little Theaters." New York Times, 15 December 1964, p. 57.

416. "New York Theater Called a 'Mess' by Edward Albee." New York Times, 8 November 1967, p. 56.

417. Newman, David. "Four Make a Wave." Esquire, 55 (April 1961), 49-51.

418. Newmark, Judy J. "Who's Afraid of Edward Albee?" St. Louis Post-Dispatch, 10 November 1977, pp. 3H, 4H. (INTERVIEW)

419. Newquist, Roy. "Edward Albee." In his Showcase, pp. 17-29. New York: Morrow, 1966. (INTERVIEW)

420. Nicoll, Allardyce. World Drama from Aeschylus to Anouilh, rev. ed., pp. 800-802. New York: Barnes & Noble, 1976.

421. Normand, J. "L'Homme mystifié: Les héros de Bellow, Albee, Styron et Mailer." Etudes anglaises, 22 (October/December 1969), 370-385.

422. Notable Names in the American Theatre, pp. 499-500. Clifton, N.J.: James T. White, 1976.

423. "Notizen: Gegenmassnahme." Theater heute, 9 (May 1968), 34.

424. Oakes, Philip. "Goings On: Don't Shoot the Playwright...." Sunday Times (London), 12 December 1976, p. 35. (INTERVIEW)

425. Oberg, Arthur K. "Edward Albee: His Language and Imagination." Prairie Schooner, 40 (Summer 1966), 139-146.

426. O'Doherty, Brian. "The Critics Meet the Playwrights." New York Times, 18 February 1963, p. 7.

427. Ōhashi. Kenzaburō; Akiro Saito, and Kichinosuke Ōhashi. Sōsetsu Amerika bungaku shi [Introduction to the history of American literature], pp. 461-462. Tokyo: Kenkyūsha, 1975.

428. "Older but Still Angry." Horizon, 21 (October 1978), 77. (INTERVIEW)

429. Paetel, Karl O. "Albee und das Absurde." Die Furche (Vienna), 2 October 1965, p. 14.

430. Pallavicini, Roberto. "Aspetti della drammaturgia contemporanea." Aut-Aut (Milan), No. 81 (May 1964), 68-73.

431. Pangalos, Mary. "Playwright Edward Albee Sees Much to Brood Over." Newsday (Garden City, N.Y.), 15 June 1961, p. 3C. (INTERVIEW)

432. Paolucci, Anne Attura. "Edward Albee and the Theater of Arrogance." Barnard Alumnae Magazine, 18 (Fall 1968), 22-24.

433. _____. From Tension to Tonic: The Plays of Edward Albee. Carbondale: Southern Illinois University Press, 1972.
    Reviewed in Booklist, 68 (15 May 1972), 789.
    Reviewed in Choice, 9 (July 1972), 666.
    Reviewed by C. J. Giankaris in Modern Drama, 15 (December 1972), 339-340.

434. _____. "Shakespeare and the Genius of the Absurd." Comparative Drama, 7 (Fall 1973), 237-246.

435. Papa, Sam. "News Around the Dials: Albee Drama Due on ABC." Daily News (New York), 17 June 1974, p. 64.

436. Parthasarathy, R. "Who's Afraid of Edward Albee? American Drama in the Sixties." Quest (Bombay), No. 55 (Autumn 1967), 52-55.

437. Peck, Joshua. "Albee Evaluates the Arts." Michigan Daily (University of Michigan, Ann Arbor), 24 February 1979, p. 5. (INTERVIEW)

438. Peck, Seymour. "Williams and The Iguana." New York Times, 24 December 1961, Sec. 2, p. 5.
    Tennessee Williams comments on Albee.

439. "People." Time, (2 October 1978), 89. (INTERVIEW)
    Albee comments on directing his own plays.

440. "People Are Talking About...." Vogue, 140 (Decmeber 1962), 120-121.

441. Phillips, Elizabeth C. "Albee and the Theatre of the Absurd." Tennessee Studies in Literature, 10 (1965), 73-80.

442. Pietropolli, Cecilia. "Il teatro di Edward Albee tra avanguardia e tradizione." Spicilegio moderno (Pisa), 4 (1975), 169-183.

443. "The Playwright as Curator." Art News, 81 (May 1982), 17-18.

444. "Playwrights Panel." In Toward Expanding Horizons and Exploring Our Art; the Proceedings of the TCG National Conference, Princeton University, June 18-24, 1980, ed. by David J. Skal, pp. 30-34. New York: Theatre Communications Group, 1980. (INTERVIEW)

445. Plett, Heinrich F. "Modern Writers: Edward Albee." Praxis
     des Neusprachlichen Unterrichts, 17 (1970), 304-311.

446. Plotinsky, Melvin L. "The Transformations of Understanding:
     Edward Albee in the Theatre of the Irresolute." Drama Sur-
     vey, 4 (Winter 1965), 220-232.

447. P[opkin], H[enry]. "Albee." In The Reader's Encyclopedia
     of World Drama, ed. by John Gassner and Edward Quinn, pp.
     10-12. New York: Crowell, 1969.

448. Popovici, Roxandra. "Edward Albee--Apariţie Originala în
     Teatrul American Contemporan." Bucharest. Universitatea.
     Annalele. Seria: Stiinte Sociale. Filologie, 16 (1967), 239-
     245. [English summary, p. 245]

449. Post, Robert M. "Cognitive Dissonance in the Plays of Edward
     Albee." Quarterly Journal of Speech, 55 (February 1969), 54-
     60.

450. Pradhan, Narindar S. Modern American Drama: A Study in
     Myth and Tradition, pp. 28-29, 47-52. New Delhi: Arnold-
     Heinemann, 1978.

451. Pree, Barry. "Richard Barr Interviewed." Transatlantic
     Review, No. 15 (Spring 1964), 10-16.
        Reprinted in Behind the Scenes: Theater and Film Inter-
     views from the Transatlantic Review, ed. by Joseph McCrindle,
     pp. 191-198. New York: Holt, Rinehart and Winston, 1971.

452. Prideaux, Tom. "The Albee Attitude, Both Sweet and Sour."
     Life, 53 (14 December 1962), 110.

453. Pryce-Jones, Alan. "The Theatre of Edward Albee."
     Listener and BBC Television Review, 76 (24 November 1966),
     763-764.

454. Przybylska, Krystyna. "Amerykański nurt awargardy."
     Dialog (Warsaw), 7 (September 1962), 90-98.

455. "Pulitzer Surprise: An Honor in Decline? Mr. Albee Has
     Second Thoughts About His Award." National Observer, 8
     May 1967, p. 4.

456. Rauter, Herbert. "Edward Albee." In Amerikanische Liter-
     atur der Gegenwart in Einzeldarstellungen, ed. by Martin
     Christadler, pp. 488-501. Stuttgart: Alfred Kröner, 1973.

457. Raymont, Henry. "Campaign by Artists." New York Times,
     14 July 1967, p. 9.
        Albee and others urge boycott of Athens music festival.

458. Razum, Hannes. "Edward Albee und die Metaphysik." In
     Theater und Drama in Amerika: Aspekte und Interpretationen,
     ed. by Edgar Lohner and Rudolf Haas, pp. 353-363. Berlin:
     E. Schmidt, 1978.

459. "A Red-Hot Hundred: A Foldout Gallery: Young Leaders of
     the Big Breakthrough." Life, 53 (14 September 1962), 4-7.

460. Reed, Michael D., and James L. Evans. "Edward Albee: An
     Updated Checklist of Scholarship, 1978-1980." In Edward
     Albee: Planned Wilderness; Interview, Essays, and Bibliog-
     raphy, ed. by Patricia De La Fuente, pp. 121-129. Edinburg,
     Tex.: School of Humanities, Pan American University, 1980.
     (Living Author Series; no. 3)

461. "Reviewers at Work." Critical Digest, 23 (12 April 1971), p.
     [3].

462. Rewald, Alice. "Albee et l'Avant-Garde." La Quinzaine
     littéraire, No. 42 (1 January 1968), 26.

463. Ribner, (Mrs.) Clayre. "Sun Stroke." [Letter] New York
     Times, 1 September 1963, Sec. 2, p. 3.

464. Rich, Alan. "Edward Albee Takes to the Air." Radio-Times:
     Journal of the British Broadcasting Corporation, 210 (27
     March/2 April 1976), 12. (INTERVIEW)

465. Robertson, Roderick. "A Theatre for the Absurd: The Pas-
     sionate Equation." Drama Survey, 2 (Spring 1962), 24-43.

466. Robinson, James A. "O'Neill and Albee." West Virginia
     University Philological Papers, 25 (February 1979), 38-45.

467. Rocha Filho, Rubem. "Albee, processo e tentativa." Tempo
     Brasileiro, No. 3 (1963), 161-172.

468. Roudané, Matthew C. "An Interview with Edward Albee."
     Southern Humanities Review, 16 (1982), 29-44. (INTERVIEW)

469. Roush, Matt. "Playwright Albee Remains Outspoken Original."
     Today (Cocoa, Fla.), 13 November 1982, pp. 1D, 3D.
     (INTERVIEW)

470. Rule, Margaret W. "An Edward Albee Bibliography."
     Twentieth Century Literature, 14 (April 1968), 35-44.

471. Rusinko, Susan. Review of The Plays, Volume Four. World
     Literature Today, 57 (Spring 1983), 292-293.

472. Rutenberg, Michael. Edward Albee: Playwright in Protest.

New York: Drama Book Specialists, 1969.
Reviewed by Murray Hartman in American Literature, 41
(January 1970), 617-618.
Reviewed by Anthony Hilfer in Journal of Modern Liter-
ature, 1 (1971), 714-716.
Reviewed by William Willeford in Modern Drama, 13 (Feb-
ruary 1971), 450-452.

473. Salmaggi, Robert. "Albee Sounds Off on Drama Critics."
World Journal-Tribune (New York), 29 March 1967.
(INTERVIEW)

474. Salvesen, Veronica. "In a Small, Quiet Room Backstage...."
Corsair (Santa Monica College), 16 April 1975, p. 3.
(INTERVIEW)

475. Samuels, Charles Thomas. "The Theatre of Edward Albee."
Massachusetts Review, 6 (Autumn/Winter 1964/65), 187-201.
Reprinted in Das amerikanische Drama von den Anfängen
bis zur Gegenwart, ed. by Hans Itschert, pp. 385-400.
Darmstadt: Wissenschaftliche Buchgesellschaft, 1972. (Ars
Interpretandi, Bd. 5)

476. Saporta, Marc. "Edward Albee." Informations & Documents
(Paris), No. 187 (15 September-1 October 1963), 20-22.
(INTERVIEW)

477. Sarotte, Georges-Michel. "Edward Albee: Homosexual Playwright in Spite of Himself." In his Like a Brother, Like a
Lover; Male Homosexuality in the American Novel and
Theater from Herman Melville to James Baldwin, translated
from the French (Comme un frère, comme un amant:
l'homosexualité masculine dans le roman et le théâtre américains
de Herman Melville à James Baldwin; Paris: Flammarion,
c1976) by Richard Miller, pp. 134-149. Garden City, N.Y.:
Anchor/Doubleday, 1978.

478. Scheller, Bernhard. "Der Figurenaufbau in den Stücken
Edward Albees." In Studien zum amerikanischen Drama nach
dem zweiten Weltkrieg, ed. by Eberhard Brüning, pp. 134-177.
Berlin: Rütten & Loening, 1977. (Neue Beiträge zur Literaturwissenschaft; Bd. 39)

479. _____. "Die Gestalt des Farbigen bei Williams, Albee und
Baldwin und ihre szenische Realisierung in DDR-Aufführungen."
Zeitschrift für Anglistik und Amerikanistik, 20 (1972), 137-157.
Reprinted with revisions in Studien zur amerikanischen
Drama nach dem zweiten Weltkrieg, ed. by Eberhard Brüning,
pp. 249-264. Berlin: Rütten & Lowning, 1977. (Neue
Beiträge zur Literaturwissenschaft; Bd. 39)

480. Schiff, Chester. "One-Act Playwright." [Letter] New York
      Times, 9 October 1966, Sec. 2, p. 11.

481. Schneider, Alan. "On." In The Arts and the Public, ed.
      by James E. Miller and Paul D. Herring, pp. 95-109. Chicago:
      University of Chicago Press, 1967.

482. _____. "What Does a Director Do?" New York Theatre
      Review, preview issue (Spring/Summer 1977), 16-17.
          Reprinted in New York Theatre Review, 1 (November 1977),
      50-51.

483. Schneider, Howard. "Albee: Hard Act for Himself to Follow."
      Los Angeles Times, 23 March 1975, Calendar sec., pp. 1, 50-51.
      (INTERVIEW)

484. _____. "Has the Tarantula Escaped?" Pittsburgh Press, 3
      February 1974, Family Magazine, pp. 6-7. (INTERVIEW)
          Reprinted in Biography News, 1 (March 1974), 246-247.
          Reprinted in Authors in the News, 1 (1976), 7-8.

485. Schneider, Paul. "Albee's Message: 'Pay Attention.'" Post-
      Standard (Syracuse, N.Y.), 4 May 1979, p. 28.

486. Schöne, Annemarie. "Edward Albee." In her Abriss der
      amerikanischen Literaturgeschichte in Tabellen, p. 276.
      Frankfurt am Main: Athenäum, 1967.

487. Schulz-Seitz, Ruth Eva. Edward Albee--der Dichterphilosoph
      der Bühne. Frankfurt am Main: Klostermann, 1966.
          Reviewed by R[udolf] Haas in Jahrbuch für Amerikastudien;
      German Yearbook of American Studies, 13 (1968), 299-303.

488. Schvey, Henry I. "Edward Albee: Innovator or Impersonator?"
      In Avant-Garde en Traditie in het Moderne Toneel, pp. 46-61.
      Muiderberg: Coutinho, 1978.

489. Schwartz, Jerry. "Government Subsidies Needed for Theater,
      Panel Members Say." Miami Herald, 16 March 1975, Sec. H,
      p. 10. (INTERVIEW)

490. Serreau, Geneviève. "Un 'Boulevard' d'avant-garde américain:
      Edward Albee, Murray Schisgal, Arthur L. Kopit, Jack
      Gelber...." In her Histoire du "Nouveau théâtre," pp. 163-
      167. Paris: Gallimard, 1966.

491. "Shakespeare liegt immer vorn--Was wird am meisten gespielt?"
      Theater heute, 8 (January 1967), 47.

492. Sharpe, Jacqueline. "No Alternative." [Letter] New York
      Times Magazine, 18 March 1962, p. 84.

493. Shelton, Frank W. "Nathanael West and the Theater of the
     Absurd: A Comparative Study." Southern Humanities Re-
     view, 10 (Summer 1976), 225-234.

494. Shepard, Richard F. "8 Albee Plays Will Tour Overseas."
     New York Times, 20 January 1979, p. 12.

495. _____. "Times Considers 2 Drama Reviews." New York
     Times, 11 October 1966, p. 55.

496. Sheppard, Eugenia. "Who's Afraid of Albee?" World-Journal
     Tribune (New York), 19 September 1966, pp. 27-28.

497. Sherman, Howard. "Playwright Directs Sculpture." Hartford
     (Conn.) Courant, 12 March, p. 52.
     Albee as curator for exhibition of works of artist Ellen Phelan.

498. Shirley, Don. "An Audience with Albee; Up the Freight
     Elevator to the Playwright's Roost." Washington Post, 18
     February 1979, Sec. K, pp. 1, 14. (INTERVIEW)

499. Silver, Lily Jay. "Edward Albee." In her Profiles in Success;
     Forty Lives of Achievement, pp. 1-12. New York: Fountain-
     head, 1965.

500. Simard, Rodney. "Harold Pinter & Edward Albee, the First
     Postmoderns." In his Postmodern Drama; Contemporary Play-
     wrights in America and Britain, pp. 25-47. Latham, Md.:
     University Press of America, 1984.

501. Simon, John. "Should Albee Have Said 'No Thanks'?" New
     York Times, 20 August 1967, Sec. 2, pp. 1, 8.
          Reprinted in his Singularities; Essays on the Theater
     1964-1974, pp. 58-64. New York: Random House, 1975.

502. "Sketches of Winners of Pulitzer Prizes for News, Scholarship
     and the Arts." New York Times, 2 May 1967, p. 40.

503. Skow, John. "Broadway's Hottest Playwright, Edward Albee."
     Saturday Evening Post, 237 (18 January 1964), 32-33.
          German translation, "Amerikas aggressivster Broadway-Star:
     Edward Albee--ein Poet des Hasses." in Die Weltwoche
     (Zurich), 31 January 1964, p. 23. (INTERVIEW)

504. Smilgis, Martha. "Stage: Edward Albee Blames His Newest
     Broadway Flop on the Critics--and Casts for Lolita on Subways."
     People Weekly, 13 (25 February 1980), 70, 73. (INTERVIEW)

505. Smith, Ardis. "Virginia Woolf Author Is a Solitary Figure."
     Buffalo Evening News, 19 October 1963, Sec. B, p. 7.
     (INTERVIEW)

506. Smith, Michael. "Edward Albee in Conversation with Michael
     Smith." Plays and Players, 11 (March 1964), 12-14.
     (INTERVIEW)

507. Solomon, Jerry. "Edward Albee: American Absurdist."
     Western Speech, 28 (Fall 1964), 230-236.

508. "Soviet Writers Found Unafraid; But Albee Says They Live in
     Literary Isolation." New York Times, 4 December 1963, p. 54.
     (INTERVIEW)

509. Spencer, Sharon D. "Edward Albee--The Anger Artist."
     Forum (Houston), 4 (Winter/Spring 1967), 25-30.

510. Stagg, Anne. "House in the Life of a Playwright: Edward
     Albee's Greenwich Village Carriage House." House and
     Garden, 132 (December 1967), 160-163.

511. Starr, John. "Albee Plus Nureyev Plus Zeffirelli Equals a
     Million Pound Mystery." Daily Mail (London), 14 April 1966,
     p. 8.

512. Stavrou, C. N. "Albee in Wonderland." Southwest Review,
     60 (Winter 1975), 46-61.

513. "Steinbeck Rips Reds; Spy Stuff Riles Albee, Too." Daily
     News (New York), 15 November 1963, p. 2.

514. Stenz, Anita Maria. Edward Albee: The Poet of Loss. The
     Hague; New York: Mouton, 1978. (Studies in American
     Literature; 32)
         Reviewed by Terry Otten in Comparative Drama, 13
     (Winter 1979/80), 381-382.

515. Stern, Daniel. "The Director's Approach--Two Views: Albee:
     'I Want My Intent Clear.'" New York Times, 28 March 1976,
     Sec. 2, pp. 1, 5. (INTERVIEW)

516. Stewart, Phyllis. "Albee Directs on LI; Joins Barr at John
     Drew Theater." Long Island Press (Jamaica, N.Y.), 9 July
     1972, magazine sec., p. 14.

517. Stewart, R. S. "John Gielgud and Edward Albee Talk About
     the Theater." Atlantic, 215 (April 1965), 61-68. (INTERVIEW)
         Reprinted in Edward Albee: A Collection of Critical Essays,
     ed. by C. W. E. Bigsby, pp. 112-123. Englewood Cliffs,
     N.J.: Prentice-Hall, 1975.
         Reprinted partially as "Sir John Gielgud and Edward Albee
     Discuss the Stage Today" in Observer (London), 18 April
     1965, p. 21.

518. Styan, J. L. The Dark Comedy; the Development of Modern Comic Tragedy, 2nd ed., pp. 216-217. Cambridge: Cambridge University Press, 1968.

519. _____. Modern Drama in Theory and Practice, Vol. 2: Symbolism, Surrealism and the Absurd, pp. 142-144. Cambridge: Cambridge University Press, 1981.

520. Sullivan, Dan. "Albee Criticizes Pulitzer Board." New York Times, 3 May 1967, p. 49.

521. _____. "Edward Albee: Playwright with More Than One Act." Los Angeles Times, 15 October 1978, Calendar sec., p. 6. (INTERVIEW)

522. Syse, Glenna. "Lady from Dubuque: Who's Afraid of Edward Albee?" Chicago Sun-Times, 17 February 1980, p. 2. (INTERVIEW)

523. "The Talk of the Town: Albee." New Yorker, 37 (25 March 1961), 30-32. (INTERVIEW)

524. "The Talk of the Town: Albee Revisited." New Yorker, 40 (19 December 1964), 31-33. (INTERVIEW)

525. "The Talk of the Town: Revisited." New Yorker, 56 (3 March 1980), 29-31. (INTERVIEW)

526. "The Talk of the Town: Theatre." New Yorker, 50 (3 June 1974), 28-30. (INTERVIEW)

527. "Talk with the Author." Newsweek, 60 (29 October 1962), 52-53. (INTERVIEW)

528. Tallmer, Jerry. "Edward Albee, Playwright." New York Post, Week-End Magazine sec., 4 November 1962, p. 10.

529. _____. "Yes, Virginia, There Is a Richard Barr." Cavalier, 13 (August 1963), 22-24, 29-30, 32.

530. Tanner, Henry. "Steinbeck and Albee Speak Out in Soviet for U.S. Professor." New York Times, 15 November 1963, pp. 1, 5.

531. Taubman, Howard. "Into the Melee: A None-Too-Innocent Bystander Comments." New York Times, 1 September 1963, Sec. 2, p. 1.

532. _____. The Making of the American Theatre, pp. 332-334. New York: Coward McCann, 1965.

533. Taylor, Robert. "Albee Shocked He's Required Reading in
      College Class." Oakland (Calif.) Tribune, 15 October 1978,
      p. 3E. (INTERVIEW)

534. Thies, Henning. Namen im Kontext von Dramen: Studien zur
      Funktion von Personennamen im englischen, amerikanischen und
      deutschen Drama, pp. 61-62, 121, 172, 293, 295. Frankfurt
      am Main: Peter Lang, 1978. (Sprache und Literatur; Bd. 13)

535. Topor, Tom. "Albee's College Script." New York Post, 9 May
      1974, p. 28.

536. Treib, Manfred. August Strindberg und Edward Albee; eine
      vergleichende Analyse moderner Ehedramen (mit einem Exkurs
      über Friedrich Dürrenmatts "Play Strindberg." Frankfurt am
      Main: Lang, 1980. (Europäische Hochschulschriften: Reihe
      18, Vergleichende Literaturwissenschaften; Bd. 23)

537. [Trewin, Ion.] "A Jinx on Albee's Plays?" Times (London),
      15 June 1967, p. 10.

538. Trotta, Geri. "On Stage: Edward Albee." Horizon, 4
      (September 1961), 78-79.

539. Turner, W. L. "Absurdist, Go Home!" Players Magazine, 40
      (February 1964), 139-140.

540. Vallbona, Rima de. "Teatro: Edward Albee: el arte y el
      público." Indice, No. 248 (1 June 1969), 32-33.

541. Van Itallie, Jean-Claude. "An Interview with Alan Schneider."
      Transatlantic Review, No. 10 (Summer 1962), 12-23.
          Reprinted in Behind the Scenes: Theater and Film Inter-
      views from the Transatlantic Review, ed. by Joseph McCrindle,
      pp. 279-292. New York: Holt, Rinehart and Winston, 1971.

542. "Villanova and Theater '65 Win Margo Jones Awards." New
      York Times, 16 February 1965, p. 40.

543. Villard, Leonie. Panorama du théâtre américain du renouveau
      1915-1962, pp. 307-312. Paris: Seghers, 1964.

544. "Visiting Scholar Series Extended; Impact on All Departments."
      Pratt Institute Quarterly News, 1 (March 1963), p. 1.

545. von Ranson, Brooks. "Edward Albee Speaks." Connecticut,
      40 (February 1977), 38-39. (INTERVIEW)

546. Vos, Nelvin. "The American Dream Turned to Nightmare:
      Recent American Drama." Christian Scholar's Review, 1
      (Spring 1971), 195-206.

Reprinted with revisions in his The Great Pendulum of
Becoming: Images in Modern Drama, pp. 43-58. Grand Rapids,
Mich.: Christian University Press, c. 1980.

547. _____. Eugene Ionesco and Edward Albee; a Critical Essay.
Grand Rapids, Mich.: Eerdmanns, 1968.
Spanish translation by Marcelo Pérez Rivas, Ionesco/Albee
y el teatro del absurdo. Buenos Aires: Ediciones Megápolis,
1970.

548. _____. The Great Pendulum of Becoming: Images in
Modern Drama, pp. 33-34, 37, 70-72, 82-87. Grand Rapids,
Mich.: Christian University Press, c1980.
See also items 546 and 549.

549. _____. "The Process of Dying in the Plays of Edward
Albee." Educational Theatre Journal, 25 (March 1973), 80-85.
Reprinted with revisions in his The Great Pendulum of
Becoming: Images in Modern Drama, pp. 110-119. Grand
Rapids, Mich.: Christian University Press, c1980.

550. Wager, Willis. "Return: Wilbur, Albee, Morris." In his
American Literature: A World View, pp. 249-273. New York:
New York University Press; London: University of London
Press, 1968.

551. Wardle, Irving. "Albee Looks at Hmself and at His Plays."
Times (London), 18 January 1969, pp. 17, 19. (INTERVIEW)

552. _____. "American Theatre since 1945." In American
Literature Since 1900, ed. by Marcus Cunliffe, pp. 242-270.
London: Barrie & Jenkins, 1975. (History of Literature in
the English Language; v. 9)

553. Wasserman, Julian N. "'The Pitfalls of Drama': The Idea of
Language in the Plays of Edward Albee." In Edward Albee;
an Interview and Essays, pp. 29-53. Houston: University of
St. Thomas, 1983.

554. Weales, Gerald. "A Bunch of Plays." Hudson Review, 14
(Summer 1961), 314-320.

555. _____. "Edward Albee: Don't Make Waves." In his The
Jumping-Off Place: American Drama in the 1960's, pp. 24-53.
New York: Macmillan, 1969.
Reprinted in Edward Albee: A Collection of Critical Essays,
ed. by C. W. E. Bigsby, pp. 10-22. Englewood Cliffs, N.J.:
Prentice-Hall, 1975.

556. _____. "Off Broadway: Its Contribution to American
Drama." Drama Survey, 2 (Spring 1962), 5-23.

Reprinted in his American Drama Since World War II, pp. 203-223. New York: Harcourt, Brace & World, 1962.

557. Weatherby, W. J. "Do You Like Cats?: Edward Albee Interviewed." Guardian (Manchester), 19 June 1962, p. 7. (INTERVIEW)

558. Weiler, A. H. "Albee to Adapt French Novel to Films." New York Times, 24 April 1969, p. 38.

559. _____. "Who's Afraid of Vaslav Nijinsky?" New York Times, 29 March 1970, Sec. 2, p. 15.
Albee to write "The Dancer" screenplay.

560. Weiner, Bernard. "Albee Is Mourning the State of Broadway." San Francisco Chronicle, 12 October 1978, p. 60. (INTERVIEW)

561. _____. "Summing Up Albee's Wordy Experiments." San Francisco Chronicle, 28 October 1978, p. 36.

562. Welland, Dennis. "Albee and After." In his The United States; a Companion to American Studies, pp. 446-450. London: Methuen, 1974.

563. Wellwarth, George E. "Hope Deferred--The New American Drama: Reflections on Edward Albee, Jack Richardson, Jack Gelber, and Arthur Kopit." Literary Review, 7 (Autumn 1963), 7-26.
Reprinted in his The Theater of Protest and Paradox: Developments in the Avant-Garde Drama, pp. 275-284. New York: New York University Press, 1964. Revision in the rev. ed., pp. 321-336. New York: New York University Press, 1971.

564. Wetzsteon, Ross. "Albee Pulls Surprise; Accepts Pulitzer Prize." Village Voice, 4 May 1967, pp. 1, 25.

565. "Where Are the Playwrights?" New York Times, 25 August 1963, Sec. 2, p. 1.

566. White, James E. "An Early Play by Albee." American Literature, 42 (March 1970), 98-99.
See item 34.

567. Whitman, Alden. "Albee to Direct in Hamptons." New York Times, 26 March 1972, Sec. 15, pp. 1, 6.

568. "Who's Afraid of Success?" Newsweek, 65 (4 January 1965), 51.

569. "Wilder Withdraws as Albee Partner." New York Times, 6 March 1968, p. 34.

570. Williams, Tennessee. "Quote, Unquote." [Letter] Newsweek,
      61 (18 February 1963), 6.

571. Wilson, Garff B. Three Hundred Years of American Drama
      and Theatre, 2nd ed., pp. 311-312. Englewood Cliffs, N.J.:
      Prentice-Hall, 1982.

572. Wilson, Robert A. "Edward Albee: A Bibliographical Check-
      list." American Book Collector, 4 (March/April 1983), 37-44.

573. Witherington, Paul. "Albee's Gothic: The Resonances of
      Cliché." Comparative Drama, 4 (Fall 1970), 151-165.

574. Woggon, Bob. "Constant Writer Still Telling Us the Truth."
      Telegraph Herald (Dubuque, Iowa), 22 March 1979, p. 7.
      (INTERVIEW)

575. _____. "The Writing Life: Avant-Garde Albee." Writer's
      Digest, 60 (October 1980), 18, 20. (INTERVIEW)

576. Wolfe, Peter. "The Social Theatre of Edward Albee."
      Prairie Schooner, 39 (Fall 1965), 248-262.

577. Wolff, Millie. "'Material Matters' Opens with Norton Gallery
      Gala." Palm Beach (Fla.) Daily News, 30 March 1980, pp. A1,
      A16. (INTERVIEW)
         Art exhibition curated by Albee.

578. "Woolf Producer Says Playwrights Are Real Stars." Buffalo
      Evening News, 22 October 1963, Sec. 2, p. 14.

579. World Authors 1950-1970, ed. by John Wakeman, pp. 22-25.
      New York: H. W. Wilson, 1975.

580. Worth, Katharine. "Edward Albee: Playwright of Evolution."
      In Essays on Contemporary American Drama, ed. by Hedwig
      Bock and Albert Wertheim, pp. 33-53. Munich: Hueber,
      1981.

581. Wunderlich, Lawrence. "Playwrights at Cross Purposes."
      Works, 1 (Winter 1968), 14-37.

582. Wyler, Siegfried. "Zu Edward Albees Bühnenschaffen."
      Reformatio; Zeitschrift für evangelische Kultur und Politik,
      16 (May 1967), 330-346.
         Reprinted in Das amerikanische Drama von den Anfängen
      bis zur Gegenwart, ed. by Hans Itschert, pp. 401-419.
      Darmstadt: Wissenschaftliche Buchgesellschaft, 1972. (Ars
      Interpretandi, Bd. 5)

583. Yates, M. S. "Changing Perspectives, the Vanishing

Character in Albee Plays." CLA Journal (College Language Association), 28 (December 1984), 210-237.

584. Zasurskii, Ia. "Vstrecha s Edvardom Olbi" [A meeting with Edward Albee] Literaturnaia Gazeta (Moscow), 24 December 1969, p. 13. (INTERVIEW)

585. Zindel, Paul, and Loree Yerby. "Interview with Edward Albee." Wagner Literary Magazine, No. 3 (1962), 1-10. (INTERVIEW)

586. Zolotow, Sam. "Albee Profiting on Fiscal Terms; 'Generous' Contract Detailed for Author of Woolf." New York Times, 25 October 1962, p. 45.

587. _____. "Albee Will Open Repertory House." New York Times, 5 August 1968, p. 46.

588. _____. "Edward Albee Is Working on 3 Plays." New York Times, 14 August 1968, p. 32.

589. _____. "Play Plan Grows into Arts Center; Albee, Barr and Wilder to Lease Broadway House." New York Times, 16 January 1968, p. 25.

590. _____. "Playwrights Get a New Workshop." New York Times, 13 November 1963, p. 34.

591. _____. "Producing Team Plans Repertory." New York Times, 5 September 1967, p. 50.

592. _____. "Repertory Group Chooses 7 Plays." New York Times, 28 August 1968, p. 39.

593. "Die Zukunft der Stückeschreiber." Theater 1969: Chronik und Bilanz eines Bühnenjahres, annual special issue of Theater heute (1969), 6. (INTERVIEW)

6. THESES AND DISSERTATIONS

References are made to abstracts available in Dissertation Abstracts (DA) or Dissertation Abstracts International (DAI)

594. Agnihotri, Satish Mohan. "Symbolism of Eugene O'Neill, Tennessee Williams and Edward Albee." Ph.D. dissertation, Panjab University (Chandigarh, India), 1976.

595. Allen, Rex Eugene. "A Production and Production Book of Edward Albee's A Delicate Balance." M.A. thesis, Baylor University, 1974.

596. Anderson, Mary Castiglie. "Ritual Structure and Romantic Vision in Edward Albee's Drama: A Study of Three Plays." Ph.D. dissertation, Michigan State University, 1981. [DAI, 42 (June 1982), 5119A]

597. Anzalone, Frank Michael. "The Relation of Love and Death in the Plays of Edward Albee." M.A. thesis, Catholic University of America, 1966.

598. Argenio, Joseph. "Tobias: A Delicate Balance." M.F.A. thesis, Smith College, 1972.

599. Baker, Burton. "Edward Albee's Nihilistic Plays." Ph.D. dissertation, University of Wisconsin-Madison, 1974. [DAI, 35 (February 1975), 5387A]

600. Beatty, Dale T. "A Production Book for All Over." M.A. thesis, University of Texas at El Paso, 1975.

601. Berger, Jere Schindel. "The Rites of Albee." Ph.D. dissertation, Carnegie-Mellon University, 1973.

602. Bigsby, C. W. E. "Confrontation and Commitment: A Study of Themes and Trends in Contemporary American Drama." Ph.D. dissertation, University of Nottingham (Eng.), 1967.

603. Blades, Larry Thomas. "Williams, Miller and Albee: A Comparative Study." Ph.D. dissertation, St. Louis University, 1971. [DAI, 32 (February 1972), 4600A]

604. Blaha, Franz. "Das amerikanische Theater des Absurden;
      Studien zu den Dramen von Edward Albee, Jack Gelber,
      Arthur L. Kopit und Murray Schisgal." Ph.D. dissertation,
      Karl-Franzens University, Graz (Austria), 1967.

605. Blankenship, Jayne. "Devaluation of Language in the Theatre
      of Pinter and Albee." M.A. thesis, University of North
      Carolina at Chapel Hill, 1968.

606. Boros, Donald. "Tiny Alice by Edward Albee: A Production
      Record and Analysis with Emphasis on Dynamic Theatrical
      Symbolism." M.A. thesis, Saint Cloud (Minn.) State College,
      1967.

607. Bourdonnay, Katherine. "The Use of Violence and Hostility
      as a Means of Communication in the Original Plays of Edward
      Albee." M.A. thesis, Catholic University of America, 1968.

608. Bourne, James Thomas. "Edward Albee: Playwright of the
      Absurd." M.A. thesis, University of South Carolina, 1968.

609. Brand, Patricia Ann. "Decline and Decay in the Plays of
      Edward Albee." Ph.D. dissertation, New York University,
      1975. [DAI, 36 (December 1975), 3708A]

610. Brede, Regine. "Die Darstellung des Kommunikationsproblems
      in der Dramatik Edward Albees; ein literarkritische Unter-
      suchung." Ph.D. dissertation, Christian-Albrechts University
      (Kiel), 1974.

611. Bristow, Donald Gene. "New Voice in the Theatre: A Struc-
      tural and Thematic Analysis of the Plays of Edward Albee."
      M.F.A. thesis, University of Oklahoma, 1964.

612. Bryson, Rhett B., Jr. "The Setting and Lighting Design for
      The Ballad of the Sad Cafe." M.F.A. thesis, University of
      Georgia, 1969.

613. Burdison, Neva Evonne. "Family Relationships in the Plays
      of Edward Albee." M.A. thesis, University of Mississippi,
      1969.

614. Burns, Carol Ann. "Seeing Double: Analogies in the Plays
      of Edward Albee." Ph.D. dissertation, State University of
      New York at Binghamton, 1978. [DAI, 39 (October 1978),
      2268A-2269A]

615. Burns, Carolyn Dolinich. "The Function of the Narrator in
      Contemporary American Drama from Wilder to Albee." M.A.
      thesis, Catholic University of America, 1968.

616. Callahan, J. Stephen. "Society, Sex, and Soul in the Plays
      of Edward Albee." M.A. thesis, University of Kansas, 1967.

617. Cavarozzi, Joyce Pennington. "An Analysis of the Plays of
      Edward Albee." M.A. thesis, Ohio State University, 1963.

618. Chubb, Kenneth Richard. "The Empty Sound: A Study of
      the Plays of Edward Albee." M.A. thesis, Carleton Univer-
      sity (Ottawa), 1970.

619. Cognard, Roger A. "Albee's Enigmatic Alice: Its Background,
      Meaning and Significance." M.A. thesis, Texas Christian
      University, 1969.

620. Coy, Juan José. "El teatro de Edward Albee, breve síntesis
      de un decenio." M.A. dissertation, University of Madrid,
      1970.

621. Daley, Ronald E. "Heroes and Antiheroes in the Plays of
      Edward Albee." M.A. thesis, Roosevelt University at Chicago,
      1968.

622. Dannenberg, William J. "A Production of The Ballad of the
      Sad Cafe, by Edward Albee." M.F.A. thesis, University of
      North Carolina at Greensboro, 1971.

623. Delatte, Ann Perkins. "Alienation, Illusion, and Confrontation:
      A Study of Edward Albee's Statement of the Condition of Man."
      M.A. thesis, University of New Orleans, 1971.

624. Dieb, Ronald. "Patterns of Sacrifice in the Plays of Arthur
      Miller, Tennessee Williams, and Edward Albee." Ph.D. disser-
      tation, University of Denver, 1969. [DAI, 30 (May 1970),
      5104A]

625. Dillon, Perry C. "The Characteristics of the French Theater
      of the Absurd in the Plays of Edward Albee and Harold
      Pinter." Ph.D. dissertation, University of Arkansas, 1968.
      [DA, 29 (July 1968), 257A-258A]

626. Doerry, Karl Wilhelm. "Edward Albee's Modern Morality Plays."
      Ph.D. dissertation, University of Oregon, 1972. [DAI, 33
      (November 1972), 2368A-2369A]

627. Drugge, Herman. "A Study of the Themes and Techniques in
      the Plays of Edward Albee." M.A. thesis, University of
      Maine, 1967.

628. Dubler, Walter. "Eugene O'Neill, Wilder, and Albee: The Uses
      of Fantasy in Modern American Drama." Ph.D. dissertation,
      Harvard University, 1964.

629. Ducker, Danny. "Hermeneutics and Literary Criticism: A Phenomenological Mode of Interpretation with Particular Application to Who's Afraid of Virginia Woolf?" Ph.D. dissertation, University of Wisconsin--Madison, 1975. [DAI, 36 (June 1976), 8045A]

630. Duncan, Nancy K. "Study, Analysis, and Discussion of Two Roles for Performance: Hecuba in The Trojan Women and Julia in A Delicate Balance." M.F.A. thesis, University of Iowa, 1969.

631. Edmondson, Doris Elaine. "Edward Albee: The Playwright's Protest Against Enslavement in Contemporary American Society." M.A. thesis, Ohio State University, 1969.

632. Elias, Michael. "The Albee Response." M.A. thesis, Emory University, 1975.

633. Ellis, Donald. "Edward Albee: A Critical Reception Study." M.A. thesis, University of Kansas, 1967.

634. Ellison, [Earl] Jerome. "God on Broadway: Deity as Reflected in the Work of Seven Playwrights Prominent in the Twentieth Century American Commercial Theater: O'Neill, Wilder, MacLeish, Williams, Miller, Albee, Chayefski." M.A. thesis, Southern Connecticut State College, 1966.

635. Engle, William Francis. "Truth Versus Illusion and Sterility in the Writings of Edward Albee: A Study of Four Plays." M.A. thesis, California State University at Fullerton, 1971.

636. English, Emma Jean Martin. "Edward Albee: Theory, Theme, Technique." Ph.D. dissertation, Florida State University, 1969. [DAI, 30 (May 1970), 5103A]

637. Farinacci, John. "A Production of The American Dream and A Phoenix Too Frequent." M.A. thesis, University of Akron, 1965.

638. Fayed, Haney S. "Edward Albee: His Planning and Influence." M.F.A. thesis, Virginia Commonwealth University, 1978.

639. Fedor, Joan Roberta. "The Importance of the Female in the Plays of Samuel Beckett, Harold Pinter, and Edward Albee." Ph.D. dissertation, University of Washington, 1976. [DAI, 38 (September 1977), 1378A]

640. Finnigan, Jacqueline S. "Protestation Against Progress and Confrontation of Reality: A Study of Dramatic Experimentation in Two Plays by Edward Albee." M.A. thesis, McNeese State College (Lake Charles, La.), 1974.

641. Fleming, William P., Jr. "Tragedy in American Drama: The
      Tragic Views of Eugene O'Neill, Tennessee Williams, Arthur
      Miller, and Edward Albee." Ph.D. dissertation, University of
      Toledo, 1972. [DAI, 33 (July 1972), 308A]

642. Fletcher, William D. "An Analysis of the Women Characters in
      Six of Edward Albee's Plays." M.A. thesis, Indiana Univer-
      sity, 1967.

643. Forney, Deanna Sue. "Three Studies in English: Donne's
      'Holy Sonnets'; A Yeats Letter; Albee's Tiny Alice." M.A.
      thesis, Pennsylvania State University, 1971.

644. French, (Brother) Paul Douglas. "The Struggle with Form
      and the Search for Theme in the Plays of Edward Albee."
      Ph.D. dissertation, Loyola University of Chicago, 1967.

645. Friedli, Max. "Another American Dream: A Study of Edward
      Albee's One-Act Play, The American Dream." M.A. thesis,
      Gonzaga University at Spokane, 1967.

646. Fritzler, James Robert. "A Production and Production Book
      of Edward Albee's Seascape." M.F.A. thesis, University of
      Texas at Austin, 1979.

647. Gaines, Robert A. "The Truth and Illusion Conflict in the
      Plays of Edward Albee." M.A. thesis, University of Maryland,
      1969.

648. Garza, Esmeralda N. "A Production and Production Book of
      Edward Albee's The Ballad of the Sad Cafe." M.F.A. thesis,
      University of Texas at Austin, 1974.

649. Glaister, Larry L. "Direct Address: Wilder, Williams, and
      Albee." M.A. thesis, Hunter College of the City University
      of New York, 1977.

650. Gontarski, Stanley E. "Albee and the Absurd." M.A. thesis,
      Long Island University, 1967.

651. Grayson-Grossman, Elizabeth. "Directing Who's Afraid of
      Virginia Woolf? for the Intimate Stage." M.F.A. thesis,
      Southern Illinois University, 1977.

652. Green, Charles Lee. "Edward Albee, an Annotated Bibliog-
      raphy, 1968-1977." M.A. thesis, University of Tennessee,
      Knoxville, 1978.
            See item 286.

653. Greiner, Patricia Ann. "Absurdity, Archetypes, and Ritual
      in Four Plays by Edward Albee." M.A. thesis, Ohio State
      University, 1976.

654. Hall, Roger Allan. "Edward Albee and His Mystery: A Struc-
      tural and Thematic Analysis of Who's Afraid of Virginia Woolf?
      and A Delicate Balance." M.A. thesis, Ohio State University,
      1972.

655. Harris, Andrew Bennett. "Storytelling in the Plays of Edward
      Albee." Ph.D. dissertation, Columbia University, 1981. [DAI,
      42 (December 1981), 2368A-2369A]

656. Harris, Phyllis Katz. "'Nouveau roman' and 'nouveau théâtre':
      A Community of Enterprise." Ph.D. dissertation, University
      of Southern California, 1981. [DAI, 42 (September 1981),
      1137A]

657. Hefling, Joel. "Who's Afraid of Virginia Woolf?: A Scene
      Design Project." M.S. thesis, Kansas State Teachers College,
      1970.

658. Hempel, Peter Andrew. "From 'Survival Kit' to Seascape:
      Edward Albee's Evolutionary Drama." Ph.D. dissertation,
      University of Texas at Austin, 1975. [DAI, 36 (April 1976),
      6683A]

659. Higgins, David M. "Existential Valuation in Five Contemporary
      Plays." Ph.D. dissertation, Bowling Green State University,
      1971. [DAI, 32 (February 1972), 412A]

660. Hill, Linda Marjenna. "Langugae as Aggression: Studies in
      the Postwar Drama." Ph.D. dissertation, Yale University,
      1974. [DAI, 35 (January 1975), 4524A]

661. Huberth, Jonathan C. "A Production of Edward Albee's The
      American Dream." B.A. thesis, Amherst College, 1966.

662. Hull, Elizabeth Anne. "A Transactional Analysis of the Plays
      of Edward Albee." Ph.D. dissertation, Loyola University of
      Chicago, 1975. [DAI, 36 (July 1975), 313A-314A]

663. Jackson, Nancy-Dabney Roosevelt. "Edward Albee: Myths
      for Our Time." Ed.D. dissertation, Columbia University
      Teachers College, 1978. [DAI, 39 (May 1979), 6399A-6400A]

664. Jánský, Ann Leah Lauf. "Albee's First Decade: An Evalua-
      tion." Ph.D. dissertation, St. Louis University, 1969. [DAI,
      30 (February 1970), 3462A]

665. _____. "Formless Form in the Plays of Edward Albee."
      M.S. thesis, St. Louis University, 1963.

666. Jenkins, J. A. "Social Comment in the Plays of Edward
      Albee." M.A. thesis, University of Texas at Arlington, 1969.

667. Jones, Donna Mae. "The Drama of Edward Albee: An Ana-
     lytical Study of His Life and Works." M.S. thesis, University
     of Wisconsin, 1964.

668. Kapur, Banarsi Lal. "Quest for Human Value in the Plays of
     Edward Albee." Ph.D. dissertation, Meerut University (Meerut,
     India), 1976.

669. Keating, William P. "Edward Albee: His Answers to Female
     Aggressiveness." M.A. thesis, Colorado State University,
     1967.

670. Kelley, Edward G. "Dominant Recurring Themes in the
     Published Plays of Edward Albee." M.A. thesis, Kent State
     University, 1966.

671. King, Alberta Demorest (Armstrong). "The American Dream
     in Selected Plays of Edward Albee." M.A. thesis, Carleton
     University (Ottawa), 1970.

672. Lallamant, Robert J. "Edward Albee: The American Dream
     and the American Reality." M.A. thesis, Boston College,
     1964.

673. Langdon, Harry. "A Critical Study of Tiny Alice by Edward
     Albee Focusing on Commanding Image and Ritual Form."
     Ph.D. dissertation, University of Iowa, 1970. [DAI, 31
     (December 1970), 3080A-3081A]

674. Larner, Daniel. "Self-Conscious Form in Modern American
     Drama." Ph.D. dissertation, University of Wisconsin, 1968.
     [DA, 29 (June 1969), 4494A-4495A]

675. Lauricella, James. "A Director's Journal for the Production of
     Two One-Act Plays: Albee's The Zoo Story and Samuel
     Beckett's Krapp's Last Tape." M.F.A. thesis, Ohio University,
     1964.

676. Levene, Victoria E. "The House of Albee: A Study of the
     Plays of Edward Albee." Ph.D. dissertation, State University
     of New York at Binghamton, 1972. [DAI, 33 (July 1972),
     317A]

677. Levy, Valerie Brussel. "Violence as Drama: A Study of the
     Development of the Use of Violence on the American Stage."
     Ph.D. dissertation, Claremont Graduate School and University
     Center, 1970. [DAI, 31 (June 1971), 6618A-6619A]

678. Leyden, William Henry. "Social Protest and the Absurd: A
     Reading of the Plays of Edward Albee." Ph.D. dissertation,
     University of Oregon, 1971. [DAI, 32 (May 1972), 6434A]

679. L'Heureux, John C. "Edward Albee and the Theatre of the
      Absurd." M.A. thesis, Boston College, 1964.

680. Lowenthal, Lawrence David. "The Absurd in Recent American
      Drama." Ph.D. dissertation, New York University, 1970.
      [DAI, 31 (March 1971), 4779A-4780A]

681. MacFarland, David. "Imitations of Existentialism: Analogies
      to Religion in Three of Edward Albee's Plays." M.A. thesis,
      Stetson University, 1966.

682. Mantel, Myrna Grace. "A Structural Analysis of Edward
      Albee's Who's Afraid of Virginia Woolf?" M.A. thesis, Ohio
      State University, 1963.

683. Martin, Emma Jean. "Edward Albee: Theory, Theme, Tech-
      nique." Ph.D. dissertation, Florida State University, 1969.

684. Mayberry, Robert Lawrence. "Theatre of Discord: The
      Dissonance of Language and Light in Selected Plays of Samuel
      Beckett, Edward Albee and Harold Pinter." Ph.D. disserta-
      tion, University of Rhode Island, 1979. [DAI, 40 (April 1980),
      5440A]

685. Mays, James L. "Edward Albee's Women: Myth Versus Reali-
      ty." M.A. thesis, Ball State University, 1968.

686. McAlester, Constance A. "Eugene Ionesco et Edward Albee:
      Deux dramaturges contemporains." M.A. thesis, Southern
      Connecticut State College, 1966.

687. McCants, Sarah Maxine. "The Shade and the Mask: Death
      and Illusion in the Works of Edward Albee." Ph.D. disserta-
      tion, University of Southern Mississippi, 1974. [DAI, 35
      (April 1975), 6722A]

688. McMurrian, Jacqueline Y. "Edward Albee: Absurdist for
      Social Reform." M.A. thesis, University of Maryland, 1966.

689. Meyer, B. Ruth. "Language: Truth and Illusion in Who's
      Afraid of Virginia Woolf?" M.A. thesis, Wichita State Univer-
      sity, 1966.

690. Miller, Robert Royce. "Tragedy in Modern American Drama:
      The Psychological, Social, and Absurdist Conditions in
      Historical Perspective." D.A. dissertation, Middle Tennessee
      State University, 1975. [DAI, 36 (December 1975), 3717A]

691. Moses, Robbie Jeanette Odom. "The Theme of Death in the
      Plays of Edward Albee." Ph.D. dissertation, University of
      Houston, 1974. [DAI, 35 (January 1975), 4443A-4444A]

692.   Myers, Charles Robert. "Game-Structure in Selected Plays."
       Ph.D. dissertation, University of Iowa, 1971. [DAI, 32
       (September 1971), 1676A-1677A]

693.   Myers, Joseph T. "A Comparison of the Two Leading Female
       Characters in Henrik Ibsen's Hedda Gabler and Edward
       Albee's Who's Afraid of Virginia Woolf?" M.A. thesis, Univer-
       sity of Mississippi, 1971.

694.   Neblett, Joseph M. "From Stage to Film: A Study of Mike
       Nichols' Who's Afraid of Virginia Woolf?" M.A. thesis, Univer-
       sity of Mississippi, 1974.

695.   Norton, Rictor C. "Studies of the Union of Love and Death:
       I. Heracles and Hylas: The Homosexual Archetype. II. The
       Pursuit of Ganymede in Renaissance Pastoral Literature.
       III. Folklore and Myth in Who's Afraid of Virginia Woolf?
       IV. The Turn of the Screw: Coincidentia Oppositorum."
       Ph.D. dissertation, Florida State University, 1972. [DAI, 33
       (March 1973), 5190A-5191A]

696.   Oi, Judith T. "The American Nightmare: An Analysis of Six
       Plays by Edward Albee." M.A. thesis, Columbia University,
       1964.

697.   Olin, Carol. "The Unique Style of Edward Albee: Creative
       Uses of the Past." M.A. thesis, University of Colorado, 1967.

698.   Ollington, Marcus H. "Edward Albee and the Theatre of the
       Absurd." M.A. thesis, University of North Carolina at
       Chapel Hill, 1967.

699.   Palazzo, Laura Maria. "The Family as Microcosm in the Plays
       of Edward Albee." M.A. thesis, Syracuse University, 1967.

700.   Pinkston, Claude A., Jr. "Identity and Existence: A Survey
       of Realities in Contemporary Dramas by Jean Genet, Edward
       Albee and Tom Stoppard." M.F.A. thesis, University of
       Florida, 1973.

701.   Plunka, Gene Alan. "The Existential Ritual in the Plays of
       Jean Genet, Peter Shaffer, and Edward Albee." Ph.D. disser-
       tation, University of Maryland, 1978. [DAI, 39 (June 1979),
       7342A-7343A]

702.   Pradhan, Narindar Singh. "Edenic Themes in Modern American
       Drama." Ph.D. dissertation, University of Utah, 1972. [DAI,
       33 (September 1972), 1178A]

703.   Preuss, Renate. "Die Einsamkeit als Grunderfahrung des
       Menschen: Untersuchung des Menschenbildes in den Dramen

Edward Albees." Ph.D. dissertation, Albert-Ludwigs University (Freiburg im Breisgau), 1976. [DAI, 43 (Summer 1982), 1563C]

704. Quetz, Jürgen. "Symbolische und allegorische Formen in der Dramatik Edward Albees; Untersuchungen zu The Zoo Story, Who's Afraid of Virginia Woolf? und Tiny Alice." Ph.D. dissertation, Johann Wolfgang Goethe University, Frankfurt am Main, 1970.

705. Redmon, Elizabeth Daron. "An Allegorical Interpretation of Edward Albee's Who's Afraid of Virginia Woolf?" M.A. thesis, California State University, Fullerton, 1977.

706. Richardson, James G. "'Division on the Groundwork': Edward Albee's Adaptation of Carson McCullers' The Ballad of the Sad Cafe." M.A. thesis, University of Florida, 1971.

707. Rios, Charlotte Rose. "Violence in Contemporary Drama: Antonin Artaud's Theater of Cruelty and Selected Drama of Genêt, Williams, Albee, Bond, and Pinter." Ph.D. dissertation, University of Notre Dame, 1981. [DAI, 41 (May 1981), 4710A-4711A]

708. Ritcher, Geraldine. "Ionesco, Albee, Pinter and Beckett: Absurd Partisans of the Self." M.A. thesis, Chico State College, 1968.

709. Rohleder, Patricia J. "Albee's American Dream." M.A. thesis, University of Tulsa, 1967.

710. Roth, Emalou. "The Family Structure of Edward Albee's Plays." M.A. thesis, University of Kansas, 1969.

711. Roudané, Matthew Charles. "Existentialist Patterns in the Theater of Edward Albee." Ph.D. dissertation, University of Oregon, 1982. [DAI, 43 (December 1982), 1974A]

712. Ruben, Paul A. "The Effect of Voluntary and Forced Theatre Attendance on Attitudes Toward the Play Who's Afraid of Virginia Woolf?, Theatre in General, and New Forms of Drama." M.A. thesis, Bowling Green State University, 1970.

713. Rudisill, Cecil Wayne. "An Analysis of the Martyr as a Dramatic Character in Three Plays by Edward Albee: Tiny Alice, The Zoo Story, and A Delicate Balance." M.A. thesis, American University, 1971.

714. Rule, Margaret Wynngate. "The Reception of the Plays of Edward Albee in Germany." Ph.D. dissertation, University of Arkansas, 1971. [DAI, 32 (August 1971), 983A-984A]

715. Russ, Carla E. "The Absurdity of Edward Albee." M.A.
      thesis, Fairleigh Dickinson University, 1969.

716. Rutenberg, Michael Elliot. "Edward Albee, Social Critic."
      D.F.A. dissertation, Yale University, 1965.

717. Sanders, Rebecca Gayle. "Misogynistic Attitudes Shown in
      Three of Edward Albee's Plays." M.A. thesis, University
      of Mississippi, 1976.

718. Sanders, Walter E. "The English Speaking Game-Drama."
      Ph.D. dissertation, Northwestern University, 1969. [DAI,
      30 (May 1970), 5001A-5002A]

719. Sapoznik, Ran. "The One-Act Plays of Thornton Wilder,
      William Saroyan and Edward Albee." Ph.D. dissertation,
      University of Kansas, 1975. [DAI, 37 (August 1976), 700A]

720. Scheller, Bernhard. "Die Rezeption nach 1945 entstandener
      englischer und amerikanischer Dramatik durch die Theater in
      der DDR von 1961 bis 1973; Probleme des Figurenaufbaus und
      der szenischen Umsetzung von Stücken des spätbürgerlich-
      kritischen Realismus." Ph.D. dissertation, Karl-Marx Univer-
      sity (Leipzig), 1974.

721. Schmalz, Wayne E. "Edward Albee: The Learning Process."
      M.A. thesis, University of Saskatchewan, 1974.

722. Schneider, Ruth Morris. "The Interpolated Narrative in
      Modern Drama." Ph.D. dissertation, State University of New
      York at Albany, 1973. [DAI, 34 (April 1974), 6605A-6606A]

723. Schupbach, Deanne Justina. "Edward Albee's America."
      Ph.D. dissertation, University of Texas at Austin, 1970. [DAI,
      32 (January 1972), 4022A-4023A]

724. Shelton, Lewis Edward. "Alan Schneider's Direction of Four
      Plays by Edward Albee: A Study in Form." Ph.D. disserta-
      tion, University of Wisconsin, 1971. [DAI, 32 (February
      1972), 4754A]

725. Shuh, Susan Elizabeth. "The Development of Albee as an Ab-
      surdist." M.A. thesis, York University (Toronto), 1968.

726. Smith, Bruce Marc. "Edward Albee's Nuclear Family." M.A.
      thesis, University of California, Santa Barbara, 1974.

727. Smith, (Sister) Gertrude. "Fantasy in Edward Albee and
      Thornton Wilder." M.A. thesis, Boston College, 1968.

728. Smith, Rebecca Louise. "Dissonance as Method in the Plays of

Edward Albee." Ph.D. dissertation, University of Alberta (Edmonton), 1975.

729. Somoza, Joseph M. "Edward Albee and Modern European Dark Comedy: A Study of Albee's Humor in Perspective." M.A. thesis, Roosevelt University at Chicago, 1966.

730. Stace, Ann Carolyn. "An Analysis and Criticism of the Work of Edward Albee." M.A. thesis, Miami University (Ohio), 1964.

731. Steadman, Dan. "An Analysis of the Plot Technique Used in Three of Edward Albee's Plays." M.A. thesis, University of Nebraska, 1969.

732. Steiner, Donald Lee. "August Strindberg and Edward Albee: The Dance of Death." Ph.D. dissertation, University of Utah, 1972. [DAI, 33 (August 1972), 766A]

733. Stephens, Suzanne Schaddelee. "The Dual Influence: A Dramaturgical Study of the Plays of Edward Albee and the Specific Dramatic Forms and Themes Which Influence Them." Ph.D. dissertation, Miami University (Ohio), 1972. [DAI, 34 (July 1973), 342A]

734. Storrer, William A. "A Comparison of Edward Albee's Who's Afraid of Virginia Woolf? as Drama and Film." Ph.D. dissertation, Ohio University, 1968. [DA, 29 (April 1969), 3544A-3545A]

735. Swan, Mary B. "Attitudes Toward the American Dream in Selected Plays of Edward Albee and Arthur Miller." M.A. thesis, University of Rhode Island, 1965.

736. Temkin, Romola. "An Analysis of the Development of the Character Agnes in A Delicate Balance." M.A. thesis, California State University, Long Beach, 1977.

737. Townley, Raymond D. "Monsters to Martyrs: The Women of Edward Albee." M.A. thesis, Hunter College, 1968.

738. Umberger, Norman C. "Edward Albee: The Development of Two Characters." M.A. thesis, West Virginia University, 1970.

739. Wagner, Marlene Strome. "The Game-Play in Twentieth-Century Absurdist Drama: Studies in a Dramatic Technique." Ph.D. dissertation, University of Southern California, 1971. [DAI, 32 (February 1972), 4637A]

740. Wallace, Robert Stanley. "The Games of Edward Albee." M.A. thesis, University of British Columbia, 1970.

741. Ware, Robert Gorton. "Edward Albee's Early Plays: A
      Dramaturgical Study." Ph.D. dissertation, Stanford Univer-
      sity, 1979. [DAI, 41 (November 1980), 1843A-1844A]

742. Welch, David A. "Edward Albee: The Language of Absurdist
      Theatre." M.A. thesis, Clark University, 1982.

743. Westerfield, William. "A Production and Thesis of Edward
      Albee's Everything in the Garden." M.A. thesis, University
      of Maryland, 1971.

744. Westermann, Susanne. "Die Krise der Familie bei Edward
      Albee." Ph.D. dissertation, Ruprecht-Karl University
      (Heidelberg), 1974.

745. Wilderman, Marie R. "The Ritual of Games in Three of Albee's
      Plays." M.A. thesis, Louisiana State University in New
      Orleans, 1971.

746. Williams, Marcellette Gay. "A Phenomenological Study of
      Place of Indeterminacy in Axël and Tiny Alice." Ph.D. disser-
      tation, Michigan State University, 1981. [DAI, 42 (February
      1982), 3590A-3591A]

747. Wilson, Raymond J. "Transactional Analysis and Literature."
      Ph.D. dissertation, University of Nebraska, Lincon, 1973.
      [DAI, 34 (June 1974), 7793A]

748. Winchell, Cedric R. "An Analysis of the Symbology in the
      Earlier Plays by Edward Albee." Ph.D. dissertation, Univer-
      sity of California, Los Angeles, 1971. [DAI, 32 (May 1972),
      6600A]

749. Wines, Mildred Halo. "Origins of the Major Elements of the
      Theatre of the Absurd with Reference to the Works of Albee,
      Gelber, and Kopit." M.A. thesis, Catholic University of
      America, 1964.

750. Yugendranath, Birakayala. "The Exploration of Neurosis in
      Edward Albee's Plays." M.Phil. thesis, Osmania University
      (Hyderabad, India), 1977.

7. CRITICISM AND REVIEWS OF INDIVIDUAL WORKS

ALL OVER

751. "Albee Play at Alley Arena Is Memorable Experience." Houston Post, 24 January 1973, p. 8/AA.

752. Auld, Hugh. [Letter] New York Times, 18 April 1971, Sec. 2, p. 7.

753. Balmer, John. "Leisure Arts." Farmington Valley Herald (Simsbury, Conn.), 6 November 1975, p. 10.

754. Barber, John. "First Night: Venom and Pain Are Play's Ingredients." Daily Telegraph (London), 1 February 1972, p. 9.

755. Barker, Felix. "Theatre: All Over." Evening News (London), 1 February 1972, p. 3.

756. Barnes, Clive. "Stage: All Over, Albee's Drama of Death, Arrives." New York Times, 29 March 1971, p. 41.
    Reprinted partially in Times (London), 30 March 1971, p. 10.

757. _____. "Stage: Subtle All Over; Hartford Offers Albee's Play About Death." New York Times, 8 November 1975, p. 23.

758. Beaufort, John. "All Over: 'Bizarre, Bitter, Comic, Literate.'" Christian Science Monitor, 29 March 1971, p. 6.

759. _____. "Viewing Things: Not So Merriwell." Christian Science Monitor, 1 May 1971, p. 6.

760. Bigsby, C. W. E. "To the Brink of the Grave: Edward Albee's All Over." In his Edward Albee: A Collection of Critical Essays, pp. 168-174. Englewood Cliffs, N.J.: Prentice-Hall, 1975.

761. Billington, Michael. "All Over at the Aldwych Theatre." Guardian (Manchester), 1 February 1972, p. 10.

762. Buck, Richard M. [Letter] New York Times, 18 April 1971,
      Sec. 2, p. 7.

763. Calta, Louis. "Albee's Latest Play Will Reach Broadway in
      Spring." New York Times, 22 December 1970, p. 38.

764. _____. "All Over Gets Reprieve through $12,500 Gift."
      New York Times, 2 April 1971, p. 32.

765. Carmines, Al. "'I Would Like to See a Revival of....'" New
      York Times, 7 April 1974, Sec. 2, pp. 1, 8.

766. Cavan, Romilly. "Scripts." Plays and Players, 19 (August
      1972), 64.

767. Cavanaugh, Arthur. "Stage: All Over." Sign, 50 (June
      1971), 50, 52.

768. Clurman, Harold. "Theatre." Nation, 212 (12 April 1971),
      476-477.
          Reprinted in his The Divine Pastime; Theatre Essays, pp.
      267-270. New York: Macmillan, 1974.

769. _____. "Theatre." Nation, 212 (3 May 1971), 571-572.
          Reprinted in his The Divine Pastime; Theatre Essays, pp.
      270-272. New York: Macmillan, 1974.

770. Coe, Richard L. "Theater: Edward Albee: Death Enacted."
      Washington Post, 6 November 1971, Sec. C, pp. 1, 5.

771. Cowie, Denise. "HSC Tackles Albee's Controversial All Over."
      Hartford (Conn.) Times, 2 November 1975, p. 29.

772. Crinkley, Richmond. "Theater: The Development of Edward
      Albee." National Review, 23 (1 June 1971), 602-604.

773. Cuthbert, David. "All Over About to Begin." Times-Picayune
      (New Orleans), 1 April 1973, Sec. 2, pp. 16, 18.

774. _____. "'Gets Us Where We Live'--Death in Albee All Over."
      Times-Picayune (New Orleans), 5 April 1973, Sec. 4, p. 11.

775. Dawson, Helen. "A Very Public Passing." Observer (London),
      6 February 1972, p. 31.

776. Donovan, Phyllis S. "From an Aisle Seat: All Over at
      Hartford Stage Company." Meriden (Conn.) Daily Journal, 3
      November 1975, p. 34.

777. Drake, Sylvie. "Stage Review: A Death Watch in All Over."
      Los Angeles Times, 28 March 1977, Sec. 4, p. 9.

778. Edwards, Jeanne L. "Albee Keeps 'Em Guessing." Norwich
(Conn.) Bulletin, 16 November 1975, p. 4.

779. Esslin, Martin. "All Over." Plays and Players, 19 (March
1972), 38-40.

780. Fearnley, John. [Letter] New York Times, 18 April 1971,
Sec. 2, p. 7.

781. Fleckenstein, Joan. "Hartford's All Over." Torrington
(Conn.) Register, 14 November 1975, p. 11.

782. Frankel, Haskel. "All Over Is Mr. Albee's Best Play, Masking
Love in Hostility." National Observer, 29 March 1971, p. 21.

783. Gianotti, Peter M. "Theatre." Curved Horn (Fordham University), 6 April 1971, p. 14.

784. Gill, Brendan. "The Theatre: Who Died?" New Yorker, 47
(3 April 1971), 95.

785. Goldfaden, Bruce. [Letter] New York Times, 18 April 1971,
Sec. 2, p. 7.

786. Gottfried, Martin. "Theater: Albee's All Over ... 'Talked to
Death.'" Women's Wear Daily, 29 March 1971.
Reprinted in New York Theatre Critics' Reviews, 32 (1971),
322-323.

787. Gram, Peter B. "Albee at Hartford Stage ... a Meaningful
Production." Manchester (Conn.) Evening Herald, 15 November
1975, Weekend suppl., p. 3.

788. Green, Harris. "On Stage: Enervated Albee, Energized
Guare." New Leader, 54 (19 April 1971), 28-29.

789. Gussow, Mel. "Albee's New All Over in Rehearsal." New
York Times, 9 February 1971, p. 32.

790. Hammerich, R[ichard] C. "That's Albee, All Over." Springfield (Mass.) Union, 3 November 1975, p. 18.

791. Harris, James Neil. "Edward Albee and Maurice Maeterlinck:
All Over as Symbolism." Theatre Research International, 3
(May 1978), 200-208.

792. Harris, Leonard. Review of All Over, WCBS television, New
York, 28 March 1971.
Reprinted in New York Theatre Critics' Review, 32 (1971),
323.

793. Hart, Tom. "Albee Play Challenges, Bores." Springfield
     (Mass.) Daily News, 6 November 1975, p. 18.

794. Hewes, Henry. "The Theater: Death Prattle." Saturday
     Review, 54 (17 April 1971), 54.
          Reprinted in Edward Albee: A Collection of Critical Essays,
     ed. by C. W. E. Bigsby, pp. 165-167. Englewood Cliffs, N.J.:
     Prentice-Hall, 1975.

795. _____. "The Theater: The London Scene." Saturday Re-
     view, 55 (8 April 1972), 8-10.

796. Hipp, Edward Sothern. "A Dance of Death, Albee-Style."
     Newark Evening News, 4 April 1971, Sec. 6, p. E4.

797. Hobson, Harold. "London Plays by Albee and Stoppard."
     Christian Science Monitor, 11 February 1972, p. 4.

798. _____. "Right on Target." Sunday Times (London), 6
     February 1972, p. 29.

799. Hoffmann, Jean K. [Letter] New York Times, 18 April 1971,
     Sec. 2, p. 11.

800. Holmes, Ann. "All Over Erratic--Splendidly Absorbing."
     Houston Chronicle, 24 January 1973, Sec. 5, p. 7.

801. Hughes, Catharine. "New York." Plays and Players, 18
     (June 1971), 30.

802. _____. "Theatre: Albee's Deathwatch." America, 124
     (5 June 1971), 593-595.

803. Hurren, Kenneth. "Theatre: The Quick and the Dead."
     Spectator, 228 (12 February 1972), 245.

804. Johnson, Malcolm L. "Albee's Difficult All Over." Hartford
     (Conn.) Courant, 9 November 1975, p. 9F.

805. _____. "Stage: Albee Disappoints." Hartford (Conn.)
     Courant, 2 November 1975, p. 11A.

806. Jones, David Richard. "Albee's All Over." In Edward Albee:
     Planned Wilderness; Interview, Essays, and Bibliography, ed.
     by Patricia De La Fuente, pp. 87-98. Edinburg, Tex.:
     School of Humanities, Pan American University, 1980. (Living
     Author Series; no. 3)

807. Kalem, T. E. "Club Bore." Time, 97 (5 April 1971), 69.
          Reprinted in New York Theatre Critics' Reviews, 32 (1971),
     320.

808. Kauffmann, Stanley. "All Over; The Proposition." New Re-
      public, 164 (17 April 1971), 24, 38-39.
          Reprinted in his Persons of the Drama; Theater Criticism
      and Comment, pp. 219-222. New York: Harper & Row, 1976.

809. Kerr, Walter. "Albee's All Over--the Living Are Dead, Too."
      New York Times, 4 April 1971, Sec. 2, pp. 1, 18.

810. Kingston, Jeremy. "Theatre." Punch, 262 (9 February 1972),
      193-194.

811. Kretzmer, Herbert. "Now Who's Afraid of Mr. Albee?" Daily
      Express (London), 1 February 1972, p. 10.

812. Kroll, Jack. "The Disconnection." Newsweek, 77 (5 April
      1971), 52.
          Reprinted in New York Theatre Critics' Reviews, 32 (1971),
      321.

813. Lahr, John. "On-Stage." Village Voice, 1 April 1971, pp.
      59, 66.

814. Lambert, J. W. "Plays in Performance." Drama; the Quarterly
      Theatre Review, No. 104 (Spring 1972), 21-22.

815. Lenz, Harold. "At Sixes and Sevens--A Modern Theatre
      Structure." Forum (Houston), 11 (1973), 72-79.

816. Lewis, Peter. "All Over, by Edward Albee." Daily Mail
      (London), 2 February 1972, p. 27.

817. Marcus, Frank. "Theatre: Firework Display." Sunday Tele-
      graph (London), 6 February 1972, p. 18.

818. M[arriott], R. B. "Tedious Albee at Aldwych." Stage and
      Television Today, No. 4738 (3 February 1972), 19.

819. Matys, Linda. "Theatre: All Over Begins at Hartford Stage."
      Hartford (Conn.) Advocate, 5 November 1975, pp. 11, 13.

820. Melloan, George. "The Theater." Wall Street Journal, 30
      March 1971, p. 18.
          Reprinted in New York Theatre Critics' Reviews, 32 (1971),
      321.

821. Mishkin, Leo. "Theater: No Opening Makes Dull Theater."
      Morning Telegraph (New York), 6 February 1971.

822. "Moreau, Ashcroft for Albee Over." Variety, 30 December
      1970, p. 41.

823.   Moses, Robbie Odom. "Death as a Mirror of Life: Edward
       Albee's All Over." Modern Drama, 19 (March 1976), 67-77.

824.   Murray, Michael. "Albee's End Game." Commonweal, 94 (23
       April 1971), 166-167.

825.   Newman, Edwin. Review of All Over, WNBC television, New
       York, 28 March 1971.
           Reprinted in New York Theatre Critics' Reviews, 32 (1971),
       324.

826.   Nightingale, Benedict. "Old Folks at Home." New Statesman,
       83 (4 February 1972), 152-153.

827.   Norton, Elliot. "Hartford Stage Has Albee's All Over."
       Boston Herald-American, 4 November 1975, p. 22.

828.   Novick, Julius. "The Distinguished Decadence of Edward Al-
       bee." Humanist, 31 (July/August 1971), 34-35.

829.   O'Connor, Garry. "All Over." Financial Times (London), 1
       February 1972, p. 3.

830.   O'Connor, John J. "TV: A Superb Production of Albee's
       All Over." New York Times, 28 April 1976, p. 83.

831.   Oppenheimer, George. "On Stage." Newsday (Garden City,
       N.Y.), 10 April 1971, magazine sec., p. 2.

832.   "Performers in Three Places." New Yorker, 47 (20 February
       1971), 32-33.

833.   Philp, Richard. "Reviews: Theater." After Dark, 4 (May
       1971), 66.

834.   Pit. "All Over." Variety, 9 February 1972, p. 72.

835.   Raidy, William A. "First Nighter: All Over Brilliant." Long
       Island Press (Jamaica, N.Y.), 29 March 1971, p. 10.

836.   [Review of All Over] Booklist, 68 (15 October 1971), 176.

837.   Roht, Helen G. [Letter] New York Times, 18 April 1971,
       Sec. 2, p. 7.

838.   Rolfe, Lee. "Sluggish Direction Mars Albee Drama." Winnipeg
       Tribune, 20 November 1976, p. 32.

839.   Rudin, Seymour. "Theatre Chronicle: Winter-Spring 1971."
       Massachusetts Review, 12 (Autumn 1971), 821-833.

840. Schubeck, John. Review of All Over, WABC television, New
      York, 28 March 1971.
           Reprinted in New York Theatre Critics' Review, 32 (1971),
      324.

841. Shorter, Eric. "Plays in Performance: Regions." Drama; the
      Quarterly Theatre Review, No. 123 (Winter 1976), 56.

842. Shulman, Milton. "Facing Death--the Mother and the Mistress."
      Evening Standard (London), 1 February 1972, p. 13.

843. Simon, John. "Of Nothing and Something." New York, 4 (5
      April 1971), 58-59.
           Reprinted in his Uneasy Stages: A Chronicle of the New
      York Theater, 1963-1973, pp. 323-326. New York: Random
      House, 1975.

844. Smith, Cecil. "The Best Is Yet to Be." Los Angeles Times,
      28 April 1976, Sec. 4, p. 19.

845. Storrer, William Allin. [Letter] New York Times, 18 April
      1971, Sec. 2, pp. 7, 11.

846. Tallmer, Jerry. "Albee's Apartment: The Opening Scene."
      New York Post, 9 February 1971, p. 24.

847. Taylor, Markland. "Albee as Albee Should Be Done." New
      Haven (Conn.) Register, 9 November 1975, pp. 1D, 4D.

848. Todd, Thomas. [Letter] New York Times, 18 April 1971,
      Sec. 2, p. 11.

849. Tompkins, June. "Albee at Hartford Stage ... Not Particu-
      larly Exciting." Manchester (Conn.) Evening Herald, 15
      November 1975, Weekend suppl., p. 3.

850. Trewin, J. C. "A Flourish of Farce." Illustrated London
      News, 260 (April 1972), 57.

851. von Ranson, Brooks. "Albee's All Over Is Lifeless but Skill-
      full [sic]." Newington (Conn.) Town Crier, 6 November 1975,
      p. 8.

852. Watt, Douglas. "Albee's All Over Is Glacial Drama About a
      Death Watch." Daily News (New York), 29 March 1971, p. 46.
           Reprinted in New York Theatre Critics' Reviews, 32 (1971),
      323.

853. _____. "Theater: Albee Labors and Brings Forth a Hollow
      Drama." Daily News (New York), 4 April 1971, Sec. 2, p. S3.

854.   Watts, Richard. "Theater: The Man Who Lay Dying." New
       York Post, 29 March 1971, p. 18.
          Reprinted in New York Theatre Critics' Reviews, 32 (1971),
       320.

855.   _____. "Theater Week: About Two Playwrights." New
       York Post, 10 April 1971, p. 16.

856.   Wimble, Barton L. Review of All Over. Library Journal, 96
       (15 September 1971), 2786-2787.

                        THE AMERICAN DREAM

857.   Adelugba, Dapo. "Theatre Critique: Faux Pas at Ibadan Uni-
       versity Arts Theatre." Ibadan, No. 26 (February 1969), 81-
       82.

858.   "Albee's Double Bill Is Staged in London." New York Times,
       25 October 1961, p. 33.

859.   Aston, Frank. "Drama: Dream Unfolds at the York.: New
       York World-Telegraph and Sun, 25 January 1961, p. 19.

860.   Atlee, Howard. "Dispossessed by Tondelayo." [Letter]
       Village Voice, 15 December 1960, pp. 4, 13.

861.   Balliett, Whitney. "Off Broadway: Three Cheers for Albee."
       New Yorker, 36 (4 February 1961), 62.

862.   Barker, Felix. "No Label for Mr. Albee." Evening News
       (London), 25 October 1961, p. 11.

863.   Bell, Muriel. "Return to Valiance." Savannah (Ga.) Morning
       News, 14 July 1963, magazine sec., p. 9.

864.   Bolton, Whitney. "Stage Review: Provocative Double Bill at
       York Theatre." Morning Telegraph (New York), 26 February
       1961.

865.   _____. "Stage Review: Welcome Return of Albee Plays."
       Morning Telegraph (New York), 6 September 1962.

866.   _____. "Theater: What! Those Old Albee Plays Again!"
       Morning Telegraph (New York), 8 December 1967.

867.   Brustein, Robert. "Fragments from a Cultural Explosion."
       New Republic, 144 (27 March 1961), 29-31.
          Reprinted in his Seasons of Discontent; Dramatic Opinions
       1959-1965, pp. 46-49. New York: Simon and Schuster, 1965.

868.   Burchard, Hank. "'Albee by Albee' Is, Uh, Albee by Albee."
        Washington Post, 23 February 1979, Weekend sec., p. 10.

869.   Canaday, Nicholas, Jr. "Albee's The American Dream and the
        Existential Vacuum." South Central Bulletin, 26 (Winter 1967),
        28-34.

870.   Christon, Lawrence. "Doctor and Dream Offered." Los
        Angeles Times, 22 June 1973, Sec. 4, p. 17.

871.   Clurman, Harold. "Theatre." Nation, 192 (11 February
        1961), 125-126.
            Reprinted in his The Naked Image; Observations on the
        Modern Theatre, pp. 15-16. New York: Macmillan, 1966.
            Reprinted in his The Divine Pastime; Theatre Essays, pp.
        109-111. New York: Macmillan, 1974.

872.   Cooke, Richard P. "The Theater: Talent at the York."
        Wall Street Journal, 26 January 1961, p. 8.

873.   Cragin, Donald H. "Four Plays of Interest." Worcester
        (Mass.) Telegram, 19 November 1961, Sec. D, p. 11.

874.   Davis, James. "Dream Weakly Comic, Bartleby Solid Work."
        Daily News (New York), 25 January 1961, p. 50.

875.   [Digest of New York newspaper reviews of The American
        Dream and Bartleby] Critical Digest, 12 (30 January 1961),
        p. [2].

876.   Dorin, Rube. "Rewarding Revival of Two Albee Plays."
        Morning Telegraph (New York), 30 May 1963, pp. 2, 8.

877.   Driver, Tom F. "Drama: The American Dream." Christian
        Century, 78 (1 March 1961), 275.

878.   Eichelbaum, Stanley. "Strong and Purposeful Staging of
        Albee One-Acts." San Francisco Examiner, 25 October 1978,
        p. 59.

879.   Fremantle, Anne. "Theatre." Jubilee, 9 (June 1961), 46-47.

880.   Funke, Lewis. "Theater: Albee Revivals." New York Times,
        29 May 1963, p. 39.

881.   Gardner, Paul. "Maharis: From Albee to 'Route 66.'" New
        York Times, 24 November 1963, Sec. 2, p. 23.

882.   Gascoigne, Bamber. "Theatre: Grandma Osmosis." Specta-
        tor, 207 (3 November 1961), 623.

883.   Gassner, John. "Broadway in Review." Educational Theatre
       Journal, 13 (May 1961), 103-111.
          Reprinted partially in his Dramatic Soundings; Evaluations
       and Retractions Culled from 30 Years of Dramatic Criticism,
       pp. 591-592. New York: Crown, 1968.

884.   Gellert, Roger. "Albee et al." New Statesman, 62 (3 Novem-
       ber 1961), 667-668.

885.   Gray, Wallace. "The Uses of Incongruity." Educational
       Theatre Journal, 15 (December 1963), 343-347.

886.   Haas, Barbara. "When Playwright Albee Directs Himself."
       Post-Standard (Syracuse, N.Y.), 4 May 1979, p. 28.

887.   Hamilton, Kenneth. "Mr. Albee's Dream." Queen's Quarterly,
       70 (Autumn 1963), 393-399.

888.   Hatch, Robert. "Theater: Arise, Ye Playgoers of the World."
       Horizon, 3 (July 1961), 116-117.

889.   Heilman, Robert B. "The Dream Metaphor: Some Ramifica-
       tions." In American Dreams, American Nightmares, ed. by
       David Madden, pp. 1-18. Carbondale: Southern Illinois
       University Press, 1970.

890.   Hewes, Henry. "Broadway Postscripts: On Our Bad Behav-
       ior." Saturday Review, 44 (11 February 1961), 54.

891.   _____. "Off Broadway." In The Best Plays of 1960-1961,
       ed. by Louis Kronenberger, pp. 36-48. New York: Dodd,
       Mead, 1961.

892.   Hill, Linda M. "Language and Society: Albee's The Ameri-
       can Dream." In her Language as Aggression: Studies in
       the Postwar Drama, pp. 38-60. Bonn: Bouvier, 1976.
       (Abhandlungen aur Kunst-, Musik- und Literaturwissen-
       schaft; Bd. 223)

893.   Hinds, Carolyn Myers. "Albee's The American Dream." Ex-
       plicator, 30 (October 1971), Item 17.

894.   Hobson, Harold. "Theatre: A View from the Bed." Sunday
       Times (London) 29 October 1961, p. 41.

895.   H[offenberg], J[oseph]. "The American Dream and The Zoo
       Story." Cue, 32 (8 June 1963), 10.

896.   Hurley, Paul J. "France and America: Versions of the Ab-
       surd." College English, 26 (May 1965), 634-640.

897.   Kali. "The American Dream and Bartleby." Variety, 15
        February 1961, p. 72.

898.   Kenn. "The American Dream." Variety, 5 June 1963, p.
        61.

899.   Keown, Eric. "At the Play." Punch, 241 (1 November 1961),
        657.

900.   Kerr, Walter. "First Night Report: The American Dream."
        New York Herald Tribune, 25 January 1961, p. 12.

901.   Knickerbocker, Paine. "The American Dream." San Francisco
        Chronicle, 24 November 1967, p. 52.

902.   Lannon, William W. "The Rise and Rationale of Post World
        War II American Confessional Theatre." Connecticut Review,
        8 (1975), 73-81.

903.   Levin, Bernard. "A Sharp Eye Stays Open as Albee Dreams."
        Daily Express (London), 25 October 1961.

904.   Livingston, Bill. "Play by Albee Attacks Modern American
        Life." Morning Advocate (Baton Rouge), 22 October 1961,
        Sec. E, p. 2.

905.   Maday, Greg. "The American Dream; The Death of Bessie
        Smith." Griffin (Canisius College, Buffalo, N.Y.), 20 Septem-
        ber 1968, p. 5.

906.   Marowitz, Charles. "Theatre Abroad: Albee Makes the
        English Scene." Village Voice, 9 November 1961, pp. 13-14.
            Reprinted in his Confessions of a Counterfeit Critic; a
        London Theatre Notebook 1958-1971, pp. 52-54. London:
        Methuen, 1973.

907.   _____. "Theatre: Dream and Zoo." Village Voice, 13
        September 1962, p. 11.

908.   McClain, John. "Off-Broadway: York Double-Header Wins a
        Split Decision." New York Journal-American, 25 January 1961,
        p. 20.

909.   Meehan, Thomas. "The American Dream." Villager (New
        York), 9 February 1961, p. 12.

910.   Miller, Jordan Y. "Myth and the American Dream: O'Neill
        to Albee." Modern Drama, 7 (September 1964), 190-198.

911.   Moore, Don D. "Albee's The American Dream." Explicator,
        30 (January 1972), Item 44.

912. Morgenstern, Joseph. "Theater News: American Dream to Start Rehearsal and Open Dec. 27." New York Herald Tribune, 28 November 1960, p. 10.

913. [Morrison], Hobe. "Death of Bessie Smith and The American Dream." Variety, 9 October 1968, p. 64.

914. Muller, Robert. "Death Blasts a Dream." Daily Mail (London), 26 October 1961, p. 3.

915. [Myers, Harold]. "The American Dream and The Death of Bessie Smith." Variety, 8 November 1961, p. 72. (signed "Myro")

916. Nadel, Norman. "Theater: 2 Albee Plays Ending Run." New York World-Telegram and Sun, 11 December 1961, p. 18.

917. _____. "Theater: Albee Pair Revived at the Cherry Lane." New York World-Telegram and Sun, 5 September 1962, p. 31.

918. Nathan, David. "Theatre: The Long and Short of It." Daily Herald (London), 25 October 1961, p. 5.

919. Newmark, Judy J. "'Albee Directs Albee' at Edison Theater." St. Louis Post-Dispatch, 6 April 1979, p. 2D.

920. Oakes, Philip. "Radio: Never Never Land." Observer (London), 13 May 1962, p. 25.

921. Oppenheimer, George. "An Empty Package." Newsday (Garden City, N.Y.), 1 February 1961, p. 9C.

922. Popkin, Henry. "Theatre Chronicle." Sewanee Review, 69 (Spring 1961), 333-345.

923. Potter, Christopher. "Four Plays Tickle Albee Fans." Michigan Daily (University of Michigan, Ann Arbor), 3 April 1979, p. 7.

924. Powers, Dennis. "New Albee Play Mourns the Death of a Dream." Oakland (Calif.) Tribune, 24 September 1961, p. 4-EL.

925. Pryce-Jones, Alan. "Alan Pryce-Jones at the Theatre." Theatre Arts, 45 (March 1961), 9-10, 68-70.

926. Radcliffe, E. B. "Playhouse Sets Sail with Real Thriller." Cincinnati Enquirer, 4 May 1966, p. 24.

927. Reinert, Otto. Drama; an Introductory Anthology, pp. 866-871. Alternate edition. Boston: Little, Brown, 1964.

928. Reuben, Elaine. "Skill but No Depth in ACT's Albee Plays."
Palo Alto (Calif.) Times, 23 November 1967, p. 33.

929. [Review of The American Dream] Booklist and Subscription
Books Bulletin, 58 (15 November 1961), 186.

930. Rissover, Fredric. "Beat Poetry, The American Dream, and the
Alienation Effect." Speech Teacher, 20 (January 1971), 36-43.

931. Roberts, Peter. "New Plays: The American Dream and The
Death of Bessie Smith." Plays and Players, 9 (December 1961),
14.

932. Rubin, Don. "Albee's Dream and a Dull Box." New Haven
(Conn.) Register, 6 October 1968, Sec. 4, p. 3.

933. Schneider, Alan. "The Human Scale." In The Off-Broadway
Experience, ed by Howard Greenberger, pp. 63-79. Englewood
Cliffs, N.J.: Prentice-Hall, 1971.

934. Shearhouse, Chris. "American Dream Is Hilarious, Hectic."
New Orleans States-Item, 22 March 1969, p. 7.

935. Shere, Charles. "Albee One-Acts Kick Off at Marines' Memo-
rial." Oakland (Calif.) Tribune, 26 October 1978, p. 27.

936. Showell, Philip S. "Sparks, No Fire; 2-in-1 Show Just
Misses." Newark Evening News, 25 January 1961, p. 54.

937. Shrapnel, Norman. "Last Night at the Theatre: The American Dream and The Death of Bessie Smith." Guardian (Manchester), 25 October 1961, p. 9.

938. Shulman, Milton. "When Screaming Seems the Only Way Out...."
Evening Standard (London), 25 October 1961.

939. Siegel, Paul N. "The Drama and the Thwarted American
Dream." Lock Haven Review, No. 7 (1965), 52-62.

940. Smith, Cecil. "American Dream Presented." Los Angeles
Times, 23 November 1967, Sec. 4, p. 17.

941. S[mith], M[ichael]. "Theatre: The Absurd (5,6)." Village
Voice, 8 March 1962, p. 12.

942. Smith, Michael. "Theatre: Two by Albee." Village Voice,
6 June 1963, p. 13.

943. Stevens, Dale. "Scripts Fail to Overcome Handicaps at Playhouse." Cincinnati Post and Times-Star, 29 April 1966, p. 21.

944. "Sydney Offering a Lunch Theater." New York Times, 20
     October 1963, p. 72.

945. Tallmer, Jerry. "Theatre: The American Dream." Village
     Voice, 2 February 1961, p. 11.

946. Taubman, Howard. "The Theatre: Albee's The American
     Dream." New York Times, 25 January 1961, p. 28.

947. Taylor, Joseph. "The American Dream Shapes Up."
     Providence (R.I.) Journal, 31 May 1964, p. W-15.

948. Trewin, J. C. "The World of the Theatre." Illustrated Lon-
     don News, 239 (11 November 1961), 836.

949. "Two by Albee." New York Guide and Theatre Magazine, 3
     (July 1961), 12-13.

950. Tynan, Kenneth. "At the Theatre: Echoes of Manhattan."
     Observer (London), 29 October 1961, p. 27.

951. "The Un-Angry." Time, 77 (3 February 1961), 53, 55.

952. "Vogue of the Double Bill in the Paris Theatre." Times
     (London), 31 December 1966, p. 5.

953. Watts, Richard. "Two on the Aisle: Another Striking Play
     by Albee." New York Post, 25 January 1961, p. 51.

954. Wax, Mel. "Sad, Wild Humor in Albee Plays." San Francisco
     Chronicle, 31 January 1963, p. 33.

955. Way, Brian. "Albee and the Absurd: The American Dream
     and The Zoo Story." In American Theatre, ed. by John R.
     Brown and Bernard Harris, pp. 189-207. New York: St.
     Martin's, 1967. (Stratford-upon-Avon Studies; 10)
        Reprinted in Edward Albee: A Collection of Critical Essays,
     ed. by C. W. E. Bigsby, pp. 26-44. Englewood Cliffs, N.J.:
     Prentice-Hall, 1975.

956. Weil, Herbert S. "Comic Structure and Tonal Manipulation in
     Shakespeare and Some Modern Plays." Shakespeare Survey, 22
     (1969), 27-33.

957. Weiner, Bernard. "'Albee Directs Albee': Playwright at the
     Helm." San Francisco Chronicle, 26 October 1978, p. 56.

958. "Well of Bitter Laughter." Times (London), 25 October 1961,
     p. 13.

959. Worsley, T[homas] C. "A Double Bill." Financial Times (Lon-
     don), 25 October 1961, p. 20.

THE BALLAD OF THE SAD CAFE

960. "Albee's Story." Critical Digest, 15 (4 November 1963),
      p. [3].

961. Anderson, Stan. "Ballad of a Sad Cafe Uneven. Cleveland
      (Ohio) Press, 21 October 1965, p. F-7.

962. "Ballad of the Sad Café." Times Literary Supplement, 6
      January 1966, p. 13.

963. Barter, Christie. "Playwright and Play: The Ballad of
      Edward Albee." Cue, 32 (26 October 1963), 11.

964. Bellamy, Peter. "Sad Cafe Here Beats Broadway." Cleveland
      (Ohio) Plain Dealer, 21 October 1965, p. 54.

965   Bigsby, C. W. E. "Edward Albee's Georgia Ballad."
      Twentieth Century Literature, 13 (January 1968), 229-236.

966. Billington, Michael. "Ballad of the Sad Café." Times (Lon-
      don), 10 March 1971, p. 11.

967. Bolton, Whitney. "Albee Turns Ballad of the Sad Cafe into
      Intense Experience." Morning Telegraph (New York), 1
      November 1963.

968. Brustein, Robert. "The Playwright as Impersonator." New
      Republic, 149 (16 November 1963), 28-29.
           Reprinted in his Seasons of Discontent: Dramatic Opinions
      1959-1965, pp. 155-158. New York: Simon and Schuster,
      1965.

969. Chapman, John. "Albee Recreates a Story: Brings McCullers'
      Ballad of Sad Cafe to Vibrant Life." Daily News (New York),
      10 November 1963, Sec. 2, p. 3.

970. _____. "Albee's Ballad of the Sad Cafe Beautiful, Exciting,
      Enthralling." Daily News (New York), 31 October 1963, p. 66.
           Reprinted in New York Theatre Critics' Reviews, 24 (1963),
      214.

971. Clurman, Harold. "Theatre." Nation, 197 (23 November
      1963), 353-354.

972. Cooke, Richard P. "The Theater: Mystery of Attachment."
      Wall Street Journal, 1 November 1963, p. 12.

973. Cotter, Jerry. "The New Plays: The Ballad of the Sad Café."
      Sign, 43 (January 1964), 30-31.

974. [Digest of New York newspaper reviews of The Ballad of the Sad Café] Critical Digest, 15 (4 November 1963), p. [2].

975. Dreele, W. H. von. "Theater: A Master Carpenter." National Review, 16 (14 January 1964), 34-35.

976. "Edward Albee Dramatizes Carson McCullers." Times (London), 25 November 1963, p. 15.

977. Gassner, John. "Broadway in Review." Educational Theatre Journal, 16 (March 1964), 70-79.
         Reprinted partially in his Dramatic Soundings; Evaluations and Retractions Culled from 30 Years of Dramatic Criticism, pp. 599-600. New York: Crown, 1968.

978. Gilman, Richard. "Albee's Sad Ballad." Commonweal, 79 (22 November 1963), 256-257.

979. Gottfried, Martin. "Theatre: The Ballad of the Sad Cafe." Women's Wear Daily, 31 October 1963, p. 28.
         Reprinted in his Opening Nights; Theater Criticism of the Sixties, pp. 49-51. New York: Putnam, 1969.

980. Hall, John. Review of The Ballad of the Sad Café. Books and Bookmen, 11 (November 1965), 42.

981. Hewes, Henry. "Broadway Postscript: Dismemberment of the Wedding." Saturday Review, 46 (16 November 1963), 54.

982. _____. "The Season in New York." In his The Best Plays of 1963-1964, pp. 3-21. New York: Dodd, Mead, 1964.

983. Hipp, Edward Sothern. "Heady Drama in Sad Cafe." Newark Evening News, 31 October 1963, p. 50.

984. Kerr, Walter. "Kerr's Critique: Ballad of the Sad Cafe." New York Herald Tribune, 31 October 1963, p. 13.
         Reprinted in New York Theatre Critics' Reviews, 24 (1963), 212-213.

985. _____. "Theater: The Barrier of The Sad Cafe." New York Herald Tribune, 17 November 1963, magazine sec., p. 31.

986. Klein, Alvin. "The Ballad of the Sad Cafe at WPA Theatre." New York Theatre Review, 2 (January 1978), 46.

987. Kostelanetz, Richard. "Albee's Sad Cafe." Swanee Review, 72 (October/December 1964), 724-726.

988. _____. "Cafe Albees Sad." In his Recyclings, a Literary Autobiography, Volume One: 1959-67, p. 29. Brooklyn, N.Y.: Assembling Press, 1974.

989. Lahr, John. "The Adaptable Mr. Albee." <u>Evergreen Review</u>,
      12 (May 1968), 37-39, 82, 84-87.
            Reprinted in his <u>Up Against the Fourth Wall: Essays on</u>
      <u>Modern Theater</u>, p. 18-34. New York: Grove Press, 1970.
            Reprinted in his <u>Acting Out America; Essays on Modern</u>
      <u>Theatre</u>, pp. 28-41. Harmondsworth, Eng.: Penguin, 1972.

990. Lask, Thomas. "Edward Albee at Ease." <u>New York Times</u>,
      27 October 1963, Sec. 2, pp. 1, 3.

991. Lewis, Theophilus. "Theatre: <u>The Ballad of the Sad Café</u>."
      <u>America</u>, 110 (4 January 1964), 26.

992. "Lonesome Lovers." <u>Time</u>, 82 (8 November 1963), 67.

993. Maddocks, Melvin. "New Plays on the Boards: <u>Ballad of the</u>
      <u>Sad Café</u>." <u>Christian Science Monitor</u>, 2 November 1963, p.
      14.

994. Maund, Rupert. "Albee New to England." <u>Times</u> (London),
      12 May 1969, p. 15.

995. McCarten, John. "The Theatre: Tormented Trio." <u>New</u>
      <u>Yorker</u>, 39 (9 November 1963), 95.

996. McClain, John. "Albee's <u>Ballad</u> Sings Rugged Drama of Love."
      <u>New York Journal-American</u>, 31 October 1963, p. 17.
            Reprinted in <u>New York Theatre Critics' Reviews</u>, 24
      (1963), 213.

997. _____. "<u>Sad Cafe</u> Revisited." <u>New York Journal-American</u>,
      10 November 1963, pp. 12S, 15S.

998. Miller, Jonathan. "On Stage: A Plausible Forgery." <u>New</u>
      <u>Leader</u>, 46 (25 November 1963), 27-28.

999. Mootz, William. "<u>Sad Cafe</u> Generates a Hypnotic Power."
      <u>Courier-Journal</u> (Louisville, Ky.), 14 March 1975, p. A-25.

1000. Morehouse, Ward. "First Nighter: Albee's <u>Ballad</u> Forceful."
      <u>Long Island Press</u> (Jamaica, N.Y.), 31 October 1963, p. 22.

1001. Morse, Ben. "Three Ballads." <u>Players Magazine</u>, 40 (Feb-
      ruary 1964), 138.

1002. Nadel, Norman. "<u>Ballad of Sad Cafe</u> Paints Poignant Tale of
      Loneliness." <u>New York World-Telegram and Sun</u>, 31 October
      1963, p. 22.
            Reprinted in <u>New York Theatre Critics' Reviews</u>, 24 (1963),
      215-216.

1003.   O'Gorman, Ned. "Uses of the Stage." Jubilee, 11 (January 1964), 55-56.

1004.   Oppenheimer, George. "Ballad of the Sad Cafe." Newsday (Garden City, N.Y.), 31 October 1963, p. 2-C.

1005.   [Review of The Ballad of the Sad Café] Choice, 1 (May 1964), 103.

1006.   Rutenberg, Michael E. "The Ballad of the Sad Café." Excerpted from his Edward Albee: Playwright in Protest (New York: Drama Book Specialists, 1969) in Edward Albee: A Collection of Critical Essays, ed. by C. W. E. Bigsby, pp. 89-98. Englewood Cliffs, N.J.: Prentice-Hall, 1975.

1007.   S., E. "Brighton: The Ballad of the Sad Café." Sunday Telegraph (London), 9 May 1979, p. 15.

1008.   Shorter, Eric. "Plays in Performance: Regions." Drama; the Quarterly Theatre Review, No. 94 (Autumn 1969), 36.

1009.   _____. "Plays in Performance: Regions." Drama; the Quarterly Theatre Review, No. 101 (Summer 1971), 37.

1010.   _____. "Regions." Drama; the Quarterly Theatre Review, No. 133 (Summer 1979), 64-65.

1011.   Simon, John. "Theatre Chronicle." Hudson Review, 17 (Spring 1964), 79-89.
          Reprinted in his Uneasy Stages: A Chronicle of the New York Theater, 1963-1973, pp. 32-35. New York: Random House, 1975.

1012.   Smith, Michael. "Albee's McCullers." Village Voice, 7 November 1963, p. 14.

1013.   Sontag, Susan. "Going to Theater." Partisan Review, 31 (Winter 1964), 95-102.

1014.   Taubman, Howard. "Nature of Love." New York Times, 10 November 1963, Sec. 2, p. 1.

1015.   _____. "Theater: The Ballad of the Sad Cafe." New York Times, 31 October 1963, p. 27.
          Reprinted in New York Theatre Critics' Reviews, 24 (1963), 214-215.

1016.   "Too Too Solid Fresh." Newsweek, 62 (11 November 1963), 76.

1017.   Ulanov, Barry. "Broadway: Brecht and Albee." Catholic World, 198 (January 1964), 263-264.

1018. Watts, Richard. "Two on the Aisle: Albee Adapts Carson
       McCullers." New York Post, 31 October 1963, p. 22.
            Reprinted in New York Theatre Critics' Reviews, 24
       (1963), 212.

1019. Winchell, Walter. "Broadway on-the-Aisle." New York
       Journal-American, 10 November 1963, p. 17L.

1020. Woolsey, F. W. "Actors Theatre Players Hit Notes on Key in
       Ballad of the Sad Cafe." Louisville (Ky.) Times, 14 March
       1975, p. B-12.

1021. Wyatt, Euphemia Van Rensselaer. "Theater: A Bleak
       Season." Lamp, 62 (January 1964), 32.

                BARTLEBY (See Bartleby in the index.)

       BOX AND QUOTATIONS FROM CHAIRMAN MAO TSE-TUNG

1022. "Albee Avoids Appraisal of His New Play Here." Buffalo
       Courier-Express, 6 March 1968, p. 37.

1023. "Albee Play Has Glittering Opening Night Here." Buffalo
       Courier-Express, 7 March 1968, p. 15.

1024. Amata, Carmie. "Edward Albee's Box-Mao-Box." Fine Arts
       (Cleveland, Ohio), 14 (18 March 1968), 5-7.

1025. Auchincloss, Louis S. "'Doctrinaire.'" [Letter] New York
       Times, 13 October 1968, Sec. 2, p. 8.

1026. Barnes, Clive. "Theater: Albee's Adventurous Plays."
       New York Times, 1 October 1968, p. 39.
            Reprinted in New York Theatre Critics' Reviews, 29
       (1968), 228.

1027. _____. "Theater: Edward Albee Takes Adventurous Step."
       New York Times, 8 March 1968, p. 48.

1028. Bigsby, C. W. E. "Box and Quotations from Chairman Mao
       Tse-Tung: Albee's Diptych." In his Edward Albee: A
       Collection of Critical Essays, pp. 151-164. Englewood Cliffs,
       N.J.: Prentice-Hall, 1975.

1029. Bolton, Whitney. "Short Plays by Albee Near Saturation
       Point." Morning Telegraph (New York), 17 October 1968,
       pp. 3, 8.

1030. Brennan, James. "Albee's Answers Leave Some Confused on
       Drama." Magnificat (Buffalo, N.Y.), 21 March 1968, p. 17.

1031. Bunce, Alan N. "Albee's Box-Mao-Box in Première at Buf-
      falo." Christian Science Monitor, 11 March 1968, p. 6.

1032. Callaghan, Barry. "Albee's Box-Mao-Box Is Intellectual but
      Tedious." Telegram (Toronto), 9 March 1968, p. 27.

1033. Carr, Jay. "Albee Sets Sail on Chartless Sea." Detroit
      News, 19 September 1968, Sec. E, pp. 5, 9.

1034. _____. "On the Aisle: Critic, Readers Argue Albee's
      Intent." Detroit News, 13 October 1968, Sec. E, pp. 5-6.

1035. Chapman, John. "Albee's Box-Mao-Box Built with Monologues."
      Daily News (New York), 1 October 1968, p. 50.
         Reprinted in New York Theatre Critics' Reviews, 29
      (1968), 228-229.

1036. _____. "Well, the Theater's Been Different Lately, Any-
      Way." Daily News (New York), 6 October 1968, Sec. 2,
      p. 3.

1037. Clurman, Harold. "Theatre." Nation, 206 (25 March 1968),
      420.

1038. Cohen, Nathan. "'I Would Have Pleased the Maharashi' at
      Premiere of Albee's Box-Mao-Box." Toronto Daily Star, 7
      March 1968, Sec. 2, p. 22.

1039. Cohn, Ruby. "Albee's Box and Ours." Modern Drama, 14
      (September 1971), 137-143.

1040. Coleman, A. D. "Theatre Afield: Buffalo Festival."
      Village Voice, 21 March 1968, pp. 40, 53.

1041. Cook, Bruce. "Box-Mao-Box: Parts for Do-It-Yourself
      Drama." National Observer, 7 October 1968, p. 22.

1042. Cooke, Richard P. "The Theater: Musical, Albee Style."
      Wall Street Journal, 2 October 1968, p. 18.
         Reprinted in New York Theatre Critics' Reviews, 29
      (1968), 229-230.

1043. "Dead Space." Time, 92 (11 October 1968), 73.

1044. [Digest of New York newspaper reviews of Box and Quotations
      from Chairman Mao Tse-tung] Critical Digest, 20 (7 October
      1968), p. [2].

1045. Doran, Terry. "Repertory Moves On: Critical Look Back."
      Buffalo Evening News, 21 September 1968, Sec. B, p. 9.

1046. Gill, Brendan. "The Theatre: Words Are the Only Certain
       Good." New Yorker, 44 (12 October 1968), 103-106.

1047. Gottfried, Martin. "Theatre: Albee's Box-Mao-Box."
       Women's Wear Daily, 11 March 1968, p. 24.
            Reprinted in his Opening Nights; Theater Criticism of the
       Sixties, pp. 57-59. New York: Putnam, 1969.

1048. _____. "Theatre: Box and Mao." Women's Wear Daily,
       1 October 1968, p. 32.
            Reprinted in New York Theatre Critics' Reviews, 29
       (1968), 230.

1049. Gussow, Mel. "Playwrights Unit Lifts Curtain on Success."
       New York Times, 4 February 1970, p. 37.

1050. Harris, Leonard. Review of Box and Quotations from Chair-
       man Mao, WCBS television, New York, 30 September 1968.
            Reprinted in New York Theatre Critics' Reviews, 29
       (1968), 231.

1051. Hewes, Henry. "The Theater." Saturday Review, 51 (19
       October 1968), 28.

1052. _____. "The Theater: Women Overbored." Saturday
       Review, 51 (23 March 1968), 34.

1053. Hilary, Jerome C. "Albee's Plays Offers [sic] Audience
       Disturbing View of Modern Life." Magnificat (Buffalo, N.Y.),
       26 September 1968, p. 15.

1054. Hopkins, Anthony. "Conventional Albee: Box and Chairman
       Mao." Modern Drama, 16 (September 1973), 141-147.

1055. James. "Box. Mao. Box." Variety, 20 March 1968, p. 72.

1056. Jefferys, Allan. Review of Box-Mao-Box. WABC television,
       New York, 30 September 1968.
            Reprinted in New York Theatre Critics' Reviews, 29
       (1968), 231.

1057. J[ohnson], G[reer]. "Box/Quotations from Chairman Mao
       Tse-tung." Cue, 37 (12 October 1968), 10.

1058. Kerensky, Oleg. "An Anti-Bayreuth Tristan by Menotti."
       Times (London), 10 July 1968, p. 8.

1059. Kerr, Walter. "Mao--But What Message?" New York Times,
       17 March 1968, Sec. 2, pp. 1, 3.

1060. _____. "Non-Sense and Nonsense." New York Times, 13

October 1968, Sec. 2, p. 5.
Reprinted in New York Theatre Critics' Reviews, 29 (1968), 213-214.

1061. Killingsworth, Kay. "Menotti Not a 'Message' Boy." Variety, 24 July 1968, pp. 27-28.

1062. K[raus], T[ed] M. "Pros & Cons." Critical Digest, 20 (7 October 1968), p. [4]. (signed "TMK")

1063. K[roll], J[ack]. "Busted Box." Newsweek, 72 (14 October 1968), 117.

1064. Kroll, Jack. "Inside the Cube." Newsweek, 71 (18 March 1968), 109-110.

1065. Mattimore, Daniel P. "Albee's Box-Mao-Box Is 'Unsuccessful Experiment.'" Magnificat (Buffalo, N.Y.), 14 March 1968, p. 10.

1066. Mayberry, Robert. "Dissonance in a Chinese Box: Edward Albee's Box and Quotations from Chairman Mao Tse-tung." In Edward Albee: Planned Wilderness; Interview, Essays, and Bibliography, ed. by Patricia De La Fuente, pp. 70-85. Edinburg, Tex.: School of Humanities, Pan American University, 1980. (Living Author Series; no. 3)

1067. Morgan, Al. "Box, Boxer, Boxed." New York, 1 (21 October 1968), 43-44.

1068. [Morrison], Hobe. "Box and Quotations from Chairman Mao Tse-Tung." Variety, 2 October 1968, pp. 64, 67.

1069. Mullin, Donald. "The 'Decline of the West' as Reflected in Three Modern Plays." Educational Theatre Journal, 28 (October 1976), 363-375.

1070. "Pay Weekly Salary for Ruth White Gab." Variety, 9 October 1968, p. 63.

1071. Popkin, Henry. "Regional Theatres Keep Broadway Interested." Times (London), 25 March 1968, p. 6.

1072. Probst, Leonard. Review of Box-Mao-Box. WNBC television, New York, 30 September 1968.
Reprinted in New York Theatre Critics' Reviews, 29 (1968), 231.

1073. Raidy, William A. "First Nighter: What's Albee Up to Now?" Long Island Press (Jamaica, N.Y.), 1 October 1968, p. 10.

1074. Rand, Calvin. "Albee's Musical Box-Mao-Box." Humanist,
      29 (January/February 1969), 27.

1075. [Review of Box and Quotations from Chairman Mao Tse-tung;
      Two Inter-Related Plays] Booklist and Subscription Books
      Bulletin, 65 (1 July 1969), 1202.

1076. [Review of Box and Quotations from Chairman Mao Tse-tung;
      Two Inter-Related Plays] Publishers Weekly, 195 (24 Feb-
      ruary 1969), 60.

1077. Sandoe, James. Review of Box and Quotations from Chairman
      Mao Tse-tung; Two Inter-Related Plays. Library Journal, 94
      (July 1969), 2635.

1078. Simon, John. "Theatre Chronicle." Hudson Review, 21 (Win-
      ter 1968/69), 703-712.

1079. _____. Uneasy Stages: A Chronicle of the New York
      Theater, 1963-1973, pp. 157-160. New York: Random House,
      1975.

1080. Smith, Ardis. "Studio Arena: Albee's Box-Mao-Box: Beauti-
      ful Poetic Fugue." Buffalo Evening News, 7 March 1968,
      Sec. 1, p. 18.

1081. _____. "Women in Albee's Play Box-Mao-Box: They Mean
      The World to Some People." Buffalo Evening News, 24
      February 1968, Sec. B, p. 9.

1082. Sokolsky, Bob. "Box Premiere Shows Talent, Few Flaws."
      Buffalo Courier-Express, 11 March 1968, p. 20.

1083. _____. "Review: Box. Mao. Box." Buffalo Courier-
      Express, 7 March 1968, p. 20.

1084. Steinfirst, Donald. "Buffalo Festival Stunning Show."
      Pittsburgh Post-Gazette, 15 March 1968, p. 6.

1085. Villano, Louis. "Albee Essays New Stage Form in Box."
      Niagara Falls (N.Y.) Gazette, 10 March 1968, p. 108.

1086. "Voices from the Cube." Times Literary Supplement, No.
      3565 (25 June 1970), 687.

1087. Washburn, Martin. "Theatre Uptown: Chic of Cliche."
      Village Voice, 10 October 1968, p. 47.

1088. Watts, Richard. "Two on the Aisle: Contrasting Theater
      Movements." New York Post, 19 October 1968, p. 20.

1089. _____. "Two on the Aisle: Edward Albee's New Experi-
      ment." New York Post, 1 October 1968, p. 24.
      Reprinted in New York Theatre Critics' Reviews, 29
      (1968), 229.

1090. Weales, Gerald. "Box Seat." Commonweal, 89 (25 October
      1968), 120, 122.

1091. Weaver, Neal. "Box and Quotations from Chairman Mao Tse-
      Tung." After Dark, 1 (November 1968), 59.

1092. West, Anthony. "Box and Quotations from Chairman Mao
      Tse-Tung, 'Mud Slide.'" Vogue, 152 (15 November 1968),
      92.

1093. Whittaker, Herbert. "Albee's Box-Mao-Box Is Largely Inter-
      esting." Globe and Mail (Toronto), 8 March 1968, p. 10.

BREAKFAST AT TIFFANY'S (HOLLY GOLIGHTLY)

1094. Funke, Lewis. "News of the Rialto: Why Albee?" New
      York Times, 27 November 1966, Sec. 2, p. 5.

1095. _____. "The Rialto: Why Holly Went Badly." New York
      Times, 25 December 1966, Sec. 2, pp. 1, 10.

1096. Harris, Radie. "On the Town: Albee to Raise His Voice--In
      Song--Over Tiffany." Newsday (Garden City, N.Y.), 23
      December 1966, p. 2-A.

1097. Kelly, Kevin. "Calling Dr. Albee: Holly Under Scalpel."
      Boston Globe, 20 November 1966, pp. A-11, A-17.

1098. Leonard, William Torbert. "Holly Golightly (a/k/a Breakfast
      at Tiffany's). In his Broadway Bound: A Guide to Shows
      That Died Aborning, pp. 206-210. Metuchen, N.J.:
      Scarecrow Press, 1983.

1099. Salmaggi, [Robert]. "Holly Calls Albee for 'Full Rewrite.'"
      World-Journal-Tribune (New York), 14 November 1966, p. 20.

1100. Sullivan, Dan. "Ill-Fated Breakfast at Tiffany's." New York
      Times, 15 December 1966, p. 60.

1101. Zolotow, Sam. "Albee Rewriting Holly." New York Times, 14
      November 1966, p. 52.   •

1102. _____. "Burrows Leaves Breakfast Job." New York Times,
      24 November 1966, p. 64.

1103. _____. "Merrick Closes 'Boring' Musical." New York Times, 15 December 1966, p. 60.

COUNTING THE WAYS

1104. Adler, Thomas P. "Theatre in Review: Counting the Ways." Educational Theatre Journal, 29 (October 1977), 407-408.

1105. "Albee's Counting the Ways Opens in London." Los Angeles Times, 10 December 1976, Sec. 4, p. 32.

1106. Barber, John. "Theatre: Disappointing Ways from Edward Albee." Daily Telegraph (London), 7 December 1976, p. 11.

1107. Barnes, Clive. "Stage: An Albee Double Bill." New York Times, 4 February 1977, Sec. C, p. 3.

1108. Billington, Michael. "Counting the Ways." Guardian (Manchester) 7 December 1976, p. 10.

1109. Boyer, Mark. "Backstage: The Eddie, Paul and Angie Show; the Principals Meet the Press." Hartford (Conn.) Advocate, 9 February 1977, p. 19. (INTERVIEW)

1110. _____. "Premier Albee: Irresistible Rhythms, Unnatural Acts." Hartford (Conn.) Advocate, 9 February 1977, pp. 19, 26.

1111. Coe, Richard L. "Counting the Ways, Counting the Seats." Washington Post, 23 February 1979, p. B3.

1112. Day, Richard. "Albee Directs Plays Adeptly; Cast Members Earn Plaudits." Bridgeport (Conn.) Post, 4 February 1977, p. 16.

1113. Eck. "Counting the Ways & Listening." Variety, 9 February 1977, p. 134.

1114. Elsom, John. "Theatre: Flatshares Limited." Listener, 96 (16 December 1976), 794-795.

1115. Esslin, Martin. "Counting the Ways." Plays and Players, 24 (February 1977), 33.

1116. Feingold, Michael. "All Fugued Up." Village Voice, 19 February 1979, p. 83.

1117. Fleckenstein, Joan. "Two Albee Plays at Hartford." Torrington (Conn.) Register, 10 February 1977, p. 9.

1118. _____. "Theatre in Review: Counting the Ways and Listening." Educational Theatre Journal, 29 (October 1977), 408-409.

1119. Glover, William. "Albee's Word Plays." Times-Picayune (New Orleans), 5 February 1977, Sec. 2, p. 2.

1120. Haas, Barbara. "Albee's Variations on a Theme." Post-Standard (Syracuse, N.Y.), 7 May 1979, p. 13.

1121. Hammerich, R[ichard] C. "Albee Stages His Own Plays." Springfield (Mass.) Union, 3 February 1977, p. 12.

1122. Johnson, Malcolm. "Albee Plays Admired, Panned." Hartford (Conn.) Courant, 20 February 1977, Sec. F, p. 2.

1123. _____. "Stage: Albee Directs Albee." Hartford (Conn.) Courant, 6 February 1977, Sec. F, p. 1.

1124. _____. "Stage: Albee Mixes Humor, Pain." Hartford (Conn.) Courant, 2 February 1977, p. 59.

1125. Kain, Laila. "Best Contemporary Plays." Springfield (Mass.) Daily News, 4 February 1977, p. 17.

1126. Kelly, Kevin. "Albee Suffers Deja Vu." Boston Globe, 10 February 1977, p. 32.

1127. Kloten, Edgar. "The Vagaries of Albee in Duplicate." West Hartford (Conn.) News, 10 February 1977, p. 4B.

1128. Kolin, Philip C. "Edward Albee's Counting the Ways: The Ways of Losing Heart." In Edward Albee; an Interview and Essays, pp. 121-140. Houston: University of St. Thomas, 1983.

1129. K[roll], J[ack]. "He and She." Newsweek, 89 (14 February 1977), 69.

1130. Levin, Bernard. "Further Lessons in How Not to Do It." Sunday Times (London), 12 December 1976, p. 35.

1131. Lewis, Peter. "Who Else But the N. T. Would Dare?" Daily Mail (London), 7 December 1976, p. 20.

1132. Minot, Stephen. "Who's Afriad of Edward Albee?" New York Times, 27 February 1977, Sec. 23, p. 17.

1133. Morley, Sheridan. "Theatre: Winning Ways." Punch, 271 (15 December 1976), 1150.

1134. "New Comedy by Albee Well Received in London." New York
      Times, 8 December 1976, Sec. 3, p. 23.

1135. Nightingale, Benedict. "'His' and 'Hers.'" New Statesman,
      92 (10 December 1976), 850.

1136. Norton, Elliot. "Albee Continues on Own Course." Boston
      Herald-American, 20 February 1977, Sec. 7, p. A31.

1137. _____. "New Albee Plays Brilliant, Flawed." Boston
      Herald-American, 12 February 1977, p. 18.

1138. Novick, Julius. "Albee Is Doing His Best." Village Voice,
      21 February 1977, p. 99.

1139. Page, Michael. Review of Counting the Ways and Listening:
      Two Plays. Library Journal, 102 (15 May 1977), 1204.

1140. Panciera, H. Victor. "Full House Welcomes Albee." Norwich
      (Conn.) Bulletin, 13 February 1977, p. 6.

1141. Pit. "Counting the Ways." Variety, 15 December 1976,
      p. 76.

1142. [Review of Counting the Ways and Listening: Two Plays]
      Booklist, 73 (1 April 1977), 1134.

1143. [Review of Counting the Ways and Listening: Two Plays]
      Choice, 14 (September 1977), 853.

1144. Ridley, Clifford A. "New, Comic Voices Assault the U.S.
      Stage." National Observer, 26 February 1977, p. 20.

1145. Rogoff, Gordon. "Theater: Albee and Mamet: The War of
      the Words." Saturday Review, 4 (2 April 1977), 36-37.

1146. Sharp, Anne. "Four Plays Tickle Albee Fans." Michigan
      Daily (University of Michigan, Ann Arbor), 3 April 1979,
      p. 7.

1147. Shulman, Milton. "Theatre." Evening Standard (London),
      7 December 1976, p. 18.

1148. Sullivan, Dan. "Stage Review: A Double Bill of Pale Albee."
      Los Angeles Times, 3 February 1977, Sec. 4, pp. 1, 13.

1149. Taylor, Markland. "Albee Explores Language, Heart and
      Mind." New Haven (Conn.) Register, 6 February 1977.

1150. Taylor, Robert. "Edward Albee's Counting the Ways Probes
      Infidelity." Oakland (Calif.) Tribune, 28 October 1978, p. 11.

1151. Thomas, Bethe. "Albee's New Plays: Wit and Disappoint-
      ment." Newington (Conn.) Town Crier, 17 February 1977,
      p. 14.

1152. Turcotte, Dick. "Stage: Listening a Good Vehicle for
      Acting." Journal Inquirer (Manchester, Conn.), 4 February
      1977, p. 25.

1153. Wardle, Irving. "Sixty-Minute, Second-Rate Doodle." Times
      (London), 7 December 1976, p. 11.

1154. Wasserman, Debbi. "Counting the Ways/Listening at the
      Hartford Stage Company." New York Theatre Review, preview
      issue (Spring/Summer 1977), 43.

1155. Watt, Douglas. "A Long Night's Journey into Albee." Daily
      News (New York), 4 February 1977, p. 27.

1156. Young, B. A. "Counting the Ways." Financial Times (Lon-
      don), 7 December 1976, p. 3.

1157. _____. "Whatever Happened to Curtain-Raisers?" Financial
      Times (London), 10 November 1976, p. 3.

THE DEATH OF BESSIE SMITH

1158. "Albee Play to Fill Own Double Bill." New York Herald
      Tribune, 26 February 1961, Sec. 4, p. 3.

1159. "Albee's Loud and Clear on Human Injustices." Medina (N.Y.)
      Journal-Register, 11 September 1968, p. 3.

1160. Aston, Frank. "Theater: York Adds Play to Albee Program."
      New York World-Telegram and Sun, 2 March 1961, p. 18.

1161. Balliett, Whitney. "Off Broadway: Empress of the Blues."
      New Yorker, 37 (11 March 1961), 114.

1162. "Bessie Wins." Berkeley Tribe, 3 (11 September 1970), 12.

1163. Bolton, Whitney. "Stage Review: New Albee Play Taut,
      Compulsive." Morning Telegraph (New York), 3 March 1961.

1164. Clurman, Harold. "Theatre." Nation, 192 (18 March 1961),
      242.
          Reprinted in his The Naked Image; Observations on the
      Modern Theatre, pp. 17-18. New York: Macmillan, 1966.
          Reprinted in his The Divine Pastime; Theatre Essays,
      pp. 111-112. New York: Macmillan, 1974.

1165. Crist, Judith. "First Night Report: The Death of Bessie Smith." New York Herald Tribune, 2 March 1961, p. 14.

1166. Daniel, Walter C. "Absurdity in The Death of Bessie Smith." CLA Journal (College Language Association), 8 (September 1964), 76–80.

1167. De Lappe, Pele. "Death of Bessie Smith Good Theater." People's World (San Francisco), 29 June 1974, p. 10.

1168. Debusscher, Gilbert. "The Death of Bessie Smith." Reprinted from his Edward Albee: Tradition and Renewal, pp. 21–30. (Brussels: American Studies Center, 1967) in Edward Albee: A Collection of Critical Essays, ed. by C. W. E. Bigsby, pp. 54–61. Englewood Cliffs, N.J.: Prentice-Hall, 1975.

1169. [Digest of New York newspaper reviews of The Death of Bessie Smith] Critical Digest, 12 (6 March 1961), p. [2].

1170. Doran, Terry. "Studio Arena: Early Plays in Albee Series Are Still Fresh, Provocative." Buffalo Evening News, 11 September 1968, Sec. 2, p. 26.

1171. Gabbard, Lucina P. "Edward Albee's Triptych on Abandonment." Twentieth Century Literature, 28 (Spring 1982), 14–33.

1172. Galano, Robert. "Two for the Road." Washington Post, 7 February 1980, p. D9.

1173. Gottfried, Martin. "Theatre: Albee Revived." Women's Wear Daily, 3 October 1968, p. 36.

1174. Grande, Luke M. "Edward Albee's Bessie Smith: Alienation/ The Color-Problem." Drama Critique, 5 (May 1962), 66–69.

1175. Hammel, Faye. "The Death of Bessie Smith." Cue, 30 (11 March 1961), 11.

1176. Jaal. "The Death of Bessie Smith." Variety, 8 March 1961, p. 72.

1177. Lukas, Mary. "Off Broadway: The Death of Bessie Smith and The American Dream." Catholic World, 193 (August 1961), 335–336.

1178. McClain, John. "Off Broadway: Exciting Night in the Theatre." New York Journal-American, 2 March 1961, p. 14.

1179. Pryce-Jones, Alan. "Alan Pryce-Jones at the Theatre." Theatre Arts, 45 (May 1961), 54–58, 76.

1180. Rosenfeld, Megan. "Bessie Smith: Unsatisfying."
       Washington Post, 23 March 1972, Sec. H, p. 13.

1181. Scutt, Ed. "Review: Death of Bessie Smith Is Timely Pro-
       duction." Lockport (N.Y.) Union-Sun and Journal, 12
       September 1968, p. 24.

1182. Siskind, Jacob. "At Centaur Theatre: Two Views of the
       Negro in America." Gazette (Montreal), 15 March 1971,
       p. 14.

1183. Sokolsky, Bob. "Review: Edward Albee Plays." Buffalo
       Courier-Express, 11 September 1968, p. 6.

1184. Sullivan, Dan. "Theater: Albee's Bessie Smith and Dream
       Revived." New York Times, 3 October 1968, p. 55.

1185. T[allmer], J[erry]. "Theatre: The Death of Bessie Smith."
       Village Voice, 9 March 1961, p. 9.

1186. Taubman, Howard. "Theatre: Intense Hour." New York
       Times, 2 March 1961, p. 19.

1187. "Taut Rhythms of Albee." Times (London), 29 June 1965,
       p. 8.

1188. Watts, Richard. "Two on the Aisle: Again Considering
       Edward Albee." New York Post, 12 March 1961, p. 13.

1189. _____. "Two on the Aisle: An Arresting Early Play by
       Albee." New York Post, 2 March 1961, p. 11.

1190- Witherington, Paul. "Language of Movement in Albee's The
  94. Death of Bessie Smith." Twentieth Century Literature, 13
       (July 1967), 84-88.

A DELICATE BALANCE

1195. "Albee Hour." Critical Digest, 18 (26 September 1966),
       p. [3].

1196. "Albee's A Delicate Balance Praised in Paris Opening." New
       York Times, 28 October 1967, p. 35.

1197. Arnold, Gary. "An Indelicate Imbalance of Intangible Angst
       and Dilemma." Washington Post, 10 December 1973, Sec. B,
       p. 18 (FILM)

1198. Bachman, Ch. R. "Albee's A Delicate Balance: Parable as
       Nightmare." Revue des langues vivantes, 38 (November/De-
       cember 1972), 619-630.

1199. Bane, Michael. "Asolo Maintains Delicate Balance." Clear-
      water (Fla.) Sun, 8 April 1974, p. 5-C.

1200. Barber, John. "First Night: Stage Dominated by Peggy
      Ashcroft." Daily Telegraph (London), 15 January 1969,
      p. 17.

1201. Bardacke, Frances. "Theatre: Mission's Move; Albee at the
      Carter; Sandy Dennis in Long Beach; a SDSU Original."
      San Diego Magazine, 31 (April 1979), 46, 48, 53-54.

1202. Barker, Felix. "A House Full of Patients ... But There's
      No Cure." Evening News (London), 15 January 1969, p. 11.

1203. Barron, Karl. "ACT Returns with a Weighty Rerun of
      Delicate Balance." San Rafael (Calif.) Independent-Journal,
      22 January 1969, p. 22.

1204. Bayer, Jerome. "A Critic's Job." [Letter] New York
      Times, 9 October 1966, Sec. 2, p. 11.

1205. Bermel, Albert. "On Stage: Mud in the Plumbing." New
      Leader, 49 (10 October 1966), 28-29.

1206. Bierhaus, E. G., Jr. "Strangers in a Room; A Delicate
      Balance Revisited." Modern Drama, 17 (June 1974), 199-
      206.

1207. Bigsby, C. W. E. "The Strategy of Madness: An Analysis
      of Edward Albee's A Delicate Balance." Contemporary
      Literature, 9 (Spring 1968), 223-235.

1208. Boardman, Kathryn. "Good Winter Reading Is Now at Hand."
      St. Paul (Minn.) Pioneer-Press, 7 January 1968, Lively Arts
      Section, p. 25.

1209. Bolton, Whitney. "Delicate Balance Albee's Latest." Morning
      Telegraph (New York), 24 September 1966.

1210. Bonin, Jane F. "A Delicate Balance." In her Prize-Winning
      American Drama: A Bibliographical and Descriptive Guide,
      pp. 190-192. Metuchen, N.J.: Scarecrow Press, 1973.

1211. Brown, Terence. "Harmonia Discord and Stochastic Process:
      Edward Albee's A Delicate Balance." Re: Arts and Letters,
      3 (Spring 1970), 54-60.

1212. Brustein, Robert. "Albee Decorates an Old House." New
      Republic, 155 (8 October 1966), 35-36.
          Reprinted in his The Third Theatre, pp. 83-86. New
      York: Knopf, 1969.

Reprinted in Edward Albee: A Collection of Critical Essays, ed. by C. W. E. Bigsby, pp. 135-137. Englewood Cliffs, N.J.: Prentice-Hall, 1975.

1213. _____. "First Nights: New York." Plays and Players, 14 (December 1966), 52.

1214. Bryden, Ronald. "Albee's Icy Vision of Hell." Observer (London), 19 January 1969, p. 27.

1215. Bunce, Alan N. "A Delicate Balance Arrives on Broadway." Christian Science Monitor, 24 September 1966, p. 4.

1216. Cardullo, Bert. "Pinter's The Homecoming and Albee's A Delicate Balance." Explicator, 42 (Summer 1984), 54-56.

1217. Champlin, Charles. "Delicate Balance: Gall in the Family." Los Angeles Times, 7 December 1973, Sec. 4, pp. 1, 24.

1218. Chapman, John. "Albee's Play, Delicate Balance, a Shimmering Start for Season." Daily News (New York), 23 September 1966, p. 47.
     Reprinted in New York Theatre Critics' Reviews, 27 (1966), 296.

1219. _____. "Edward Albee Growing Up; Delicate Balance Has Fine Cast and Is Beautifully Written." Daily News (New York), 2 October 1966, Sec. 2, p. 3.

1220. Chernowitz, Rose M. "Psychic Drama." [Letter] New York Times, 9 October 1966, Sec. 2, pp. 10-11.

1221. Clurman, Harold. "Theatre." Nation, 203 (10 October 1966), 361-363.

1222. C[ocks], J[ay]. "Tableaux of Ice." Time, 103 (14 January 1974), 39. (FILM)

1223. Cohen, Marshall. "Theater 67." Partisan Review, 34 (Summer 1967), 436-444.

1224. Cohen, Nathan. "Albee's Newest Gives the Broadway Season a Dreary Start." Toronto Daily Star, 24 September 1966, Sec. 2, p. 1.

1225. Coleman, John. "Films." New Statesman, 91 (2 April 1976), 444-445. (FILM)

1226. Cooke, Richard P. "The Theater: Albee's Latest." Wall Street Journal, 26 September 1966, p. 18.
     Reprinted in New York Theatre Critics' Reviews, 27 (1966), 296-297.

1227. Croce, Arlene. "Theater: New-Old, Old-New, and New."
      National Review, 19 (24 January 1967), 99-100.

1228. Cross, Mary Ellen. "Albee Play Examines Human Ties."
      Anderson (Ind.) Herald, 27 December 1978, p. 22.

1229. "A Delicate Balance." Life, 61 (28 October 1966), 119.

1230. "Dialogue Takes Charge in New Albee Play." Times (London),
      10 October 1966, p. 6.

1231. [Digest of New York newspaper reviews of A Delicate Balance]
      Critical Digest, 18 (3 October 1966), p. [2].

1232. Donnelly, Tom. "Albee on the Real Thing (Theater) Versus
      a Film." Washington Post, 28 October 1973, Sec. L, pp. 1-2.
      (FILM)

1233. _____. "What Came Later: The Real Ending to Albee's
      A Delicate Balance." Washington Post, 11 December 1973,
      Sec. B, p. 11.

1234. Donovan, Phyllis S. "From an Aisle Seat: A Delicate Balance,
      Hartford Stage Company." Meriden (Conn.) Journal, 31
      October 1969, p. 7.

1235. Downer, Alan S. "The Doctor's Dilemma: Notes on the New
      York Theater, 1966-1967." Quarterly Journal of Speech, 53
      (October 1967), 213-223.

1236. Drutman, Irving. "No Journalists?" [Letter] New York
      Times, 10 September 1967, Sec. 2, p. 8.

1237. Eichelbaum, Stanley. "A Delicate Balance Vitally Staged."
      San Francisco Examiner, 29 March 1968, p. 22.

1238. Fitzgerald, John E. "Edward Albee: Growing into Great-
      ness?" Ave Maria, 105 (7 January 1967), 7-9.

1239. Fleischer, Leonard. "Season of Discontent." Congress Bi-
      Weekly, 34 (8 May 1967), 20-21.

1240. French, Philip. "The State of the Union." Plays and
      Players, 16 (March 1969), 16-19.

1241. Fumerton, M. Patricia. "Verbal Prisons: The Language of
      Albee's A Delicate Balance." English Studies in Canada, 7
      (Summer 1981), 201-211.

1242. Gardella, Kay. "Albee's Delicate Balance Opening Night
      Prospect." Daily News (New York), 6 December 1967, p. 125.

1243. Gassner, John. "Broadway in Review." Educational Theatre
       Journal, 18 (December 1966), 450-454.
           Reprinted partially in his Dramatic Soundings; Evaluations
       and Retractions Culled from 30 Years of Dramatic Criticism,
       pp. 603-607. New York: Crown, 1968.

1244. G[eagley], B. Review of film soundtrack recording of A
       Delicate Balance. Listening Post, 5 (June 1974), 24.
       (FILM)

1245. George, Kathleen. Rhythm in Drama, pp. 36-42. Pittsburgh:
       University of Pittsburgh Press, 1980.

1246. Gottfried, Martin. "Theatre: A Delicate Balance."
       Women's Wear Daily, 23 September 1966, p. 29.
           Reprinted in New York Theatre Critics' Reviews, 27
       (1966), 297.

1247. Gow, Gordon. "A Delicate Balance." Films and Filming, 22
       (March 1976), 30-31. (FILM)

1248. Green, Benny. "Cinema: Very Good, Eddie." Punch, 270
       (7 April 1976), 640. (FILM)

1249. Guarino, Ann. "Talk Trips the Delicate Balance." Daily
       News (New York), 10 December 1973, p. 54. (FILM)

1250. Gussow, Mel. "Stage: Delicate Balance Is Revived in
       Princeton." New York Times, 9 April 1983, p. 19.

1251. Hardwick, Elizabeth. "Straight Play." New York Review of
       Books, 7 (20 October 1966), 4-5.

1252. _____. "Theatre." Vogue, 143 (1 January 1964), 20.

1253. Harper, Jay. [Letter] New York Times, 9 October 1966,
       Sec. 2, p. 10.

1254. Haskell, Molly. "Film: The Long Night of the Suburban
       Soul." Village Voice, 13 December 1973, p. 93. (FILM)

1255. Hawk[ins, Robert F.] "A Delicate Balance." Variety, 19
       February 1969, pp. 70, 72.

1256. Herridge, Frances. "Albee's Balance Goes on Screen."
       New York Post, 10 December 1973, p. 45. (FILM)

1257. Hewes, Henry. "Bests of the 1966-67 Theater Season."
       Saturday Review, 50 (10 June 1967), 18-22.

1258. _____. "The Theater: The Family That Stayed Separate."
       Saturday Review, 49 (8 October 1966), 90.

1259. Hipp, Edward Sothern. "A Delicate Balance; New Albee Play
      Staged at Martin Beck." Newark Evening News, 23 September
      1966, p. 54.

1260. _____. "Stage: Albee Drama in Progress." Newark
      Evening News, 2 October 1966, Sec. 6, pp. E1, E4.

1261. Hobson, Harold. "Arts: Entertainment." Christian Science
      Monitor, 22 January 1969, p. 10.

1262. _____. "A Dazzling Parisian Cast in Delicate Balance."
      Christian Science Monitor, 6 November 1967, p. 6.

1263. _____. "Theatre: Dream Children." Sunday Times
      (London), 19 January 1969, p. 57.

1264. _____. "Theatre: In the Shadow of the Rock." Sunday
      Times (London), 26 January 1969, p. 57.

1265. Holland, Mary. "Plays." Queen, 432 (5 February 1969),
      21.

1266. Hope-Wallace, Philip. "Albee on a Collision Course."
      Manchester Guardian Weekly, 23 January 1969, p. 20.

1267. _____. "Aldwych Theatre: A Delicate Balance." Guardian
      (Manchester), 15 January 1969, p. 6.

1268. Hull, Elizabeth Anne. "A Popular Psychology Illuminates an
      'Elite' Art Medium: A Look at Albee's A Delicate Balance
      through Transactional Analysis." In Proceedings of the Sixth
      National Convention of the Popular Culture Association,
      Chicago, Ill., April 22-24, 1976, comp. by Michael T.
      Marsden, pp. 1071-1086. (Presented papers microfilmed by
      Northwest Ohio--Great Lakes Research Center) Bowling
      Green: Bowling Green State University Popular Press, 1976.

1269. Jacob, Bonnie. "Delicate Balance Tipped." Boston After
      Dark, 27 June 1972, Sec. 2, p. 14.

1270. Kahn, Carole. "Stage Performs Flawless Albee." Hartford
      (Conn.) Times, 19 October 1969, Sec. C, p. 12.

1271. Kemper, Robert Graham. "Drama: A Weekend with the
      'Can Do' Family." Christian Century, 83 (23 November 1966),
      1447.

1272. Kerr, Walter. "Only Time Really Happens to People." New
      York Times, 2 October 1966, Sec. 2, p. 1.

1273. _____. "The Theater: Albee's A Delicate Balance at the

Martin Beck." New York Times, 23 September 1966, p. 44.
Reprinted in New York Theatre Critics' Reviews, 27
(1966), 294.

1274. _____. "Theater: The Common Tongue." New York
Herald Tribune, 24 November 1963, magazine, p. 27.

1275. Kihss, Peter. "Albee Wins Pulitzer Prize; Malamud Novel Is
Chosen." New York Times, 2 May 1967, pp. 1, 40.

1276. Kingston, Jeremy. "At the Theatre." Punch, 256 (22
January 1969), 138.

1277. Kitching, Jessie. Review of A Delicate Balance. Publishers
Weekly, 190 (10 October 1966), 72-73.

1278. Klein, Alvin. "Princeton: An Abstruse Albee." New York
Times, 10 April 1983, Sec. 11, p. 18.

1279. Kloten, Edgar. "On Stage: Albee and Stage Co. Rank High."
West Hartford (Conn.) News, 23 October 1969, p. 15.

1280. _____. "On Stage: UofH, CCSC, and HOT Plays." West
Hartford (Conn.) News, 22 July 1976, p. 4-B.

1281. Knickerbocker, Paine. "An Absorbing Production of A
Delicate Balance." San Francisco Chronicle, 30 March 1968,
p. 28.

1282. Kramer, Carol. "Movies: Albee's Case Against Compromise."
Chicago Tribune, 28 October 1973, Sec. 6, p. 13. (FILM)

1283. K[raus,], T[ed] M. "Pros & Cons." Critical Digest, 18 (3
October 1966), p. [4]. (signed "TMK")

1284. Lambert, J. W. "Plays in Performance." Drama; the Quarterly Theatre Review, No. 92 (Spring 1969), 17-19.

1285. Lee, Robert C. "Albee in Paris." Drama Critique, 11
(Winter 1968), 38-39.

1286. Lewis, Peter. "Loneliness, Fear and the Delicate Balance of
Love." Daily Mail (London), 15 January 1969, p. 6.

1287. _____. "Snake in the Drawing Room." Daily Mail (London), 15 January 1969, p. 10.

1288. Lewis, Theophilus. "Theatre: A Delicate Balance." America,
115 (8 October 1966), 432-433.

1289. L[imbacher], J[ames] L. Review of A Delicate Balance

soundtrack recording. Previews, 3 (September 1974), 29.
(signed "JLL") (FILM)

1290. Liston, William T. "IRT's Delicate Balance Strong, Fully
Professional." Muncie (Ind.) Star, 24 December 1978, Sec. B,
p. 7.

1291. Lowell, Sondra. "Stage Review: A Delicate Balance at the
Cast Theater." Los Angeles Times, 16 January 1978, Sec. 4,
p. 10.

1292. Luc[chese, S]. "A Delicate Balance." Variety, 31 October
1973, p. 26. (FILM)

1293. Mallery, David. "Film." Independent School Bulletin, 33
(May 1974), 59. (FILM)

1294. Marcus, Frank. "Theatre: A Balance Disturbed." Sunday
Telegraph (London), 19 January 1969, p. 14.

1295. M[arriott], R. B. "A Delicate Balance at the Aldwych."
Stage and Television Today, No. 4579 (16 January 1969), 16.

1296. Marriott, R. B. "A Delicate Balance: Edward Albee Fresh
and Also Familiar." Stage and Television Today, No. 4580
(23 January 1969), 13.

1297. Matthews, Anne McIlhenney. "Delicate Balance Just That."
Buffalo Courier-Express, 14 February 1968, p. 39.

1298. Mattimore, Daniel P. "Bright, Sensitive Comedy Polishes
Albee's Image." Magnificat (Buffalo, N.Y.), 22 February
1968, p. 16.

1299. McCarten, John. "The Theatre: Six on a Seesaw." New
Yorker, 42 (1 October 1966), 121.

1300. McElfresh, Tom. "Brilliant, Comic, Tragic, Rueful, Protean
Albee at Playhouse." Cincinnati Enquirer, 2 February 1973,
p. 10.

1301. Meyer, Eve R. "Life Balance." [Letter] Village Voice, 6
October 1966, p. 4.

1302. Micklin, Bob. "On the Isle: Laughs in Play at Mineola
Balance Out Indelicately." Newsday (Garden City, N.Y.),
12 July 1967, p. 43-W.

1303. Miers, Virgil. "With Witchy Albee Puzzle, Center Season Is
Cut Into." Dallas Times Herald, 29 September 1967, Sec. B,
p. 8.

1304. Millar, S. "A Delicate Balance." Monthly Film Bulletin
      (British Film Institute, London), 43 (March 1976), 50–51.
      (FILM)

1305. "Montherlant Play Worth Waiting 16 Years For." Times (Lon-
      don), 3 January 1968, p. 6.

1306. [Morrison], Hobe. "A Delicate Balance." Variety, 28 Sep-
      tember 1966, p. 62.

1307. Morriss, Frank. "Show Beat." Winnipeg Tribune, 4 April
      1968, p. 23.

1308. Nadel, Norman. "Diffusion of Focus Disturbs Edward Albee's
      Delicate Balance." World-Journal-Tribune (New York), 2
      October 1966, Sec. 5, p. 6.

1309. _____. "The New Play: A Delicate Balance Lacks It."
      World-Journal-Tribune (New York), 23 September 1966, p. 28.
          Reprinted in New York Theatre Critics' Reviews, 27 (1966),
      295.

1310. Nathan, David. "Theatre: Albee Explores Hostile Land."
      Sun (London), 15 January 1969, p. 9.

1311. Neville, John. "Stage in Review: DTC Balances Albee Neatly."
      Dallas Morning News, 29 September 1967, p. 12-A.

1312. Nightingale, Benedict. "Family Friends." New Statesman, 77
      (24 January 1969), 128–129.

1313. Paolucci, Anne. "A Vision of Baal: A Delicate Balance."
      Reprinted from her From Tension to Tonic: The Plays of
      Edward Albee, pp. 105–122 (Carbondale: Southern Illinois
      University Press, 1972) in Edward Albee: A Collection of
      Critical Essays, ed. by C. W. E. Bigsby, pp. 138–150.
      Englewood Cliffs, N.J.: Prentice-Hall, 1975.

1314. P[arker], T[heodore] H. "Albee Play Brilliant at Stage Co."
      Hartford (Conn.) Courant, 18 October 1969, p. 17.

1315. Patrick, Corbin. "The Lively Arts: IRT Has Winner in
      Albee's Play, A Delicate Balance." Indianapolis Star, 18
      December 1978, p. 24.

1316. Pearre, Howard. "How to Be Graceful with Noblesse Oblige."
      Nashville (Tenn.) Banner, 2 December 1966, p. 36.

1317. Perry, Virginia I. "Disturbing Our Sense of Well-Being:
      The 'Uninvited' in A Delicate Balance." In Edward Albee:
      An Interview and Essays, pp. 55–64. Houston: University
      of St. Thomas, 1983.

1318. "Playboy After Hours: Theater." Playboy, 13 (December 1966), 34, 39.

1319. Porter, M. Gilbert. "Toby's Last Stand: The Evanescence of Commitment in A Delicate Balance." Theatre Journal, 31 (October 1979), 398-408.

1320. Post, Robert M. "Fear Itself: Edward Albee's A Delicate Balance." CLA Journal (College Language Association), 13 (December 1969), 163-171.

1321. Powell, Dilys. "Films: Spirit of the Times." Sunday Times (London), 4 April 1976, p. 36. (FILM)

1322. Prideaux, Tom. "A Cry of Loss: Dilemma Come Back!" Life, 61 (28 October 1966), 120.

1323. Rachow, Louis A. Review of A Delicate Balance. Library Journal, 92 (1 February 1967), 594.

1324. Raidy, William A. "First Nighter: Albee Play Fascinating." Long Island Press (Jamaica, N.Y.), 23 September 1966, p. 16.

1325. Reed, Rex. "No One But Hepburn Can Fill Her Shoes." Daily News (New York), 14 December 1973, p. 106. (FILM)

1326. R[eilly], C[harles] P[hillips]. "A Delicate Balance." Films in Review, 24 (December 1973), 624-625. (FILM)

1327. [Review of A Delicate Balance] Booklist and Subscription Books Bulletin, 63 (1 February 1967), 558-559.

1328. [Review of A Delicate Balance] Publishers Weekly, 192 (27 November 1967), 45.

1329. Rothstein, Irma. "On Balance." [Letter] New York Times, 10 September 1967, Sec. 2, p. 13.

1330. _____. "Subject Was Friends." [Letter] New York Times, 9 October 1966, Sec. 2, p. 11.

1331. Roud, Richard. "Successful Failure." Guardian (Manchester), 13 October 1966, p. 9.

1332. Rutenberg, Michael. "Edward Albee: Playwright in Protest." Players Magazine, 44 (October/November 1968), 28-34. Excerpted from his Edward Albee: Playwright in Protest (New York: DBS Publications, 1969).

1333. Ryan, Terry. "Albee Play Theatrically Pleasing." Palo Alto (Calif.) Times, 22 January 1969, p. 28.

1334. Sainer, Arthur. "Where Are the Producers?" Village Voice,
       16 November 1972, pp. 68, 70.

1335. Salmaggi, Robert. "Another Opening of an Albee Show."
       World-Journal-Tribune (New York), 18 September 1966,
       Sec. 5, p. 10.

1336. Sayre, Nora. "Screen: Albee's A Delicate Balance." New
       York Times, 11 December 1973, p. 52. (FILM)

1337. Schaap, Dick. "Edward Albee--Or Not to Be." World-
       Journal-Tribune (New York), 22 September 1966, p. 13.

1338. Schieber, Larry. "Studio Arena Review: Best of Season
       Delicate Balance Is Outstanding." Kensington Topics/Cheek-
       towaga Journal (West Seneca, N.Y.), 21 February 1968, p. 7.

1339. Sheed, Wilfrid. "Liquor Is Thicker." Commonweal, 85 (14
       October 1966), 55-56.
          Reprinted in his The Morning After; Selected Essays and
       Reviews, pp. 165-167. New York: Farrar, Straus &
       Giroux, 1971.

1340. Shorey, Kennth Paul. "Albee Work Memorable, Acting
       Superb, Precise." Birmingham (Ala.) News, 27 January 1976,
       p. 4. (FILM)

1341. Shuster, Alvin. "Reaction in Wrong Places Closes 3 Plays in
       Prague." New York Times, 3 February 1970, p. 5.

1342. Siegel, Jack. "Misadventure." [Letter] New York Times, 9
       October 1966, Sec. 2, p. 11.

1343. Simon, John. "How to Fall Between Stools." New York, 6
       (22 October 1973), 101. (FILM)

1344. _____. "Theatre Chronicle." Hudson Review, 19 (Winter
       1966-67), 627-636.
          Reprinted in his Uneasy Stages: A Chronicle of the New
       York Theater, 1963-1973, pp. 96-99. New York: Random
       House, 1975.

1345. "Skin Deep." Newsweek, 68 (3 October 1966), 98.

1346. Smith, Ardis. "Studio Arena: Story, Stars Combine for
       Smash of Season: A Delicate Balance." Buffalo Evening
       News, 9 February 1968, p. 14.

1347. Smith, Cecil. "Albee Play Totally Absorbing." Los Angeles
       Times, 18 May 1967, Sec. 4, pp. 1, 12.

1348. Smith, Liz. "Cosmo Goes to the Movies." Cosmopolitan, 176
      (February 1974), 24. (FILM)

1349. Smith, Michael. "Theatre Journal: A Delicate Balance."
      Village Voice, 29 September 1966, pp. 21-22.

1350. Sokolsky, Bob. "At Studio Arena: A Delicate Balance."
      Buffalo Courier-Express, 9 February 1968, p. 9.

1351. Spurling, Hilary. "Theatre: Off Balance." Spectator, 222
      (24 January 1969), 116-117.

1352. Staff, Charles. "Showtime: Delicate Balance: IRT Best."
      Indianapolis News, 19 December 1978, p. 30.

1353. "Stage Co. to Begin Series with Albee Play." Hartford
      (Conn.) Courant, 13 November 1969, p. 63.

1354. Stein, Jerry. "Theater: When Your Cat Dislikes You."
      Cincinnati Post, 2 February 1973, p. 27.

1355. Sterritt, David. "...And She Also Shines in Delicate
      Balance." Christian Science Monitor, 14 December 1973,
      p. 24. (FILM)

1356. Syse, Glenna. "Albee, Cast Grip Audience in A Delicate
      Balance." Chicago Sun-Times, 21 March 1967, p. 36.

1357. Szeliski, John J. von. "Albee: A Rare Balance."
      Twentieth Century Literature, 16 (April 1970), 123-130.

1358. Thompson, Howard. "Albee's A Delicate Balance Goes into
      Rehearsal." New York Times, 16 August 1966, p. 35.

1359. Toohey, John L. "A Delicate Balance." In his A History of
      the Pulitzer Prize Plays, pp. 334-339. New York: Citadel,
      1967.

1360. Trewin, J. C. "Friends and Relations." Illustrated London
      News, 254 (25 January 1969), 28.

1361. Vaughan, S. B. "A Delicate Balance: Open Allegory."
      Audience (New York), 6 (December 1973), 3-4. (FILM)

1362. Walker, Alexander. "Albee's World of Fear." Evening
      Standard (London), 15 January 1969, p. 19.

1363. Wardle, Irving. "London Sees the New Albee." Times
      (London), 15 January 1969, p. 6.

1364. Watts, Richard. "Two on the Aisle: The Development of
      Edward Albee." New York Post, 8 October 1966, p. 22.

1365. _____. "Two on the Aisle: Good News from Edward
       Albee." New York Post, 23 September 1966, p. 22.
            Reprinted in New York Theatre Critics' Reviews, 27
       (1966), 295-296.

1366. Weales, Gerald. "Stop the Balance, I Want to Get Off."
       Reporter, 35 (20 October 1966), 52-53.

1367. Weintraub, Stanley. Review of A Delicate Balance. Books
       Abroad, 41 (Summer 1967), 346.

1368. West, Anthony. "A Delicate Balance, 'Self-Indulgent.'"
       Vogue, 148 (1 November 1966), 150.

1369. "Whisky before Breakfast." Time, 88 (30 September 1966),
       88.

1370. Witt, Erwin. A. "Language a la Kerr." [Letter] New
       York Times, 9 October 1966, Sec. 2, p. 10.

1371. Young, B. A. "A Delicate Balance." Financial Times (Lon-
       don), 16 January 1969), p. 3.

1372. Zimmerman, Paul D. "Theater in the Camera." Newsweek,
       82 (3 December 1973), 113-114, 116. (FILM)
            Reprinted in Film 73/74; an Anthology by the National
       Society of Film Critics, ed. by Jay Cocks and David Denby,
       pp. 281-282. New York: Bobbs-Merrill, 1974.

ENVY (in THE SHOW OF THE SEVEN DEADLY SINS/FAUSTUS IN HELL)

1373. Gussow, Mel. "Stage: A New Look at 7 Deadly Sins." New
       York Times, 3 February 1985, Sec. 1, p. 55.

1374. Klein, Alvin. "A Sinful Pastiche at McCarter Theatre."
       New York Times, 3 February 1985, Sec. 11, p. 17.

1375. Mart. "Faustus in Hell." Variety, 30 January 1985, p. 88.

EVERYTHING IN THE GARDEN

1376. Abel, Leionel. "The Empty Theater." New American Review,
       No. 3 (1968), 247-256.

1377. Barnes, Clive. "The Theater: Everything in the Garden
       Arrives." New York Times, 30 November 1967, p. 60.
            Reprinted in New York Theatre Critics' Reviews, 28
       (1967), 211.

1378. Bermel, Albert. "On Stage: Gifts and Borrowings." New
      Leader, 50 (18 December 1967), 22-23.

1379. Bolton, Whitney. "Everything in the Garden Isn't All Roses."
      Morning Telegraph (New York), 1 December 1967.

1380. Brustein, Robert. "Albee at the Crossroads." New Republic,
      157 (16 December 1967), 25-27.
         Reprinted in his The Third Theatre, pp. 87-90. New
      York: Knopf, 1969.

1381. Bunce, Alan N. "Everything in the Garden by Albee on
      Broadway." Christian Science Monitor, 8 December 1967,
      p. 14.

1382. Cavanaugh, Arthur. "Stage: Everything in the Garden."
      Sign, 47 (February 1968), 30.

1383. Clurman, Harold. "Theatre." Nation, 205 (18 December
      1967), 669.

1384. Cooke, Richard P. "The Theater: Money as the Root."
      Wall Street Journal, 1 December 1967, p. 16.
         Reprinted in New York Theatre Critics' Reviews, 28
      (1967), 213.

1385. Diesel, Leota. "The Theatre: Everything in the Garden."
      Villager (New York), 30 November 1967, p. 12.

1386. [Digest of New York newspaper reviews of Everything in the
      Garden] Critical Digest, 19 (4 December 1967), p. [2].

1387. Forbes, Anthony. "New Play Advances Albee's Reputation."
      Nashville (Tenn.) Banner, 26 April 1968, p. 28.

1388. Gapsis. "Eddie in Tennies." Helix (Seattle), 10 (20 Novem-
      ber 1969), 17, 19.

1389. Gottfried, Martin. "The Theatre: Everything in the Garden."
      Women's Wear Daily, 30 November 1967, p. 36.
         Reprinted in New York Theatre Critics' Reviews, 28
      (1967), 212.

1390. Hewes, Henry. "The Theater: A Hothouse Is Not a Home."
      Saturday Review, 50 (16 December 1967), 24.

1391. Hipp, Edward Sothern. "New Albee Play." Newark Evening
      News, 30 November 1967, p. 66.

1392. Kerr, Walter. "The Artifice in Albee's Garden." New York
      Times, 10 December 1967, Sec. 2, pp. 1, 15.

Reprinted in New York Theatre Critics' Reviews, 28
(1967), 204-205.
Reprinted in his Thirty Plays Hath November; Pain and
Pleasure in the Contemporary Theater, pp. 210-214. New
York: Simon and Schuster, 1969.

1393. K[raus,] T[ed] M. "Pros & Cons." Critical Digest, 19 (4
December 1967), p. [4]. (signed "TMK")

1394. Kroll, Jack. "Poisoned Quills." Newsweek, 70 (11 December
1967), 96.

1395. Lahr, John. "Mr. Albee Adapts Art to Lies." Westside News
and Free Press (New York), 7 December 1967, pp. 5, 8.

1396. Lesser, Betty. "Garden at Regent Not Bed of Roses."
Daily Orange (Syracuse University, Syracuse, N.Y.), 20
March 1970, p. 9.

1397. Lewis, Theophilus. "Theatre: Everything in the Garden."
America, 118 (6 January 1968), 19-20.

1398. O'Brian, Jack. "O'Neill Play Prospers Despite Brutal Reviews." Arkansas Gazette (Little Rock), 4 December 1967,
Sec. B, p. 5.

1399. "Playboy After Hours: Theater." Playboy, 15 (February
1968), 32.

1400. Popkin, Henry. "Edward Albee Americanizes Giles Cooper."
Times (London), 15 January 1968, p. 5.

1401. Prideaux, Tom. "Why Must I Worry About Albee?" Life,
64 (2 February 1968), 16.

1402. Raidy, William A. "First Nighter: Everything Not Grade A."
Long Island Press (Jamaica, N.Y.), 30 November 1967, p. 30.

1403. [Review of Everything in the Garden] Publishers Weekly, 193
(5 February 1968), 62.

1404. Sandoe, James. Review of Everything in the Garden.
Library Journal, 93 (August 1968), 2895.

1405. Short, Kathryn. "Same Old Snake? Weird Solution in Albee's
Play." Morning Advocate (Baton Rouge), 14 July 1968, Sec.
E, p. 2.

1406. Simon, John. "Albee's Necrosis." Commonweal, 87 (12
January 1968), 444.
Reprinted in his Uneasy Stages: A Chronicle of the New

York Theater, 1963-1973, pp. 121-123. New York: Random
House, 1975.

1407. Smith, Michael. "Theatre Journal: Everything in the Garden." Village Voice, 7 December 1967, pp. 33-34.

1408. Sullivan, Dan. "Albee's Home Is the Setting for a First Rehearsal." New York Times, 24 October 1967, p. 50.

1409. "Tattletale-Grey Comedy." Time, 90 (8 December 1967), 96.

1410. Villa, Jacquie. "Dinner-Theater: Albee Play at Thanos."
Long Island Press (Jamaica, N.Y.), 2 March 1976, p. 14.

1411. Wardle, Irving. "English Critic on Broadway's Theatrical
Straitjacket: Cooper Americanized." Times (London), 21
February 1968, p. 13.

1412. Watt, Douglas. "Everything in the Garden Is a Chiller
Disguised as a Comedy." Daily News (New York), 30 November 1967, p. 88.
      Reprinted in New York Theatre Critics' Reviews, 28
(1967), 213.

1413. Watts, Richard. "Two on the Aisle: More Good News of
Edward Albee." New York Post, 9 December 1967, p. 22.

1414. _____. "Two on the Aisle: The Afternoons of Some
Ladies." New York Post, 30 November 1967, p. 54.
      Reprinted in New York Theatre Critics' Reviews, 28
(1967), 212.

1415. Weales, Gerald. "Working Wives." Reporter, 37 (28 December 1967), 38-39.

1416. West, Anthony. "Everything in the Garden, 'Albee's Innocence.'" Vogue, 151 (15 January 1968), 28.

1417. Zolotow, Sam. "Albee Adaptation Acquired by Fox." New
York Times, 9 October 1967, p. 60.

1418. _____. "Albee to Transplant a British Comedy." New
York Times, 7 March 1967, p. 45.

FAM & YAM

1419. Aston, Frank. "Theater: ANTA Series Is Resumed." New
York World-Telegram and Sun, 26 October 1960, p. 38.

1420. Gelb, Arthur. "Theatre: 3 One-Acters." New York Times,
26 October 1960, p. 44.

1421. Herridge, Frances. "Across the Footlights: Albee and
       Beckett in Trio at DeLys." New York Post, 26 October 1960,
       p. 66.

1422. Munroe, Richard C. [Letter] Newsweek, 61 (18 February
       1963), 6.

1423. Schmidt, Sandra. "Theatre: ANTA Triptych." Village
       Voice, 3 November 1960, pp. 7, 12.

                        FINDING THE SUN

1424. Ben-Zvi, Linda. "Finding the Sun." Theatre Journal, 36
       (March 1984), 102-103.

1425. Sullivan, Dan. "Finding the Sun." Los Angeles Times, 26
       May 1984, Sec. 5, p. 2.

                     THE LADY FROM DUBUQUE

1426. Adler, Thomas P. "The Pirandello in Albee: The Problem
       of Knowing in The Lady from Dubuque." In Edward Albee:
       An Interview and Essays, pp. 109-119. Houston: Univer-
       sity of St. Thomas, 1983.

1427. "Asides and Adlibs." Variety, 2 April 1980, p. 89.

1428. Barnes, Clive. "'Hardening of the Arteries' on B'way."
       New York Post, 7 February 1980, pp. 29, 37.

1429. Barr, Richard. "Barr Paid No Advance to Studio Arena,
       Buff." Variety, 18 April 1979, p. 184.

1430. Beaufort, John. "Albee's New Drama: A Game of 'Who Am
       I?'" Christian Science Monitor, 1 February 1980, p. 19.
           Reprinted in New York Theatre Critics' Reviews, 41 (1980),
       387.

1431. Brustein, Robert. "Self-Parody and Self-Murder." New
       Republic, 182 (8 March 1980), 26.

1432. Caltabiano, Frank P. Review of The Lady from Dubuque.
       World Literature Today, 55 (Summer 1981), 473-474.

1433. Carr, Jay. "Stage: An Elegant But Hollow Musing on Death."
       Detroit News, 6 February 1980, Sec. E, p. 1.

1434. Chadbourne, Malcolm K. "Lady from Dubuque Hasn't Got
       Virginia's Class." Journal Inquirer (Manchester, Conn.),
       10 June 1980, p. 21.

1435. Clarke, Gerald. "Theater: Night Games." Time, 115 (11 February 1980), 69.
 Reprinted in New York Theatre Critics' Reviews, 41 (1980), 388.

1436. Clurman, Harold. "Theater." Nation, 230 (23 February 1980), 221.

1437. Cunningham, Dennis. Review of The Lady from Dubuque, WCBS television, New York, 31 January 1980.
 Reprinted in New York Theatre Critics' Reviews, 41 (1980), 389.

1438. Currie, Glenne. "The Lady from Dubuque Grows Old Quickly." Telegraph Herald (Dubuque, Iowa), 8 February 1980, p. 1.

1439. De Meo, Raymond. "Theater: Hartford Has a Winner; Lady from Dubuque Asks Meaningful Questions." West Hartford (Conn.) News, 12 June 1980, "Goodtimes" suppl., p. 2.

1440. Frankel, Haskel. "Weidner Leaves with Lady from Dubuque." New York Times, 15 June 1980, Sec. 23, p. 16.

1441. Garrity, Pat. "Lady from Dubuque Supremely Entertaining." Springfield (Mass.) Daily News, 18 June 1980, p. 22.

1442. Gill, Brendan. "The Theatre: Out There and Down Here." New Yorker, 55 (11 February 1980), 63-64.

1443. Gussow, Mel. "Albee Prepares Play in 'Woolf' Mode." New York Times, 23 May 1978, Sec. 3, pp. 1, 4.

1444. "Hartford Stage Actor Nominated for Tony." Shore Line Times (Guilford, Conn.), 27 May 1980, pp. 15, 19.

1445. Holley, Tim. "Lady from Dubuque--Edward Albee Stings Us Again." Bridgeport (Conn.) Post, 1 February 1980, p. 25.

1446. Johnson, Malcolm L. "Albee's Lady Dies Too Soon." Hartford (Conn.) Courant, 10 February 1980, pp. 1G, 4G.

1447. _____. "Edward Albee's Dubuque in Memorable Production." Hartford (Conn.) Courant, 1 June 1980, p. 43.

1448. Keezing, Henry M. "Albee's Lady from Dubuque Is Provocative, But Disappointing." Herald (New Britain, Conn.), 6 June 1980, p. 15.

1449. Kemper, Steve. "Theatre: New Life for the Lady: A Fine

Production of a Flawed Play." Hartford (Conn.) Advocate, 4 June 1980, pp. 24-25.

1450. Kerr, Walter. "Stage: Albee's Lady from Dubuque." New York Times, 1 February 1980, p. C5.
Reprinted in New York Theatre Critics' Reviews, 41 (1980), 384.

1451. Kissel, Howard. "Theater: The Lady from Dubuque." Women's Wear Daily, 1 February 1980, p. 24.
Reprinted in New York Theatre Critics' Reviews, 41 (1980), 386.

1452. Klein, Alvin. "Theater Season Offering Few Surprises." New York Times, 26 September 1982, Sec. 21, p. 15.

1453. Kroll, Jack. "Going to Hell with Albee." Newsweek, 95 (11 February 1980), 102-103.
Reprinted in New York Theatre Critics' Reviews, 41 (1980), 387.

1454. Lawson, Carol. "News of the Theater: Albee's Play Delayed." New York Times, 19 December 1979, p. C23.

1455. _____. "News of the Theater: Dubuque in Rehearsal." New York Times, 2 January 1980, p. C21.

1456. _____. "News of the Theater: Dubuque Still in Limbo." New York Times, 26 December 1979, p. C16.

1457. McCormick, John. "The Lady from Dubuque to Hit Broadway This Fall." Telegraph Herald (Dubuque, Iowa), 13 May 1979, p. 23.

1458. McEnroe, Colin. "Actor Hyman Pours Himself into His Roles." Hartford (Conn.) Courant, 15 June 1980, pp. 1G, 3G.

1459. Montgomery, Roger. "Albee's Lady Is Brilliant Experience." Day (New London, Conn.), 10 June 1980, p. 22.

1460. [Morrison], Hobe. "The Lady from Dubuque." Variety, 6 February 1980, p. 132.

1461. Novick, Julius. "Mr. Albee's Pavane." Village Voice, 11 February 1980, p. 77.

1462. Pacheco, Patrick. "Reviews: On Broadway and Off." After Dark, 12 (April 1980), 22-23.

1463. [Review of The Lady from Dubuque] Choice, 18 (January 1981), 654.

1464. Roudané, Matthew C. "On Death, Dying, and the Manner of Living: Waste as Theme in Edward Albee's The Lady from Dubuque." In Edward Albee: An Interview and Essays, pp. 65-81. Houston: University of St. Thomas, 1983.

1465. Schlueter, June. "Is It 'All Over' for Edward Albee?: The Lady from Dubuque." In Edward Albee: Planned Wilderness; Interview, Essays, and Bibliography, ed. by Patricia De La Fuente, pp. 112-119. Edinburg, Tex.: School of Humanities, Pan American University, 1980. (Living Author Series; no. 3)

1466. Siegel, Joel. Review of The Lady from Dubuque, WABC television, New York, 31 January 1980.
    Reprinted in New York Theatre Critics' Reviews, 41 (1980), 389.

1467. Silverman, Stephen M. "Puzzle of a Strange Lady in Town." New York Post, 31 January 1980, pp. 29, 36.

1468. Simon, John. "Theater: From Hunger, Not Dubuque." New York, 13 (11 February 1980), 74-75.

1469. "Sked Lady from Dubuque for Hartford Stage Co." Variety, 23 April 1980, p. 85.

1470. Watt, Douglas. "Albee on the Chill of Death and Loss." Daily News (New York), 1 February 1980, "Friday" sec., p. 5.
    Reprinted in New York Theatre Critics' Reviews, 41 (1980), 385.

1471. Weatherby, W. J. "So Who's Afraid of The Lady from Dubuque?" Guardian Weekly (Manchester) 3 February 1980, 1980, p. 21.

1472. Wilson, Edwin. "Theater: Edward Albee's The Lady from Dubuque." Wall Street Journal, 8 February 1980, p. 15.
    Reprinted in New York Theatre Critics' Reviews, 41 (1980), 388-389.

LISTENING

1473. Brown, James. "Radio: Albee's Listening to Open 'Earplay.'" Los Angeles Times, 3 October 1976, Calendar sec., p. 78.

1474. Collis, John. "Radio." Listener, 95 (1 April 1976), 414.

1475. Curtis, Anthony. "Radio 3: Listening." Financial Times (London), 29 March 1976, p. 3.

112   Edward Albee

1476. Derrickson, Howard. "Shocker Climaxes 3-Night Edison
       Stand." Clayton Citizen (St. Louis), 11 April 1979, p. 9A.

1477. Fraser, C. Gerald. "New Albee Play Assists in Rebirth of
       Radio Drama." New York Times, 2 February 1976, p. 46.

1478. Milofsky, David. "Radio Plays Stage a Comeback." New
       York Times, 14 March 1976, Sec. 2, p. 25.

1479. Porter, Peter. "Radio: Talkies." New Statesman, 91 (18
       June 1976), 825.

1480. Roe, G. F. "Listening." [Letter] Times Literary Supple-
       ment, No. 3866 (16 April 1976), 465.

1481. Steele, Mike. "Curtain Rises Again for Radio Theater."
       Minneapolis Tribune, 18 April 1976, pp. 1D, 7D.

1482. Sullivan, Dan. "Stage: Radio Drama and the Way We Sound
       Now." Los Angeles Times, 31 October 1976, Calendar sec.,
       p. 50.

1483. "Voices Off." Times Literary Supplement, No. 3864 (2 April
       1976), 372.

1484. Wade, David. "Radio: Other People's Traumas." Times
       (London), 3 April 1976, p. 10.

1485. _____. "Radio: Taking Wing." Times (London), 27
       March 1976, p. 8.

                              LOLITA

1486. "Aurochs and Angels." Horizon, 24 (April 1981), 10, 12.

1487. Beaufort, John. "Theater." Christian Science Monitor, 25
       March 1981, p. 18.
          Reprinted in New York Theatre Critics' Reviews, 42
       (1981), 314-315.

1488. Berkvist, Robert. "Nabokov's Lolita Becomes a Play by
       Albee." New York Times, 1 March 1981, Sec. 2, pp. 1, 4.

1489. Blau, Eleanor. "News of the Theater: Problem with
       Lolita?" New York Times, 11 March 1981, p. C19.

1490. Blum, "Lolita." Variety, 4 February 1981, p. 170.

1491. Brustein, Robert. "The Trashing of Edward Albee." New
       Republic, 184 (11 April 1981), 27-28.

1492. Cameron, Ben. "Who's Afraid of Vladimir Nabokov?; Edward
      Albee's Lolita." Theater (Yale University), 12 (Summer/Fall
      1981), 77-80.

1493. Corry, John. "Broadway." New York Times, 6 February
      1981, p. C2.

1494. _____. "Broadway." New York Times, 20 February 1981,
      p. C2.

1495. _____. "Broadway." New York Times, 27 February 1981,
      p. C2.

1496. Donovan, Mark. "Lolita, Broadway's Bomb of the Year,
      Detonates Edward Albee, Bemuses Donald Sutherland and Il-
      luminates a Lovely Survivor, Blanche Baker." People Weekly,
      15 (6 April 1981), 44-46.

1497. Feingold, Michael. "Sitting Ducks." Village Voice, 25 March
      1981, pp. 95-96.

1498. Fremont-Smith, Eliot. "Quilty Verdict." Village Voice, 25
      March 1981, p. 29.

1499. Gill, Brendan. "The Theatre: Dead Souls." New Yorker,
      57 (30 March 1981), 62.

1500. Gilman, Richard. "Lolita." Nation, 232 (18 April 1981),
      474-476.

1501. Kalem, T. E. "Lo and Hum as Ho and Hum." Time, 117
      (30 March 1981), 65.
         Reprinted in New York Theatre Critics' Reviews, 42 (1981),
      316-317.

1502. Kauffmann, Stanley. "Theater: Lolita Undone." Saturday
      Review, 8 (May 1981), 78-79.

1503. Kerr, Walter. "Critic's Notebook: The Unsolved Mysteries
      that Baffle a Theatergoer." New York Times, 9 April 1981,
      p. C19.

1504. _____. "Stage View: How Albee Avoided Lolita." New
      York Times, 29 March 1981, Sec. 2, pp. 3, 24.

1505. Klemesrud, Judy." "'Lolita Syndrome' Is Denounced." New
      York Times, 3 March 1981, p. B14.

1506. Kroll, Jack. "Albee's Humbert Humbug." Newsweek, 97
      (30 March 1981), 85.
         Reprinted in New York Theatre Critics' Reviews, 42
      (1981), 317.

1507. Rich, Frank. "Critic's Notebook: The Sound of One Voice
       Talking." New York Times, 16 April 1981, p. C17.

1508. _____. "Stage: Albee's Adaptation of Lolita Opens."
       New York Times, 20 March 1981, p. C3.
           Reprinted in New York Theatre Critics' Reviews, 42
       (1981), 315.

1509. Rosenthal, David. "Growing Pains: Lolita Comes to Broad-
       way." New York, 14 (16 March 1981), 35-39.

1510. Siegel, Joel. Review of Lolita, WABC television, New York,
       19 March 1981.
           Reprinted in New York Theatre Critics' Reviews, 42
       (1981), 318.

1511. Simon, John. "Theater: Low Litter." New York, 14 (30
       March 1981), 34.

1512. Wilson, Edwin. "Theater: Bacall Shines But Rest of Broad-
       way Goes Dull." Wall Street Journal, 31 March 1981, p. 32.
           Reprinted in New York Theatre Critics' Reviews, 42
       (1981), 30-31.

1513. Yakir, Dan. "Sutherland Seduced." After Dark, 13 (March
       1981), 30-31.

MALCOLM

1514. Battelle, Phyllis. "Albee ... After the Flop." New York
       Journal-American, 21 January 1966, p. 23.

1515. Bolton, Whitney. "Theater: Day of Automation in Theater
       Is Here." Morning Telegraph (New York), 21 December 1965.

1516. _____. "Theater: Some Pro, Some Con on Playwright
       Albee." Morning Telegraph (New York), 18 January 1966.

1517. Brien, Alan. "Theatre: Period Pratfalls." Daily Telegraph
       (London), 16 January 1966, p. 12.

1518. Brustein, Robert. "Albee's Allegory of Innocence." New
       Republic, 154 (29 January 1966), 34, 36.
           Reprinted in The Third Theatre, pp. 79-82. New
       York: Knopf, 1969.

1519. Calta, Louis. "Malcolm Cast Meets Director." New York
       Times, 24 November 1965, p. 35.

1520. _____. "Zeffirelli Talks About Show Here." New York
       Times, 15 January 1966, p. 15.

1521. Chapin, Louis. "Last Gasp for Malcolm." Christian Science Monitor, 15 January 1966, p. 6.

1522. Chapman, John. "Malcolm's Life Without Father." Daily News (New York), 12 January 1966, p. 64.
Reprinted in New York Theatre Critics' Reviews, 27 (1966), 394-395.

1523. Cooke, Richard P. "The Theater: Mr. Albee's Adaptation." Wall Street Journal, 13 January 1966, p. 12.

1524. Corrigan, Robert W. "Malcolm 'Didn't Mean Very Much.'" Vogue, 147 (15 February 1966), 56.

1525. Dash, Tom. "Quo Vadis--Edward Albee." Show Business, 24 (22 January 1966), 8.

1526. Deuel, Pauline B. Review of Malcolm. Book Abroad, 41 (Winter 1967), 90.

1527. [Digest of New York newspaper reviews of Malcolm] Critical Digest, 17 (17 January 1966), p. [2].

1528. Gottfried, Martin. "Theatre." Women's Wear Daily, 14 January 1966, p. 49.
Reprinted in his Opening Nights; Theater Criticism of the Sixties, pp. 54-57. New York: Putnam, 1969.

1529. Guernsey, Otis L. "The Season in New York." In his The Best Plays of 1965-1966, pp. 3-41. New York: Dodd, Mead, 1966.

1530. Hardwick, Elizabeth. "The Theater of Decadence." New York Review of Books, 6 (28 April 1966), 8-9.

1531. Hipp, Edward Sothern. "Albee, Whistling in Dark." Newark Evening News, 23 January 1966, Sec. 6, pp. 1, 3.

1532. _____. "New Play by Albee." Newark Evening News, 12 January 1966, p. 58.

1533. Hoffman, Leonard. "The New York Play: Malcolm." Hollywood Reporter, 189 (12 January 1966), 3.

1534. Kauffmann, Stanley. "Theater: Edward Albee's Malcolm." New York Times, 12 January 1966, p. 29.
Reprinted in New York Theatre Critics' Reviews, 27 (1966), 392.

1535. Kerr, Walter. "Kerr Reviews Malcolm." New York Herald Tribune, 12 January 1966, p. 10.

Reprinted in New York Theatre Critics' Reviews, 27
(1966), 393-394.

1536. K[raus,] T[ed] M. "Pros & Cons." Critical Digest, 17
(17 January 1966), p. [4]. (signed "TMK")

1537. Little, Stuart W. "An Albee Option: Purdy's Malcolm."
New York Herald Tribune, 30 September 1963, p. 14.

1538. _____. "3 Treadmills, 39 Scenes; Malcolm: Play on the
Move." New York Herald Tribune, 13 December 1965, p. 15.

1539. McCarten, John. "The Theatre: Innocent Astray." New
Yorker, 41 (22 January 1966), 74.

1540. McClain, John. "An Elaborate Bore." New York Journal-
American, 12 January 1966, p. 14.
Reprinted in New York Theatre Critics' Reviews, 27
(1966), 395.

1541. Mishkin, Leo. "Stage Review: Edward Albee's Malcolm."
Morning Telegraph (New York), 13 January 1966.

1542. [Morrison], Hobe. "Malcolm." Variety, 19 January 1966,
p. 76.

1543. "The Murk of Albee." Newsweek, 67 (24 January 1966), 82.

1544. Nadel, Norman. "Albee Stumbles in Malcolm." New York
World-Telegram and Sun, 12 January 1966, p. 15.
Reprinted in New York Theatre Critics' Reviews, 27
(1966), 392.

1545. Oppenheimer, George. "Malcolm Was Really That Bad."
Newsday (Garden City, N.Y.), 29 January 1966, p. 33-W.

1546. Raidy, William A. "First Nighter: Malcolm Is Fascinating."
Long Island Press (Jamaica, N.Y.), 12 January 1966, p. 26.

1547. [Review of Malcolm] Booklist and Subscription Books Bulletin,
62 (15 July 1966), 1072.

1548. [Review of Malcolm] Choice, 3 (September 1966), 534.

1549. [Review of Malcolm] Virginia Quarterly Review, 43 (Winter
1967), xxi.

1550. Schaap, Dick. "Albee in Wonderland." New York Herald
Tribune, 29 November 1965, p. 23.

1551. _____. "Who's Afraid?" New York Herald Tribune, 10
January 1966, p. 13.

1552. Sheed, Wilfrid. "Notes on Albee." Commonweal, 83 (18 February 1966), 584-585.

1553. Smith, Michael. "Theatre Journal: Malcolm." Village Voice, 20 January 1966, pp. 19-20.

1554. "Tiny Albee." Time, 87 (21 January 1966), 50.

1555. Wallach, Allan. "Albee's Malcolm Trips Over the Obvious." Newsday (Garden City, N.Y.), 12 January 1966, p. 3C.

1556. Watts, Richard. "Random Notes on This and That." New York Post, 18 January 1966, p. 47.

1557. _____. "Two on the Aisle: Edward Albee Has a Catastrophe." New York Post, 12 January 1966, p. 38.
        Reprinted in New York Theatre Critics' Reviews, 27 (1966), 394.

1558. _____. "Two on the Aisle: The Worst from One of the Best." New York Post, 23 January 1966, p. 18.

1559. Wortis, Irving. Review of Malcolm. Library Journal, 91 (1 June 1966), 2868.

1560. Zolotow, Sam. "Malcolm to Quit Saturday Night; Producers Charge Closing to Adverse Reviews." New York Times, 13 January 1966, p. 46.

1561. _____. "New Albee Play Fills Chief Role." New York Times, 21 October 1965, p. 56.

THE MAN WHO HAD THREE ARMS

1562. Adler, Thomas P. "The Man Who Had Three Arms." Theatre Journal, 35 (March 1983), 124.

1563. Arnold, Christine. "Albee Goes Out on a Limb and Succeeds." Miami Herald, 12 June 1982, p. 28A.

1564. Beaufort, John. "Satiric Allegory from Edward Albee." Christian Science Monitor, 14 April 1983, p. 16.
        Reprinted in New York Theatre Critics' Reviews, 44 (1983), 325.

1565. Cunningham, Dennis. Review of The Man Who Had Three Arms, WCBS television, New York, 5 April 1983.
        Reprinted in New York Theatre Critics' Reviews, 44 (1983), 326.

1566. Gill, Brendan. "The Theatre: Bellyacher." New Yorker,
       59 (18 April 1983), 130, 132.

1567. Hughes, Catharine. "The Pulitzer Puzzle." America, 148
       (7 May 1983), 361.

1568. Kerr, Walter. "Stage View: How to Win an Audience."
       New York Times, 17 April 1983, Sec. 2, pp. 3, 7.

1569. Kroll, Jack. "Edward Albee's Hymn of Self-Disgust."
       Newsweek, 101 (18 April 1983), 54.
       Reprinted in New York Theatre Critics' Reviews, 44
       (1983), 325.

1570. Mor. "The Man Who Had Three Arms." Variety, 27 October
       1982, p. 85.

1571. Rich, Frank. "Stage: Drama by Albee, Man Who Had 3
       Arms." New York Times, 6 April 1983, p. C15.
       Reprinted in New York Theatre Critics' Reviews, 44
       (1983), 322.

1572. Siegel, Joel. Review of The Man Who Had Three Arms, WABC
       television, New York, 5 April 1983.
       Reprinted in New York Theatre Critics' Reviews, 44
       (1983), 325.

1573. Simon, John. "Theater: Dubious Blessings." New York,
       16 (25 April 1983), 92.

1574. Weales, Gerald. Review of The Man Who Had Three Arms.
       Georgia Review, 37 (Fall 1983), 605-606.

THE SANDBOX

1575. Alpert, Arthur. "Two Plays on Cherry Lane Stage." New
       York World-Telegram and Sun, 19 February 1962, p. 16.

1576. "American Playwrights." Times Literary Supplement, No.
       3145 (8 June 1962), 428.

1577. Anderson, Jack. "Encore Hosts The Sandbox by Workshop."
       Oakland (Calif.) Tribune, 31 July 1961, p. D-33.

1578. Barrows, Marjorie Wescott. "Edward Albee." In her The
       American Experience: Drama, pp. 356-358. New York:
       Macmillan, 1968.

1579. Cubeta, Paul M. "Commentary." In his Modern Drama for
       Analysis, 3rd ed., pp. 598-604. New York: Holt, Rinehart
       and Winston, 1962.

1580. Eichelbaum, Stanley. "A New Albee Play at the Workshop."
      San Francisco Examiner, 23 May 1961, p. 27.

1581. Farra, Harry E. "Good Plays for Coffeehouses." Christian
      Advocate, 13 (3 April 1969), 9-10.

1582. Gelb, Arthur. "'4 in 1' Bill of One-Act Plays Opens at the
      Jazz Gallery." New York Times, 17 May 1960, p. 42.

1583. Gussow, Mel. "Stage: Acting Company's 'Pieces of 8.'"
      New York Times, 9 March 1984, p. C3.

1584. Kelly, Kevin. "Albee Double-Bill: Theater Co. of Boston
      Has Distinct Promise." Boston Globe, 13 July 1963, p. 12.

1585. Kerr, Walter. "Off Broadway: Three New One-Act Plays
      Presented at Jazz Gallery." New York Herald Tribune, 17
      May 1960, p. 22.

1586. K[nickerbocker], P[aine]. "Actor's Workshop: Two Chal-
      lenging Dramas at Encore." San Francisco Chronicle, 24
      May 1961, p. 43.

1587. Robb, Pat. "Albee's Sandbox Grimly Funny." News-Call
      Bulletin (San Francisco), 23 May 1961, p. 22.

1588. S[mith], M[ichael]. "Theatre: The Absurd (2)," Village
      Voice, 22 February 1962, p. 10.

1589. T[allmer], J[erry]. "Theatre: 4 in 1." Village Voice,
      18 May 1960, pp. 9, 10.

1590. Thompson, David. "Editor's Note." In his Theatre Today,
      pp. 168-169. London: Longman, 1965.

1591. West, Anthony. "The Subhuman Theatre." Show, 2 (July
      1962), 27-28.

SEASCAPE

1592. Adler, Thomas P. "Albee's Seascape: Humanity at the
      Second Threshold." Renascence, 31 (Winter 1979), 107-114.

1593. Bardacke, Frances L. "Theatre." San Diego Magazine, 29
      (April 1977), 36.

1594. _____. "Theatre." San Diego Magazine, 28 (September
      1976), 51.

1595. Barnes, Clive. "Albee's Seascape Is a Major Event." New

York Times, 27 January 1975, p. 20.
Reprinted in New York Theatre Critics' Reviews, 36
(1975), 368.

1596. Beaufort, John. "New Albee Comedy on Broadway."
       Christian Science Monitor, 30 January 1975, p. 10.
       Reprinted in New York Theatre Critics' Reviews, 36
       (1975), 371.

1597. Bernstein, Samuel J. "Seascape, Edward Albee." In his
       The Strands Entwined; a New Direction in American Drama,
       pp. 111-135. Boston: Northeastern University Press, 1980.

1598. Brendle, Mary. "Anti-Clutter." [Letter] New York Times,
       23 February 1975, Sec. 2, p. 7.

1599. Buck, Richard M. Review of Seascape. Library Journal,
       100 (15 June 1975), 1236.

1600. Christiansen, Richard. "A Smooth Seascape." Chicago Daily
       News, 12 January 1977, p. 16.

1601. Christon, Lawrence. "Stage Review: Albee and Weill in a
       Double Bill." Los Angeles Times, 12 May 1979, Sec. 2, pp.
       10-11.

1602. Clurman, Harold. "Theatre." Nation, 220 (15 March 1975),
       314.

1603. Coe, Richard L. "Albee: Striving for Originality...."
       Washington Post, 8 December 1974, Sec. E, p. 8.

1604. Collins, William B. "In Seascape Albee Is in Trim Again."
       Philadelphia Inquirer, 5 January 1975, Sec. H, p. 7.

1605. _____. "Seascape Is Witty Albee-it Wise; More than Foot-
       notes on the Sand of Time." Philadelphia Inquirer, 31 De-
       cember 1974, Sec. B, p. 5.

1606. _____. "Stage Review: Lizards Have All the Lines."
       Los Angeles Times, 15 January 1975, Sec. 4, p. 14.

1607. Davis, James. "Deborah Kerr to Star in Albee Play."
       Daily News (New York), 12 August 1974, p. 44.

1608. Donnelly, Tom. "What's It All About, Albee?" Washington
       Post, 15 December 1974, Sec. F, pp. 1, 16.

1609. Eichelbaum, Stanley. "Upbeat Albee--His Best in Years."
       San Francisco Examiner & Chronicle, 2 March 1975, Sunday
       Scene section, p. 10.

1610. Fletcher, Florence. "Deborah Kerr: A Figure in an Enig-
      matic Seascape." Cue, 44 (27 January 1975), 64.

1611. Freemon, Bill. "Talking Lizards Spark Make-Believe Sea-
      scape." San Gabriel Valley Tribune (Covina, Calif.), 5 April
      1975, p. A8.

1612. Gabbard, Lucina P. "Albee's Seascape: An Adult Fairy
      Tale." Modern Drama, 31 (September 1978), 307-317.

1613. Gill, Brendan. "The Theatre: Among the Dunes." New
      Yorker, 50 (3 February 1975), 75-77.

1614. Glackin, William. "Theater: A Funny, Brilliant Seascape."
      Sacramento Bee, 13 April 1975, Scene sec., pp. 1-2.
      Reprinted in Contemporary American Theater Critics: A
      Directory and Anthology of Their Works, comp. by M. E.
      Comtois and Lynn F. Miller, pp. 267-269. Metuchen, N.J.:
      Scarecrow Press, 1977.

1615. Glover, William. "Articulate Lizards in Albee's Latest Play."
      San Francisco Examiner, 28 January 1975, p. 20.

1616. Gottfried, Martin. "Theater: Edward Albee's Latest." New
      York Post, 27 January 1975, p. 23.
      Reprinted in New York Theatre Critics' Reviews, 36
      (1975), 369-370.

1617. Gray, Beverly. "Stage." Coast (Beverly Hills, Calif.), 16
      (July 1975), 59-60.

1618. Griffin, William. "Stage: Seascape." Sign, 54 (April 1975),
      18.

1619. Gussow, Mel. "Recalling Evolution of Seascape Play, Albee
      Sees Tale Not of Lizard, But of Life." New York Times, 21
      January 1975, p. 40.

1620. Hewes, Henry. "Theater: Albee Surfaces." Saturday Re-
      view, 2 (8 March 1975), 40.

1621. Higgins, John. "Edward Albee's Lesson from the Lizards."
      Times (London), 30 January 1975, p. 8.

1622. Holland, Glenn. "Seascape." Daily Bruin (University of
      California at Los Angeles), 10 April 1975, p. 17.

1623. Hughes, Catharine. "Albee's Seascape." America, 132
      (22 February 1975), 136-137.
      Reprinted in Contemporary American Theater Critics:
      A Directory and Anthology of Their Works, comp. by

M. E. Comtois and Lynn F. Miller, pp. 264-366. Metuchen, N.J.: Scarecrow Press, 1977.

1624. _____. "New York." Plays and Players, 22 (May 1975), 34-35.

1625. "Human Beings to Get Half of Albee's Roles." New York Times, 23 May 1969, p. 36.

1626. K[alem], T. E. "Primordial Slime." Time, 105 (10 February 1975), 57.
Reprinted in New York Theatre Critics' Reviews, 36 (1975), 372.

1627. Kauffmann, Stanley. "Stanley Kauffmann on Theater: Seascape." New Republic, 172 (22 February 1975), 22, 33-34.
Reprinted in his Persons of the Drama; Theater Criticism and Comment, pp 222-224. New York: Harper & Row, 1976.

1628. Kaufman, Michael T. "Langella Hones His Craft as Star in the Lizard's Skin." New York Times, 13 February 1975, p. 42.

1629. Kerr, Walter. "Albee's Unwritten Part; McNally's Missing Joke." New York Times, 2 February 1975, Sec. 2, p. 5.

1630. Kihss, Peter. "Contrasting Biographies, Albee Play Win Pulitzers." New York Times, 6 May 1975, pp. 1, 34.

1631. Kissel, Howard. "Seascape." Women's Wear Daily, 27 January 1975, p. 10.
Reprinted in New York Theatre Critics' Reviews, , 36 (1975), 370-371.

1632. K[raus,] T[ed] M. "Pros & Cons." Critical Digest, 26 (3 February 1975), [4]. (signed "TMK")
Reprinted in Contemporary American Theater Critics: A Directory and Anthology of Their Works, comp. by M. E. Comtois and Lynn L. Miller, pp. 448-449. Metuchen, N.J.: Scarecrow Press, 1977.

1633. Kroll, Jack. "Leapin' Lizards." Newsweek, 85 (10 February 1975), 75.
Reprinted in New York Theatre Critics' Reviews, 36 (1975), 372-373.

1634. Lerner, Max. "The Best Plays." New York Post, 9 May 1975, p. 41.

1635. Loynd, Ray. "Stage Review: Albee's View from the Sea."
       Los Angeles Herald-Examiner, 4 April 1975, p. C-3.

1636. Luce. "Seascape." Variety, 27 November 1974, pp. 80, 83.

1637. Luft, Herbert G. "As We See It: Playgoing!" B'nai B'rith
       Messenger (Los Angeles), 11 April 1975, p. 12.

1638. Madd[en, John]. "Seascape." Variety, 29 January 1975,
       p. 68.

1639. McCaslin, Walt. "Albee and Ionesco Draw No Raves for 2
       Tedious Works." Journal Herald (Dayton, Ohio), 25 March
       1980, p. 18.

1640. McMorrow, Tom. "Return of the Woolf Man." Daily News
       (New York), 26 January 1975, Sec. 3, p. 1.

1641. Moran, Rita. "Seascape Presents Albee in a Philosophical
       Mood." Ventura County Star-Free Press (Ventura, Calif.),
       5 April 1975, p. B-5.

1642. Morrison, Hobe. "Seascape's Pulitzer Is a '24-Carat
       Howler.'" Herald-News (Passaic, N.J.), 12 May 1975, p. 8.

1643. Novick, Julius. "Mr. Albee's Leaping Lizards." Village
       Voice, 3 February 1975, p. 84.

1644. "On the Beach." Cue, 44 (27 January 1975), 6.

1645. Oppenheimer, George. "A Seascape to Please the Eye and
       Mind." Newsday (Garden City, N.Y.), 9 February 1975,
       Sec. 2, p. 9.

1646. Pacheco, Patrick. "Reviews: Theater." After Dark, 7
       (March 1975), 27-28.

1647. Pennington, Ron. "Stage Review: Shubert Theatre:
       Seascape." Hollywood Reporter, 235 (4 April 1975), 33.
            Reprinted in Contemporary American Theater Critics:
       A Directory and Anthology of Their Works, comp. by.
       M. E. Comtois and Lynn F. Miller, pp. 635-636. Metuchen,
       N.J.: Scarecrow Press, 1977.

1648. "Playboy After Hours: Theater." Playboy, 22 (May 1975),
       42.

1649. Probst, Leonard. Review of Seascape, NBC television, 27
       January 1975.
            Reprinted in New York Theatre Critics' Reviews, 36
       (1975), 373.

124   Edward Albee

1650. Purdon, Liam O. "The Limits of Reason: <u>Seascape</u> as
       Psychic Metaphor." In <u>Edward Albee: An Interview and
       Essays</u>, pp. 141-153. Houston: University of St. Thomas,
       1983.

1651. Raidy, William A. "First Nighters: <u>Seascape</u>'s Elusive."
       <u>Long Island Press</u> (Jamaica, N.Y.), 27 January 1975, p. 14.

1652. Ridley, Clifford A. "The Jokes Are Serious from Simon,
       Albee." <u>National Observer</u>, 28 October 1974, p. 16.

1653. Sanders, Kevin. Review of <u>Seascape</u>, WABC television, New
       York, 26 January 1975.
       Reprinted in <u>New York Theatre Critics' Reviews</u>, 36
       (1975), 373.

1654. Schaffer, Quentin. "Western Debut of <u>Seascape</u>: Albee
       Visits LA Unafraid of Critics." <u>Daily Trojan</u> (University of
       Southern California), 4 April 1975, p. 5. (INTERVIEW)

1655. Schier, Ernest. "Albee's <u>Seascape</u>--A Curiosity Piece."
       <u>Evening Bulletin</u> (Philadelphia), 31 December 1974, p. 24.

1656. "Set 70-30% Deal for Backers on Barr & Woodward <u>Seascape</u>."
       <u>Variety</u>, 18 September 1974, pp. 89, 92.

1657. Simon, John. "Evolution Made Queasy." <u>New York</u>, 8 (10
       February 1975), 55.

1658. Sloan, Robin Adams. "The Gossip Column." <u>Daily News</u>
       (New York), 16 March 1975, Sec. 3, p. 2.

1659. Smither, Kitty Harris. "A Dream of Dragons: Albee as Star
       Thrower in <u>Seascape</u>." In <u>Edward Albee: Planned Wilderness;
       Interview, Essays, and Bibliography</u>, ed. by Patricia De La
       Fuente, pp. 99-110. Edinburg, Tex." School of Humanities,
       Pan American University, 1980. (Living Author Series; no.
       3)

1660. Sullivan, Dan. "Stage Review: Miss Kerr in <u>Seascape</u>."
       <u>Los Angeles Times</u>, 4 April 1975, pp. 1, 19.

1661. Syse, Glenna. "Edward Albee's Lizards That Make You
       Think." <u>Chicago Sun-Times</u>, 13 January 1977, p. 98.

1662. Thompson, Howard. "News of the Stage: Albee Play to Star
       Deborah Kerr." <u>New York Times</u>, 11 August 1974, Sec. 1,
       p. 51.

1663. Warfield, Polly. "Actress, Playwright Discuss Their Craft
       and Latest Play." <u>Gardena</u> (Calif.) <u>Valley News</u>, 10 April
       1975, p. 5. (INTERVIEW)

1664. _____. "Seascape." Gardena (Calif.) Valley News, 10
       April 1975, p. 14.

1665. Watt, Douglas. "Seascape: The Lizard Has the Lines."
       Daily News (New York), 27 January 1975, p. 41.
       Reprinted in New York Theatre Critics' Reviews, 36
       (1975), 369.

1666. _____. "Theater: Seascape Isn't Exactly a Beach Ball."
       Daily News (New York), 9 February 1975, Sec. 2, p. 3.

1667. Watts, Richard. "Theater Week: Ed Mullins' Best Play."
       New York Post, 10 May 1975, p. 16.

1668. _____. "Theater Week: Seascape: Albee at Top of
       Form." New York Post, 8 February 1975, p. 14.
       Reprinted in Contemporary American Theater Critics:
       A Directory and Anthology of Their Works, comp. by
       M. E. Comtois and Lynn F. Miller, pp. 909-911. Metuchen,
       N.J.: Scarecrow Press, 1977.

1669. Weiner, Bernard. "Albee's Play Without a Play." San
       Francisco Chronicle, 27 February 1975, p. 43.

1670. Williams, Nick B. "Joe the Unreluctant Dragon (Well, Okay,
       Lizard) High-Tails It Just in Time." Los Angeles Times, 26
       March 1979, Sec. 2, p. 7.

1671. Wilson, Earl. "Deborah Kerr--No Rest for a Star." New
       York Post, 15 February 1975, p. 22.

1672. _____. "It Happened Last Night: Limping Lizard...."
       New York Post, 10 March 1975, p. 16.

1673. Wilson, Edwin. "Disturbing Creatures from the Deep."
       Wall Street Journal, 28 January 1975, p. 16.
       Reprinted in New York Theatre Critics' Reviews, 36
       (1975), 370.

1674- Winer, Linda. "Theater: Seascape: Sweetness Distilled from
75.   Albee's Salt." Chicago Tribune, 12 January 1977, Sec. 2,
       p. 5.

TINY ALICE

1676. "ACT-Albee Feud Goes On--So Does the Play." San Francisco
       Examiner, 21 October 1975, p. 25.

1677. "Albee Forced Changes in Staging of Alice for B'way (and
       S.F. Return)." Variety, 8 October 1969, p. 63.

1678. "Albee Hasn't Sued Yet." Oakland (Calif.) Tribune, 9 October 1975, p. 23.

1679. "Albee Play Puzzles New York." Times (London), 7 January 1965, p. 7.

1680. "Albee vs. Ball-Continued." San Francisco Examiner, 28 October 1975, p. 25.

1681. Anderson, Mary Castiglie. "Staging the Unconscious: Edward Albee's Tiny Alice." Renascence, 32 (Spring 1980), 178-192.

1682. Anderson, Robert. "Who's to Blame? The Albee Debate." [Letter] New York Times, 25 April 1965, Sec. 2, p. 4.

1683. Ashford, Gerald. "Tiny Alice Enormously Difficult, Well Performed." San Antonio (Tex.) Express, 14 December 1967, p. 11-H.

1684. Bail. "Tiny Alice." Variety, 21 January 1970, p. 68.

1685. Ballew, Leighton M. "Who's Afraid of Tiny Alice?" Georgia Review, 20 (Fall 1966), 292-299.

1686. Bannon, Anthony. "The Alice Bit: What's It All About, Albee?" Buffalo Evening News, 12 November 1969, Sec. 4, p. 81.

1687. Barber, John. "About the Theatre: Alice, Albee, and Abstraction." Daily Telegraph (London), 19 January 1970, p. 12.

1688. _____. "Fascinating Conundrum that Fails." Daily Telegraph (London), 16 January 1970, p. 16.

1689. Barker, Felix. "Tiny Alice: Aldwych." Evening News (London), 16 January 1970, p. 2.

1690. Barnes, Clive. "The Stage: American Conservatory Presents Albee's Tiny Alice." New York Times, 30 September 1969, p. 42.
    Reprinted in New York Theatre Critics' Reviews, 30 (1969), 254.

1691. Barron, Karl. "Performances." San Francisco, 18 (January 1976), 34.

1692. Belsnick, Morris. [Letter] New York Review of Books, 4 (8 April 1965), 37.

1693. Bender, Marilyn. "Designer Seeks Effect of Beauty Without Chic." New York Times, 18 December 1964, p. 38.

1694. Benedictus, David. "Plays." Queen, 435 (17 February 1970), 64.

1695. Bermel, Albert. "On Stage: Alice in Underhand." New Leader, 48 (18 January 1965), 26-27.

1696. Bigsby, C. W. E. "Curiouser and Curiouser: A Study of Albee's Tiny Alice." Modern Drama, 10 (December 1967), 258-266.

1697. _____. "Tiny Alice." Excerpted from his Albee (Edinburgh: Oliver & Boyd, 1969) in his Edward Albee: A Collection of Critical Essays, pp. 124-134. Englewood Cliffs, N.J.: Prentice-Hall, 1975.

1698. Bladen, Barbara. "Hell-Fire-Damnation Zeal in Tiny Alice." San Mateo (Calif.) Times, 7 October 1975, p. 23.

1699. _____. "Master Gunfighter a Sick, Lurid Film." San Mateo (Calif.) Times, 8 October 1975, p. 29.

1700. Bolton, Whitney. "Albee's Talent Flares Anew in Fascinating Tiny Alice." Morning Telegraph (New York), 31 December 1964.

1701. _____. "Theater: In Rebuttal of Albee's Blast at Critics." Morning Telegraph (New York), 22 November 1967.

1702. Booth, Wayne C. A Rhetoric of Irony, pp. 266-267. Chicago: University of Chicago Press, 1974.

1703. Brennan, Thomas. "Tiny Alice." Villager (New York), 2 October 1969, p. 8.

1704. Brien, Alan. "Alan Brien at the New York Theatre: The Truth Is a Puzzle." Sunday Telegraph (London), 3 January 1965, p. 10.

1705. Brustein, Robert. "Three Plays and a Protest." New Republic, 152 (23 January 1965), 32-34, 36.
    Reprinted in his Seasons of Discontent; Dramatic Opinions 1959-1965, pp. 304-311. New York: Simon and Schuster, 1965.

1706. Bryden, Ronald. "The Tiny Ghost in Albee's Fantasy Castle." Observer (London), 18 January 1970, p. 32.

1707. Bunce, Alan. "New York Theater: The Season's Pace Quickens." Christian Science Monitor, 25 October 1969, p. 14.

1708. Cahn, Judah. "Tiny Alice--Symbol or Symptom?" Reconstruc-
       tionist, 31 (14 May 1965), 22-27.

1709. Calta, Louis. "Albee Lectures Critics on Taste." New York
       Times, 23 March 1965, p. 33.

1710. Campbell, Mary Elizabeth. "The Statement of Edward Albee's
       Tiny Alice." Papers on Language and Literature, 4 (Winter
       1968), 85-100.

1711. _____. "Tempters in Albee's Tiny Alice." Modern Drama,
       13 (May 1970), 22-23.

1712. Casper, Leonard. "Tiny Alice: The Expense of Joy in the
       Persistence of Mystery." In Edward Albee: An Interview
       and Essays, pp. 83-92. Houston: University of St. Thomas,
       1983.

1713. Cavan, Romilly. "Scripts." Plays and Players, 19 (July
       1972), 81.

1714. Cavanaugh, Arthur. "Play Reviews: Tiny Alice." Sign,
       44 (March 1965), 27.

1715. C[hapin], L[ouis]. "Albee's Broadside." Christian Science
       Monitor, 27 March 1965, p. 4.

1716. Chapin, Louis. "Albee's Latest: Tiny Alice." Christian
       Science Monitor, 2 January 1965, p. 6.

1717. Chapman, John. "Edward Albee's Tiny Alice, or The Temp-
       tation of John Gielgud." Daily News (New York), 30 December
       1964, p. 36.
          Reprinted in New York Theatre Critics' Reviews, 25
       (1964), 97.

1718. _____. "Revival of Tiny Alice: Still Metafuzzical Bore."
       Daily News (New York), 30 September 1969, p. 60.
          Reprinted in New York Theatre Critics' Reviews, 30
       (1969), 256.

1719. Christiansen, Richard. "Albee's Tiny Alice Returns to Hull
       House." Chicago Daily News, 31 January 1978, p. 21.

1720. Clum, John M. "Religion and Five Contemporary Plays: The
       Quest for God in a Godless World." South Atlantic Quarterly,
       77 (Autumn 1978), 418-432.

1721. Clurman, Harold. "Theatre." Nation, 200 (18 January 1965),
       65.
          Reprinted in his The Naked Image; Observations on the

Modern Theatre, pp. 21-24. New York: Macmillan, 1966.
Reprinted in his The Divine Pastime; Theatre Essays, pp.
116-118. New York: Macmillan, 1974.

1722. _____. "Theatre." Nation, 209 (27 October 1969), 451.

1723. Coe, Richard M. "Beyond Absurdity: Albee's Awareness
of Audience in Tiny Alice." Modern Drama, 18 (December
1975), 371-383.

1724. "Comment: Theology on Broadway." Christian Advocate, 9
(25 February 1965), 2.

1725. Cook, Joy. "People in the News." New York Post, 6 October 1975, p. 7.

1726. Cooke, Richard P. "The Theater: Metaphysical Mystery."
Wall Street Journal, 31 December 1964, p. 6.

1727. _____. "The Theater: Tiny Alice at ANTA." Wall Street
Journal, 1 October 1969, p. 18.
Reprinted in New York Theatre Critics' Reviews, 30
(1969), 255.

1728. Crinkley, Richmond. "Theater: The Loss of Privacy."
National Review, 21 (30 December 1969), 1334-1335.

1729. "Curiouser and Curiouser." Newsweek, 65 (5 April 1965),
53.

1730. Curry, Ryder H., and Porte, Michael. "The Surprising
Unconscious of Edward Albee." Drama Survey, 7 (Winter
1968-69), 59-68.

1731. Cuthbert, David. "Cryptic Albee Drama: Tiny Alice in a
Church: Respectable, Unfulfilled." Times-Picayune (New
Orleans), 3 June 1973, Sec. 1, p. 43.

1732. Darlington, W. A. "Alice in Albee-Land." Daily Telegraph
(London), 21 March 1966, p. 56.

1733. Davison, Richard A. "Edward Albee's Tiny Alice: A Note
of Re-Examination." Modern Drama, 11 (May 1968), 54-60.

1734. Day, Richard. "Tiny Alice; Good Friday with Albee."
Bridgeport (Conn.) Post, 13 April 1968, p. 7.

1735. [Digest of New York newspaper reviews of Tiny Alice]
Critical Digest, 16 (28 December 1964), p. [2].

1736. "Director Rebuffs Playwright." Oakland (Calif.) Tribune, 7
October 1975, p. 20.

1737. Doran, Terry. "Studio Arena: Tiny Alice's Puzzles Unsolved, But Here's Honors-Grade Study." Buffalo Evening
News, 7 November 1969, Sec. 2, p. 22.

1738. Dorin, Rube. "Writer, Director of Tiny Alice: Albee and
Schneider on 'Play as Creation.'" Morning Telegraph (New
York), 20 January 1965.

1739. "Dramatic Decline." Times Literary Supplement, No. 3352
(26 May 1966), 472.

1740. Dukore, Bernard F. "Tiny Alice." Drama Survey, 5 (Spring
1966), 60-66.

1741. Dundy, Elaine. "What Means Tiny Alice?" New York Herald
Tribune, 31 January 1965, magazine, pp. 16-17, 27.

1742. Dusay, John M. "The Games Alice Plays: A Transactional
Analysis." A.C.T. 2 Backstage Newsletter (American Conservatory Theatre, San Francisco), 1 (February 1967), 2,
10.

1743. Eichelbaum, Stanley. "Albee vs. Ball--Act II." San Francisco Examiner, 7 October 1975, p. 23.

1744. _____. "An Incendiary Tiny Alice Returns." San Francisco Examiner, 6 October 1975, p. 26.

1745. _____. "Play Was Rewritten: Albee Disowns ACT's
Alice." San Francisco Exmainer and Chronicle, 5 October
1975, pp. 1, 11.

1746. Elliott, George P. "Destroyers, Defilers, and Confusers of
Men." Atlantic, 221 (December 1968), 74-80.

1747. Ellison, [Earl] Jerome. "Albee: Tiny Alice." In his God
on Broadway, pp. 57-63. Richmond, Va.: John Knox
Press, 1971.

1748. Emerson, Paul. "ACT Masterful in Alice." Palo Alto (Calif.)
Times, 17 January 1968, p. 31.

1749. Fanning, Garth. "Albee's Alice Is Stunning; Church, God,
Man Are Probed in ACT Production." Sacramento Bee, 21
January 1968, pp. L6, L31.

1750. Fleischer, Leonore. Review of Tiny Alice. Publishers
Weekly, 189 (21 February 1966), 195.

1751. Franzblau, Abraham. "A Psychiatrist Looks at Tiny Alice."
Saturday Review, 48 (30 January 1965), 39.

Reprinted in Edward Albee: A Collection of Critical
Essays, ed. by C. W. E. Bigsby, pp. 110-111. Englewood
Cliffs, N.J.: Prentice-Hall, 1975.

1752. Freedley, George. Review of Tiny Alice. Library Journal,
90 (15 March 1965), 1343.

1753. Funke, Lewis. "West Coast Tiny Alice Passes Albee's
Scrutiny Here." New York Times, 29 September 1969, p. 52.

1754. Gardner, Paul. "Tiny Alice Mystifies Albee, Too." New
York Times, 21 January 1965, p. 22.

1755. Gassner, John. "Broadway in Review." Educational Theatre
Journal, 17 (October 1965), pp. 257-270.
Reprinted partially in his Dramatic Soundings; Evaluations
and Retractions Culled from 30 Years of Dramatic Criticism,
pp. 601-602. New York: Crown, 1968.

1756. Gelmis. "Albee Hurls Tiny Bit of Malice at the Critics."
Newsday (Garden City, N.Y.), 23 March 1965, p. 3C.

1757. Gielgud, John. "In the Words of Sir John Gielgud." Cue,
39 (7 November 1970), 8-9.

1758. Gill, Brendan. "The Theatre: In Old Vienna." New Yorker,
45 (11 October 1969), 85-86.

1759. [Gilman, Richard.] "Chinese Boxes." Newsweek, 65 (11
January 1965), 75.
Reprinted in his Common and Uncommon Masks; Writings
on Theatre 1961-1970, pp. 137-139. New York: Random
House, 1971.

1760. Glackin, William C. "Alice Is Worth the Uproar." Sacramento
Bee, 12 October 1975, Scene section, pp. 1, 10.

1761. Glenn, Jules. "The Adoption Theme in Edward Albee's Tiny
Alice and The American Dream." Psychoanalytic Study of the
Child, 29 (1974), 413-429.
Reprinted in Lives, Events, and Other Players; Directions
in Psychobiography, ed. by Joseph T. Coltrera, pp. 255-269.
New York: Aronson, 1981. (Downstate Psychoanalytic
Institute Twenty-Fifth Anniversary Series)

1762. Gottfried, Martin. "Theatre: Tiny Alice." Women's Wear
Daily, 30 December 1964, p. 40.
Reprinted in his Opening Nights; Theater Criticism of the
Sixties, pp. 51-54. New York: Putnam, 1969.

1763. _____. "Theatre: Tiny Alice." Women's Wear Daily, 30

September 1969, p. 31.
Reprinted in New York Theatre Critics' Reviews, 30
(1969), 256.

1764. Griffiths, Stuart. "First Night: Man's Doubt a Sacrifice to
Albee's Cruel Power Games." Evening Standard (London), 16
January 1970, p. 20.

1765. Guernsey, Otis L. "The Season in New York." In his The
Best Plays of 1964-1965, pp. 3-20. New York: Dodd, Mead,
1965.

1766. Gussow, Mel. "Theater: Albee's Alice." New York Times,
17 April 1972, p. 46.

1767. Guthke, Karl S. "A Stage for the Anti-Hero: Metaphysical
Farce in Modern Theatre." Studies in the Literary Imagination, 9 (Spring 1976), 119-137.

1768. Hagopian, John V. [Letter] New York Review of Books, 4
(8 April 1965), 37.

1769. Harris, Leonard. Review of Tiny Alice, WCBS television,
New York, 29 September 1969.
Reprinted in New York Theatre Critics' Reviews, 30
(1969), 257.

1770. Harris, Sydney J. "The Critics, Albee, and Tiny Alice."
Chicago Daily News, 27 March 1965, Panorama sec., p. 13.

1771. Henry, William A. "Reviewer's Stand: Tiny Alice Probes
Faith." Yale Daily News (New Haven, Conn.), 11 April
1968, p. 3.

1772. Hewes, Henry. "Broadway Postscript: The Tiny Alice
Caper." Saturday Review, 48 (30 January 1965), 38-39, 65.
Reprinted in Edward Albee: A Collection of Critical
Essays, ed. by C. W. E. Bigsby, pp. 99-104. Englewood
Cliffs, N.J.: Prentice-Hall, 1975.

1773. _____. "Broadway Postscript: Through the Looking
Glass, Darkly." Saturday Review, 48 (16 January 1965), 40.

1774. _____. "Broadway Postscript: Upon Your Imaginary
Forces, ACT!" Saturday Review, 48 (4 September 1965), 43.

1775. _____. "The Theater: Theater Paprika." Saturday Review, 52 (18 October 1969), 20.

1776. Hipp, Edward Sothern. "New Albee Drama: John Gielgud,
Irene Worth in Tiny Alice." Newark Evening News, 30
December 1964, p. 12.

1777. _____. "Tiny Alice Again." Newark Evening News, 30
September 1969, p. 54.

1778. Hobson, Harold. "New Director Clarifies Albee's Alice--
Maybe." Christian Science Monitor, 23 January 1970, p. 4.

1779. _____. "Theatre: Mr. Albee's Secret." Sunday Times
(London), 9 February 1964, p. 33.

1780. _____. "Theatre: The Path of Temptation." Sunday
Times (London), 18 January 1970, p. 57.

1781. Holmstrom, John. "Tiny Alice." Plays and Players, 17
(March 1970), 38-42.

1782. Hope-Wallace, Philip. "Tiny Alice." Guardian (Manchester),
16 January 1970, p. 8.

1783. Hopper, Stanley Romaine. "How People Live Without Gods:
Albee's Tiny Alice." American Poetry Review, 2 (March/April
1973), 35-38.

1784. Jackson, Katherine Gauss. "Books in Brief: Tiny Alice."
Harper's Magazine, 230 (May 1965), 146.

1785. Johnson, Helen. "Who Is Tiny Alice?" Together (Nashville,
Tenn.), 9 (July 1965), 57.

1786. Jones, Jimmie. "Strictly Show Biz!" Vallejo (Calif.) Times-
Herald, 8 October 1975, p. 23.

1787. Kauffmann, Stanley. "A Patriot for Me: American Conservatory Theater." New Republic, 161 (1 November 1969), 22,
33.
    Reprinted in his Persons of the Drama; Theater Criticism
and Comment, pp. 31-32. New York: Harper & Row, 1976.

1788. Kelly, Herbert L. "'And an Ancient Theme It Is....'"
[Letter] Christian Science Monitor, 10 April 1970, p. B-17.

1789. Kelly, Kevin. "Albee Play in N.Y.: Tiny Alice Is Drama of
Size and Substance." Boston Globe, 30 December 1964, p. 8.

1790. Kerr, Walter. "Albee's Tiny Alice--Walter Kerr's Review."
New York Herald Tribune, 30 December 1964, p. 10.
    Reprinted in New York Theatre Critics' Reviews, 25
(1964), 98.

1791. _____. "Edward Albee's World of Chance." New York
Herald Tribune, 17 January 1965, magazine, p. 25.

134   Edward Albee

1792. _____. "An Improved Alice, A Flattened Flea." New
       York Times, 12 October 1969, Sec. 2, p. 9.
       Reprinted in New York Theatre Critics' Reviews, 30
       (1969), 251-252.

1793. _____. "Theater: Cerebral Plays for the Non-Thinking
       Man." New York Herald Tribune Magazine, 18 July 1965,
       p. 27.
       Reprinted in his Thirty Plays Hath November; Pain and
       Pleasure in the Contemporary Theater, pp. 207-210.
       New York: Simon and Schuster, 1969.

1794. _____. "Theater: O'Neill's Daydream vs. Albee's Truth."
       New York Herald Tribune Magazine, 24 January 1965, p. 23.

1795. Kingston, Jeremy. "At the Theatre." Punch, 258 (21
       January 1970), 116-117.

1796. Kloten, Edgar. "O'Neill for Real; Albee for Symbol." West
       Hartford (Conn.) News, 11 April 1968, p. 6.

1797. _____. "On Stage: Tiny Alice Becomes Tinier and
       Tinier." West Hartford (Conn.) News, 6 April 1972, p. 6B.

1798. K[raus,] T[ed] M. "Pros & Cons." Critical Digest, 16 (11
       January 1965), p. [4]. (signed "TMK")

1799. Kretzmer, Herbert. "Why the Holy Hush for This Over-
       weight White Elephant?" Daily Express (London), 16 January
       1970, p. 14.

1800. Kroll, Jack. "ACT in New York." Newsweek, 74 (13
       October 1969), 125.

1801. Lahr, John. "On Stage." Village Voice, 9 October 1969,
       pp. 45, 58.

1802. Lambert, J. W. "Plays in Performance." Drama; the Quar-
       terly Theatre Review, No. 96 (Spring 1970), 15-17.

1803. Lamport, Felicia. "Das Ist Alice." [Poem] Harper's
       Magazine, 230 (May 1965), 20.

1804. Laschever, Barnett D. "Extraordinary Drama: Of Men and
       Failings." Hartford (Conn.) Times, 1 April 1972, p. 3.

1805. Lerner, Max. "Who's Afraid of Edward Albee?" New York
       Post, 3 February 1965, p. 37.

1806. Lewis, Emory. "The Theatre: Albee, Babes in the Wood,
       and Others." Cue, 34 (9 January 1965), 14.

1807. Lewis, Peter. "Albee Drives Even the Young to Distraction."
      Daily Mail (London), 16 January 1970, p. 10.

1808. Lewis, Theophilus. "Theatre: Tiny Alice." America, 112
      (6 March 1965), 336-337.

1809. _____. "Theatre: Tiny Alice." America, 121 (18 October
      1969), 342-343.

1810. Lipton, Edmond. "The Tiny Alice Enigma." [Letter]
      Saturday Review, 48 (20 February 1965), 21.

1811. Little, Stuart W. "Albee Slugs Back at the Critics." New
      York Herald Tribune, 23 March 1965, p. 14.

1812. _____. "Albee Talks--but Doesn't Tell Meaning of Tiny
      Alice." New York Herald Tribune, 20 January 1965, p. 16.

1813. _____. "Albee's New One Is Called Tiny Alice--Meaning???"
      New York Herald Tribune, 16 November 1964, p. 16.

1814. _____. "Theater News: Producers: Tiny Alice a Hit."
      New York Herald Tribune, 31 December 1964, p. 7.

1815. _____. "Tonight, First Public Preview of Tiny Alice."
      New York Herald Tribune, 21 December 1964, p. 10.

1816. Livingston, Howard. "Albee's Tiny Alice: Symbols of
      Symbols." North American Review, 252 (New Series 4) (May
      1967), 3.

1817. "London Puzzles Over Tiny Alice." New York Times, 17
      January 1970, p. 24.

1818. Loney, Glenn M. "Broadway in Review." Educational
      Theatre Journal, 17 (March 1965), 56-69.

1819. Lowell, Sondra. "Stage Beat: Tiny Alice at Theatrecraft."
      Los Angeles Times, 9 July 1976, Sec. 4, p. 16.

1820. Lucey, William F. "Albee's Tiny Alice: Truth and Appear-
      ance." Renascence, 21 (Winter 1969), 76-80, 110.

1821. Mandanis, Alice. "Symbol and Substance in Tiny Alice."
      Modern Drama, 12 (May 1969), 92-98.

1822. Maravel, Harry. "Short Cut." [Letter] New York Times,
      25 April 1965, Sec. 2, p. 4.

1823. Marcus, Frank. "Theatre." Daily Telegraph (London), 18
      January 1970, p. 16.

1824. Markson, John W. "Tiny Alice: Edward Albee's Negative
       Oedipal Enigma." American Imago, 23 (Spring 1966), 3-21.

1825. Markus, Thomas B. "Tiny Alice and Tragic Cartharsis."
       Educational Theatre Journal, 17 (October 1965), 225-233.

1826. Marriott, R. B. "Glitter, Glamour, But What Does It Add Up
       To?" Stage and Television Today, No. 4632 (22 January
       1970), 13.

1827. Martin, Paulette. "A Theater of Mystery: From the Absurd
       to the Religious." Commonweal, 84 (16 September 1966),
       582.

1828. McCarten, John. "The Theatre: Mystical Manipulations."
       New Yorker, 40 (9 January 1965), 84.

1829. McClain, John. "Albee's Secret Is Safe." New York Journal-
       American, 30 December 1964, p. 13.
       Reprinted in New York Theatre Critics' Reviews, 25
       (1964), 96.

1830. _____. "Audiences Also Have Rights." New York Journal-
       American, 4 April 1965, pp. 9S-10S.

1831. _____. "An Intellectual Fraud." New York Journal-
       American, 10 January 1965, p. 32-L.

1832. McKinnon, George. "Tiny Alice: Creditable Acting in
       Albee's Drama." Boston Globe, 4 January 1967, p. 54.

1833. Meehan, Thomas. "Edward Albee and a Mystery." New York
       Times, 30 December 1964, Sec. 2, pp. 1, 16.

1834. Michelson, Herb. "Ball Rewrites Albee's Alice; It's a San
       Francisco Scandal." Variety, 8 October 1975, pp. 73, 75.

1835. Miller, Jeanne. "'Once You Stop Trying to Figure It
       Out....'" San Francisco Examiner, 19 September 1975, p. 29.

1836. Minahen, Betty. "An Enigmatic Opening for ACT's New
       Season." Vallejo (Calif.) Times-Herald, 12 October 1975, p.
       W-7.

1837. Mishkin, Leo. "ACT Repertory: Tiny Alice." Morning Tele-
       graph (New York), 1 October 1969, p. 3.

1838. [Morrison], Hobe. "Tiny Alice." Variety, 1 October 1969,
       p. 70.

1839. Morrison, Kristin. "Pinter, Albee, and 'The Maiden in Shark
       Pond.'" American Imago, 35 (Fall 1978), 259-274.

1840. Muggeridge, Malcolm. "Books." Esquire, 63 (April 1965), 58, 60.

1841. Nadel, Norman. "The Theater: Tiny Alice Is a Large and Worthy Play." New York World-Telegram and Sun, 11 January 1965, p. 8.

1842. _____. "Tiny Alice Lofty and Profound." New York World-Telegram and Sun, 30 December 1964, p. 10. Reprinted in New York Theatre Critics' Reviews, 25 (1964), 95.

1843. Neville, John. "Stage in Review: Albee's Alice Raises Questions." Dallas Morning News, 14 October 1966, p. 12-A.

1844. Nightingale, Benedict. "Cunundrum Castle." New Statesman, 79 (23 January 1970), 125.

1845. Novick, Julius. Beyond Broadway: The Quest for Permanent Theatres, pp. 228-229. New York: Hill and Wang, 1968.

1846. Oppenheim, Irene. "Who's Afraid of Edward Albee?" San Francisco Bay Guardian, 10 October 1975, p. 29.

1847. Oppenheimer, George. "Gielgud Stars in Albee's Tiny Alice." Newsday (Garden City, N.Y.), 30 December 1964, p. 3-C.

1848. _____. "San Francisco Troupe Presents Tiny Alice." Newsday (Garden City, N.Y.), 30 September 1969, p. 28-A.

1849. P[arker], T[heodore] H. "Albee's Tiny Alice Given by Stage Company." Hartford (Conn.) Courant, 1 April 1972, p. 11.

1850. Pease, Donald. Tiny Alice (Edward Albee). [Sound recording of lecture] Deland, Fla.: Everett/Edwards, 1971. (audio cassette, 40 min.)

1851. P[erlin], J[udith Ann]. "The Truth About Alice." A.C.T. 2 Backstage Newsletter (American Conservatory Theatre, San Francisco), 1 (February 1967), 1, 3.

1852. "Playboy After Hours: Theater." Playboy, 12 (April 1965), 20, 22.

1853. Popkin, Henry. "Some American Attitudes to Chekhov." Times (London), 17 December 1969, p. 15.

1854. _____. "Tiny Alice, 'Preposterous Lack of Proportion.'" Vogue, 145 (15 February 1965), 50.

1855. Porter, Bob. "Tiny Alice Visits Center." Dallas Times Herald, 14 October 1966, p. A19.

1856. Post, Robert M. "Albee's Alice." Western Speech, 31 (Fall 1967), 260-265.

1857. Powers, James. "Play Review: Tiny Alice." Hollywood Reporter, 189 (13 January 1966), 3.

1858. Prideaux, Tom. "Who Needs Answers for Albee?" Life, 58 (29 January 1965), 14.

1859. Probst, Leonard. Review of Tiny Alice, WNBC television, New York, 29 September 1969.
      Reprinted in New York Theatre Critics' Reviews, 30 (1969), 257.

1860. Pumphrey, Bryon. "Theater." Arts and Architecture, 83 (April 1966), 34-35.

1861. "Puppet Shows." Time, 94 (17 October 1969), 72.

1862. Raidy, William A. "Modern Morality Play." Long Island Press (Jamaica, N.Y.), 30 December 1964, p. 6.

1863. [Review of Tiny Alice] Booklist and Subscription Books Bulletin, 61 (1 June 1965), 946.

1864. [Review of Tiny Alice] Choice, 2 (July-August 1965), 309.

1865. R[ichards], L[eila]. "Tiny Alice." Park East (New York), 16 October 1969, p. 12.

1866. Richter, Judy. "Tiny Alice Is to Enjoy--Not Interpret." Fairfield (Calif.) Daily Republic, 8 October 1975, p. 24.

1867. Riley, Clayton. "Tiny Alice: A Personal Confession." Manhattan Tribune (New York), 11 October 1969, p. 9-10.

1868. Rogoff, Gordon. "The Trouble with Alice." Reporter, 32 (28 January 1965), 53-54.

1869. Roth, Philip. "The Play That Dare Not Speak Its Name." New York Review of Books, 4 (25 February 1965), 4.
      Reprinted in Edward Albee: A Collection of Critical Essays, ed. by C. W. E. Bigsby, pp. 105-109. Englewood Cliffs, N.J.: Prentice-Hall, 1975.

1870. _____. [Reply to letters] New York Review of Books, 4 (8 April 1965), 37.

1871. Sachs, Lloyd. "Albee's Tiny Alice in a Wise but Labored Production." Chicago Sun-Times, 1 February 1978, p. 81.

1872. Sales, Grover, Jr. "The A.C.T. First Season ... The Plight of Non-Subsidized Theater in America." San Francisco, 9 (August 1967), 30-31, 78-83.

1873. "Say, What's Going On?" South Buffalo-West Seneca News (Buffalo, N.Y.), 20 November 1969, p. 1.

1874. Schultze, Edward W. "Boos and Bouquets." Wethersfield (Conn.) Post, 18 April 1968, p. 12.

1875. Shaw, Howard N. "Mr. Albee's Error." [Letter] New York Times, 25 April 1965, Sec. 2, p. 4.

1876. Sheed, Wilfrid. "Mirror, Mirror." Commonweal, 81 (22 January 1965), 543-544.

1877. Sheppard, Eugenia. "Inside Fashion: The Richest Woman." New York Herald Tribune, 29 December 1964, p. 13.

1878. Sherman, Thomas B. "Reading & Writing: Dissertation on Faith? Albee Play Has the Reek of Sewage." St. Louis Post-Dispatch, 7 March 1965, p. 4B.

1879. Simon, John. "Theatre Chronicle." Hudson Review, 18 (Spring 1965), 81-90.
      Reprinted in his Uneasy Stages: A Chronicle of the New York Theater, 1963-1973, pp. 62-66. New York: Random House, 1975.

1880. _____. "Theatre: Reviving a Cadaver." New York, 2 (13 October 1969), 53.

1881. Simpson, Herbert M. "Tiny Alice: Limited Affirmation in a Conflict Between Theatre and Drama." Forum (Houston), 6 (Fall/Winter 1968), 43-46.

1882. Skir, Leo. [Letter] New York Review of Books, 4 (8 April 1965), 37.

1883. Skloot, Robert. "The Failure of Tiny Alice." Players Magazine, 43 (February/March 1968), 79-81.

1884. Smith, Donna. "Review: Tiny Alice." Griffin (Canisius College, Buffalo, N.Y.), 14 November 1969, p. 9.

1885. Smith, Michael. "Theatre Journal." Village Voice, 9 October 1969, pp. 43, 57.

1886. _____. "Theatre Uptown: Tiny Alice." Village Voice, 14 January 1965, pp. 13, 17.

1887. Sokolsky, Bob. "Review: Albee's Tiny Alice." Buffalo
       Courier-Express, 7 November 1969, p. 7.

1888. Spurling, Hilary. "Once a Real Turtle." Spectator, 224
       (24 January 1970), 115-116.

1889. Stark, John. "Camping Out: Tiny Alice and Susan Sontag."
       Players Magazine, 47 (April-May 1972), 166-169.

1890. Stone, Judy. "How It All Began." San Francisco Chronicle,
       6 October 1975, p. 40.

1891. Stugrin, Michael. Edward Albee's Tiny Alice and Other
       Works; a Critical Commentary. New York: Monarch Press,
       c1973. (Monarch Notes; 00913)

1892. Stutzin, Leo. "On Stage." Modesto (Calif.) Bee, 12 October
       1975, Sec. C, p. 10.

1893. Sullivan, Dan. "ACT Opens on Broadway with Alice." Los
       Angeles Times, 1 October 1969, pp. 1, 15.

1894. Sullivan, (Rev.) Patrick Sullivan, S.J. "Tiny Alice Offers
       Viewers Choice of Relaxing or Probing." Magnificat (Buffalo,
       N.Y.), 13 November 1969, p. 14.

1895. Syse, Glenna. "Critic At-Large: Hull House in New League."
       Chicago Sun-Times, 30 November 1965, p. 49.

1896. "A Tale Within a Tail." Time, 85 (15 January 1965), 68, 70.

1897. Tallmer, Jerry. "Across the Footlights: Albee on Alice and
       Critics." New York Post, 23 March 1965, p. 54.

1898. _____. "Across the Footlights: Things Will Never Be the
       Same." New York Post, 7 December 1965, p. 64.

1899. Taubman, Howard. "Are the Critics to Blame?" New York
       Times, 11 April 1965, Sec. 2, p. 1.

1900. _____. "Enigma That Runs Down." New York Times, 10
       January 1965, Sec. 2, p. 1.

1901. _____. "Theater: Albee's Tiny Alice Opens." New York
       Times, 30 December 1964, p. 14.
           Reprinted in New York Theatre Critics' Reviews, 25
       (1964), 95-96.

1902. Taylor, Robert. "Albee's Tiny Alice by ACT: Overwritten,
       Underwrought." Oakland (Calif.) Tribune, 7 October 1975,
       p. 20.

1903. Terrien, Samuel. "Albee's Alice." Christianity and Crisis, 25 (28 June 1965), 140-143.

1904. "Tinny Allegory." Time, 85 (8 January 1965), 32.

1905. "Tiny Alice Is Branded Offensive in Singapore." New York Times, 24 July 1969, p. 13.

1906. "Tiny Alice to Close May 22; Will Try London in Summer." New York Times, 10 May 1965, p. 38.

1907. "Tiny Alice to Continue." Vallejo (Calif.) Times-Herald, 9 October 1975, p. 9.

1908. Tolpegin, Dorothy Dunlap. "The Two-Petaled Flower: A Commentary on Edward Albee's Play, Tiny Alice." Cimarron Review, No. 14 (January 1971), 17-30.

1909. Trewin, J. C. "Albee Fogbound." Illustrated London News, 256 (31 January 1970), 31.

1910. Tucker, John Bartholomew. Review of Tiny Alice, WABC television, New York, 29 September 1969.
       Reprinted in New York Theatre Critics' Reviews, 30 (1969), 257.

1911. Ulanov, Barry. "Play of the Month: Luv and Tiny Alice." Catholic World, 200 (March 1965), 383-384.

1912. Unger, Michael D. "Albee Tries to Define Intent of Tiny Alice." Newark Evening News, 23 April 1965, p. 62.

1913. Valgemae, Mardi. "Albee's Great God Alice." Modern Drama, 10 (December 1967), 267-273.

1914. Wardle, Irving. "Albee Presents a Poser." Times (London), 16 January 1970, p. 13.

1915. _____. "Giles Havergal's Miniature National Theatre." Times (London), 13 December 1971, p. 10.

1916. _____. "Waiting for Alice." Times (London), 10 January 1970, pp. I, III.

1917. Washer, Ben. "The New York Play: Tiny Alice, ANTA Theatre." Hollywood Reporter, 207 (1 October 1969), 3.

1918. Watts, Richard. "Two on the Aisle: Edward Albee Stirs Up Debates." New York Post, 17 January 1965, p. 22.

1919. _____. "Two on the Aisle: Edward Albee's Enigmatic Parable." New York Post, 11 October 1969, p. 20.

142   Edward Albee

1920.   _____. "Two on the Aisle: Edward Albee's Home of
          Secrets." New York Post, 30 December 1964, p. 14.
          Reprinted in New York Theatre Critics' Reviews, 25
          (1964), 97.

1921.   _____. "Two on the Aisle: The Mysteries of Tiny Alice."
          New York Post, 30 September 1969, p. 71.
          Reprinted in New York Theatre Critics' Reviews, 30
          (1969), 255.

1922.   _____. "Two on the Aisle: To Get Right Back to Edward
          Albee." New York Post, 7 February 1965, p. 16.

1923.   Weiner, Bernard. "ACT's Tiny Alice--Diary of a Controver-
          sy." San Francisco Chronicle, 6 October 1975, p. 40.

1924.   Weintraub, Stanley. Review of Tiny Alice. Books Abroad,
          39 (Autumn 1965), 459.

1925.   White, James E. "Albee's Tiny Alice, an Exploration of
          Paradox." Literatur in Wissenschaft und Unterricht, 6
          (1973), 247-258.

1926.   _____. "Santayanian Finesse in Albee's Tiny Alice."
          Notes on Contemporary Literature, 3 (May 1973), 12-13.

1927.   Willeford, William. "The Mouse in the Model." Modern Drama,
          12 (September 1969), 135-145.

1928.   Young, B. A. "Tiny Alice." Financial Times (London), 16
          January 1970, p. 3.

1929.   Zeiger, Henry A. "On Stage: Three from ACT, Plus One."
          New Leader, 52 (27 October 1969), 23-25.

1930.   Zolotow, Sam. "Box-Office Queue for Tiny Alice." New York
          Times, 31 December 1964, p. 14.

                              WALKING

1931.   Sullivan, Dan. "Walking." Los Angeles Times, 26 May 1984,
          Sec. 5, p. 2.

                 WHO'S AFRAID OF VIRGINIA WOOLF?

1932.   "2 New Censors Unhappy About Ban on Woolf." Sunday
          Times (Johannesburg), 6 October 1963, p. 15.

1933.   "5 Pinkertons Weed Out Juves Trying to See Woolf." Daily
          Variety, 132 (24 June 1966), 1, 4. (FILM)

1934. "1,000 in South Africa Wait in Vain to See Albee's Play."
      New York Times, 3 October 1963, p. 31.

1935. "$75,000 to Charity at Woolf New York Debut." Motion Pic-
      ture Daily, 99 (24 June 1966), 1, 3. (FILM)

1936. "$1,300,000 for Virginia Woolf First Week...." Hollywood Re-
      porter, 191 (6 July 1966), 1. (FILM)

1937. Acharya, Shanta. "Edward Albee: Beyond the Absurd."
      Bulletin of the Department of English (University of Calcutta),
      13 (1977/78), 22-29.

1938. "Actor Shuffles in Woolf Casts; Who's on First?" Variety, 19
      June 1963, p. 65.

1939. "Actor to Await Censors' Decision." Rand Daily Mail (Johan-
      nesburg), 19 October 1963, p. 3.

1940. "Actors to Discuss Play's Suspension." Sunday Express
      (Johannesburg), 6 October 1963, p. 11.

1941. Adler, Thomas P. "Albee's Who's Afraid of Virginia Woolf?:
      A Long Night's Journey into Day." Educational Theatre
      Journal, 25 (March 1973), 66-70.

1942. "Advanced Tactics in Marital Warfare." Times (London), 7
      February 1964, p. 15.

1943. Agel, Julie. "Probable?" [Letter] New York Times, 2 De-
      cember 1962, Sec. 2, p. 5.

1944. Agnihotri, S. M. "Child-Symbol and Imagery in Edward
      Albee's Who's Afraid of Virginia Woolf?" Punjab University
      Research Bulletin (Arts), 3 (October 1972), 107-111.

1945. Agueros, Jack. "Quien le teme a Virginia Woolf?" Village
      Voice, 26 October 1972, p. 62.

1946. Aguglia, John. "Virginia Woolf Is Ending Note for Old
      Studio Arena Theatre." Griffin (Canisius College, Buffalo,
      N.Y.), 14 April 1978, p. 3.

1947. "Albee Gets It Wrong?" Observer (London), 5 March 1967,
      p. 23. (FILM)

1948. "Albee Integrates Audience Abroad." New York Times, 11
      September 1963, p. 46.

1949. "Albee Nixes Homo Virginia Woolf." Variety, 18 November
      1970, pp. 1, 76.

1950. "Albee Play Divides Stockholm Critics." New York Times, 6
       October 1963, p. 68.

1951. "Albee Play in Paris Closed by Dispute Between Stars." New
       York Times, 3 December 1965, p. 45.

1952. "Albee Play Seen by Few Africans." New York Times, 24
       September 1963, p. 45.

1953. "Albee Play Wins British Award." Daily News (New York), 6
       January 1965, p. 28.

1954. "Albee Seeking to Close All-Male Woolf." New York Times, 3
       August 1984, p. C5.

1955. "Albee Tailors Woolf to Suit Boston." New York Post, 5
       September 1963, p. 17.

1956. "The Albee Whodunnit." Observer (London), 12 March 1967,
       p. 23. (FILM)

1957. "Albee's Woolf Scores in London." New York Post, 9 Feb-
       ruary 1964, p. 17.

1958. "Albee's World." Critical Digest, 14 (22 October 1962), p.
       [3].

1959. Allen, E. [Letter] Nashville (Tenn.) Banner, 23 July 1966,
       p. 4.

1960. Angell, Richard C. [Letter] Reporter, 30 (30 January
       1964), 12.

1961. Atkinson, Brooks, and Albert Hirschfeld. "Edward Albee:
       Who's Afraid of Virginia Woolf?" In their The Lively Years,
       1920-1973, pp. 277-280. New York: Association Press,
       1973.

1962. "Aussie Pic Censors Unafraid of Woolf." Variety, 17 August
       1966, p. 15. (FILM)

1963. "Author Agrees: Virginia Bows to Censor Edict." Boston
       Globe, 4 September 1963, p. 19.

1964. "Author Halts Montreal Production." Body Politic (Toronto),
       11 (January 1974), 4.

1965. Avery, Nicholas C. "The Exorcism of a Tabooed Wish: An
       Analysis of Who's Afraid of Virginia Woolf?" Seminars in
       Psychiatry, 5 (August 1973), 347-357.

1966. "Award Given to Virginia Woolf." New York Times, 26 April
       1963, p. 25.

1967. Axel, Marian. "Trap of Success." [Letter] New York Herald
       Tribune, 26 May 1963, Sec. 4, p. 3.

1968. B., C. "The Play is Horrible But the Acting Superb."
       Natal Mercury (Durban, South Africa), 18 September 1963,
       p. 13.

1969. Baker, Robb. "Surviving Without Paragraphs." Soho Weekly
       News (New York), 15 April 1976, pp. 33, 36.

1970. "Ban on Virginia Woolf Film." Times (London), 19 July 1966,
       p. 19. (FILM)

1971. "The Banning of Virginia Woolf." Stage and Television Today,
       No. 4305 (17 October 1963), 15.

1972. Bannon, Barbara A. Review of Who's Afraid of Virginia
       Woolf? Publishers Weekly, 189 (13 June 1966), 131.

1973. Barker, Felix. "Terrifying--and What a Grand Play."
       Evening News (London), 7 February 1964, p. 7.

1974. Barnes, Clive. "Stage: Virginia Woolf." New York Times,
       2 April 1976, p. 20.
       Reprinted in New York Theatre Critics' Reviews, 37
       (1976), 310.

1975. Barr, Richard, and Clinton Wilder. "Boston Has Special
       Definition of Deity?" [Letter] Variety, 18 September 1963,
       p. 68.

1976. Bart, Peter. "What Big Eyes You Have, Grandma." New
       York Times, 11 July 1965, Sec. 2, p. 5. (FILM)

1977. _____. "Woolf at Hollywood's Door." New York Times,
       12 July 1964, Sec. 2, p. 7. (FILM)

1978. Bates, John. "Hope?" [Letter] New York Times, 4 Novem-
       ber 1962, Sec. 2, p. 3.

1979. Baumhover, Betty. "Courageous Protest." [Letter]
       Telegraph-Herald (Dubuque, Iowa), 10 September 1966,
       p. 4. (FILM)

1980. Baxandall, Lee. "Theatre and Affliction." Encore, 10
       (May/June 1963), 8-13.

1981. Beaufort, John. "Who's Afraid of Virginia Woolf in Potent

146   Edward Albee

Revival." Christian Science Monitor, 9 April 1976, p. 19.
Reprinted in New York Theatre Critics' Reviews, 37
(1976), 313.

1982. Bell, Eleanor. "Edward Albee: Human Conduct Under
      Scrutiny." Cincinnati Post and Times-Star, 29 June 1966,
      p. 32. (FILM)

1983. Bellamy, Peter. "Be Left Limp But Don't Be Afraid of
      Woolf." Cleveland Plain Dealer, 17 March 1966, p. 55.

1984. "Berlin Festival Charges Edward Albee Betrayal on Priority
      to Woolf." Variety, 23 October 1963, p. 63.

1985. Bigsby, C. W. E. "Who's Afraid of Virginia Woolf?: Edward
      Albee's Morality Play." Journal of American Studies, 1
      (October 1967), 257-268.

1986. Blank, Edward L. "Something to Be Afraid of: Camelot's
      Virginia Woolf." Pittsburgh Press, 7 April 1978, p. A-12.

1987. Blau, Herbert. The Impossible Theater; a Manifesto, pp.
      39-42. New York: Macmillan, 1964.

1988. Blevins, Phebe. "Barter Actors Pass Tough Test in Experi-
      mental Theatre Drama." Roanoke (Va.) Times, 2 July 1965,
      p. 12.

1989. Blinken, Donald M. "Unpleasant." [Letter] New York
      Times, 1 September 1963, Sec. 2, p. 3.

1990. "Blood Sport." Time, 80 (26 October 1962), 84, 86.

1991. Blum, Harold P. "A Psychoanalytic View of Who's Afraid of
      Virginia Woolf?" Journal of the American Psychoanalytic
      Association, 17 (July 1969), 888-903.
          Reprinted in Lives, Events, and Other Players: Direc-
      tions in Psychobiography, ed. by Joseph T. Coltrera, pp.
      271-283. New York: Aronson, 1981. (Downstate Psycho-
      analytic Institute Twenty-Fifth Anniversary Series)

1992. Bobker, Lee R. "Albee vs. Chester." [Letter] Commentary,
      36 (October 1963), 274-275.

1993. Boge, Elaine. "Noteworthy Aspects." [Letter] Telegraph-
      Herald (Dubuque, Iowa), 6 September 1966, p. 4. (FILM)

1994. Bolton, Whitney. "Stage Review: Atelje 212 Troupe in
      Virginia Woolf." Morning Telegraph (New York), 5 July
      1968.

1995. _____. "Theatre: Cummings Convincing as Virginia
Woolf." Morning Telegraph (New York), 26 September 1964,
p. 2.

1996. _____. "Theatre: Further Evaluation of Virginia Woolf,
Still Effective, with Single-Track Theme." Morning Telegraph (New York), 5 November 1962, p. 2.

1997. _____. "Theatre: Introduce British Actors Resolution on
Characters in Virginia Woolf." Morning Telegraph (New York),
11 February 1963.

1998. _____. "Theatre: 'It Was Gigantic When I First Read It';
Hagen Talks of Role in Virginia Woolf." Morning Telegraph
(New York), 16 January 1963, p. 2.

1999. _____. "Theatre: Season Hasn't Lived Up to It's [sic] fore-
cast; Woolf Is Most Substantial Offering." Morning Telegraph
(New York), 8 November 1962, p. 2.

2000. Bone. "Who's Afraid of Virginia Woolf?" Variety, 3 March
1976, p. 89.

2001. Bonin, Jane F. Major Themes in Prize-Winning American
Drama, pp. 46-48, 134-136. Metuchen, N.J.: Scarecrow
Press, 1975.

2002. _____. "Who's Afraid of Virginia Woolf?" In her Prize-
Winning American Drama: A Bibliographical and Descriptive
Guide, pp. 171-174. Metuchen, N.J.: Scarecrow Press,
1973.

2003. "Boston Censor Asks Cuts in Albee Play." New York Times,
4 September 1963, p. 35.

2004. "Boston, the Cradle of Censorship, Trims Virginia Woolf
as 'Cesspool'; Dailies, Liberties Union Protest." Variety, 11
September 1963, pp. 79, 84.

2005. Boyd, Malcolm. "Movies: Purgatorial." Christian Century,
83, (27 July 1966), 937-938. (FILM)

2006. Branche, Bill. "Beyond the Shock, Virginia Is Comedy."
Niagara Gazette (Niagara Falls, N.Y.), 8 April 1978, p. 4A.

2007. Branigan, Alan. "Vivid Combat: Cummings, Clark Head
Fine Virginia Woolf Cast." Newark Evening News, 25
August 1964, p. 54.

2008. "Broadway and Hollywood Acclaim Who's Afraid of Virginia
Woolf?" Motion Picture Daily, 99 (24 June 1966), 4-5. (FILM)

148   Edward Albee

2009. Brody, Benjamin. "Psychology and the Arts: Who's Afraid
       of Virginia Woolf?" Psychology Today, 10 (October 1976),
       26.

2010. Brown, John Lindsay. "Pictures of Innocence." Sight and
       Sound, 41 (Spring 1972), 101-103. (FILM)

2011. Bruer, Thomas. "And Men Died for This Freedom."
       [Letter] Nashville (Tenn.) Tennessean, 21 July 1966, p. 16.
       (FILM)

2012. Brustein, Robert. "Albee and the Medusa-Head." New
       Republic, 147 (3 November 1962), 29-30.
       Reprinted in his Seasons of Discontent; Dramatic Opinions
       1959-1965, pp. 145-148. New York: Simon and Schuster,
       1965.

2013. _____. "Death Rattles Down on Broadway." Observer
       (London), 25 November 1962, p. 25.

2014. Bryant, Hallman R. "Let the People Do the Deciding."
       [Letter] Nashville (Tenn.) Tennessean, 23 July 1966, p. 4.
       (FILM)

2015. Buchanan, D. E. "Who's Afraid of Virginia Woolf." Film
       (London), No. 48 (Spring 1967), 38. (FILM)

2016. Buckley, Tom. "Who's Afraid of Broadway? Not Ben
       Gazzara." New York Times, 23 May 1976, Sec. 2, p. 7.

2017. Bunce, Alan N. "... and Molière." Christian Science
       Monitor, 12 July 1968, p. 4.

2018. Burgess, Martha K. P. "Human Values." [Letter] New
       York Times, 1 September 1963, Sec. 2, p. 3.

2019. "Burns Balks at Pfohl Plan for Legal Action on Film."
       Telegraph-Herald (Dubuque, Iowa), 26 August 1966, p. 1.
       (FILM)

2020. Byars, John A. "Taming of the Shrew and Who's Afraid of
       Virginia Woolf?" Cimarron Review, No. 21 (October 1972),
       41-48.

2021. Cain, Alex Matheson. "Eating People Is Wrong." Tablet,
       218 (15 February 1964), 190.

2022. "Call Me Elizabeth." Newsweek, 66 (13 September 1965),
       86. (FILM)

2023. Callenbach, Ernest. "Who's Afraid of Virginia Woolf." Film
       Quarterly, 20 (Fall 1966), 45-48. (FILM)

2024. "Calls Sgt. Cobb 'Ignorant Busybody.'" <u>Variety</u>, 27 July
       1966, p. 23. (FILM)

2025. Calta, Louis. "<u>Virginia Woolf</u> to Close May 16; Albee Hit
       Leaves Broadway After 660 Performances." <u>New York Times</u>,
       5 May 1964, p. 53.

2026. Cameron, Kate. "Magnificent Acting in <u>Virginia Woolf</u>."
       <u>Daily News</u> (New York), 24 June 1966, p. 72. (FILM)

2027. Canby, Vincent. "Public Not Afraid of Big Bad <u>Woolf</u>;
       2,000 See Film of Albee Play and Emerge Unshocked." <u>New
       York Times</u>, 25 June 1966, p. 21. (FILM)

2028. _____. "Valenti Is Facing First Film Crisis; Movie Asso-
       ciation Refuses Seal to <u>Virginia Woolf</u>." <u>New York Times</u>, 28
       May 1966, p. 12. (FILM)

2029. _____. "<u>Virginia Woolf</u> Given Code Seal; Industry's
       Censors Exempt Film from Speech Rules." <u>New York Times</u>,
       11 June 1966, p. 21. (FILM)

2030. Candide. "The Theatre: <u>Who's Afraid of Virginia Woolf?</u>"
       <u>Villager</u> (New York), 25 October 1962, p. 12.

2031. Carnes, Del. "It's Monumental Film; Albee Can't Cry
       'Woolf.'" <u>Denver Post</u>, 30 June 1966, p. 46. (FILM)

2032. Carney, Brian R. "Mind Boggles at the Thought." [Letter]
       <u>Nashville</u> (Tenn.) <u>Tennessean</u>, 22 July 1966, p. 12. (FILM)

2033. Carr, Duane R. "St. George and the Snapdragons: The
       Influence of Unamuno on <u>Who's Afraid of Virginia Woolf?</u>"
       <u>Arizona Quarterly</u>, 29 (Spring 1973), 5-13.

2034. Carruth, Grant F. [Letter] <u>Nashville</u> (Tenn.) <u>Banner</u>, 23
       July 1966, p. 4. (FILM)

2035. Cassidy, Claudia. "On the Aisle: Afraid of <u>Virginia Woolf</u>,
       Pulitzer Snubs the Stage Despite Equity's Golden Jubilee."
       <u>Chicago Tribune</u>, 7 May 1963, Sec. 2, p. 1.

2036. "Catholic Office's A-4 Rating to <u>Woolf</u>; Industry's Own Seal
       Still Not Bestowed." <u>Variety</u>, 1 June 1966, p. 7. (FILM)

2037. "Catholics Define <u>Woolf</u> Attitude." <u>Variety</u>, 1 June 1966,
       p. 7. (FILM)

2038. "Censors Ban Woolf as Offensive." <u>Rand Daily Mail</u> (Johan-
       nesburg), 11 October 1963, p. 2.

2039. "Censors Have Read Virginia Woolf." Star (Johannesburg),
       7 October 1963, p. 1.

2040. Champlis, Charles. "Virginia Woolf Was Afraid." Washington
       Post, 7 August 1966, Sec. G, p. 1.

2041. Chapman, John. "For Dirty-Minded Females Only; the
       Women Begin to Patronize Lewd, Vulgar, Obscene Shows."
       Daily News (New York), 21 October 1962, Sec. 2, p. 1.

2042. _____. "A Play Lies Under the Muck in Who's Afraid of
       Virginia Woolf?" Daily News (New York), 15 October 1962,
       p. 46.
       Reprinted in New York Theatre Critics' Reviews, 23
       (1962), 251.

2043. _____. "Show Business: Virginia Woolf DOESN'T Win a
       Pulitzer Prize; No Drama Cited." Daily News (New York),
       7 May 1963, p. 53.

2044. "Characters' Sexes Restored: Who's Afraid to Re-Open
       Tomorrow." Gazette (Montreal), 3 December 1963, p. 21.

2045. Chester, Alfred. "Edward Albee: Red Herrings and White
       Whales." Commentary, 35 (April 1963), 296-301.

2046. Chiari, Joseph. Landmarks of Contemporary Drama, pp. 157-
       160. London: Herbert Jenkins, 1965.

2047. Chiaromonte, Nicolo. "Albee Damned." New York Review
       of Books, 1 (special issue 1963), 16.

2048. Choudhuri, A. D. "Who's Afraid of Virginia Woolf?: Death
       of an Illusion." In his The Face of Illusion in American
       Drama, pp. 129-143. Atlantic Highlands, N.J.: Humanities,
       1979.

2049. Christiansen, Richard. "Ivanhoe Woolf a Knockout."
       Chicago Daily News, 23 September 1970, p. 39.

2050. Christie, Roy. "Warning by Virginia Woolf Stars: Crisis
       Threat to S.A. Theatre." Sunday Times (Johannesburg),
       6 October 1963, p. 1.

2051. Clark, Glenn. "Nichols, May Not Afraid of Virginia Wolfe
       [sic]." West Haven (Conn.) News, 17 April 1980, p. 13.

2052- Clark, Margy. "Albee's Virginia Woolf--Still Has the Shocks."
53.   Kingsport (Tenn.) Times-News, 9 July 1967, Sec. B, p. 5.

2054. Clay, Carolyn. "A Night on Bitch Mountain: Albee: Still

Savage After All These Years." Boston Phoenix, 15 May
1979, Sec. 3, p. 5.

2055. Clurman, Harold. "Theatre." Nation, 195 (27 October 1962),
273-274.
        Reprinted in his The Naked Image; Observations on the
Modern Theatre, pp. 18-21. New York: Macmillan, 1966.
        Reprinted in his The Divine Pastime; Theatre Essays,
pp. 112-115. New York: Macmillan, 1974.
        Reprinted in Edward Albee: A Collection of Critical Es-
says, ed. by C. W. E. Bigsby, pp. 76-79. Englewood Cliffs,
N.J.: Prentice-Hall, 1975.

2056. _____. "Theatre." Nation, 222 (24 April 1976), 507-508.

2057. "Code Review Board Overrules Shurlock, Gives Woolf Seal."
Daily Variety, 132 (13 June 1966), 1. (FILM)

2058. Coe, Richard L. "One on the Aisle: Did Academe Strike
Back?" Washington Post, 8 May 1963, p. C8.

2059. _____. "One on the Aisle: 'Ginny Woolf' Now on Discs."
Washington Post, 1 June 1963, p. A-12.

2060. _____. "One on the Aisle: Nancy Kelly in Albee's
Drama." Washington Post, 28 April 1964, p. B-10.

2061. _____. "Public Corrects Pulitzer Oversight; 'Ginny' Is
One Not to Be Ignored." Washington Post, 10 May 1964,
Sec. G, p. 1.

2062. _____. "Who's Afraid of Theatricality? Not Virginia
Woolf?" Washington Post, 28 October 1962, Sec. G, p. 1.

2063. Cole, Douglas. "Albee's Virginia Woolf and Steele's Tatler."
American Literature, 40 (March 1968), 81-82.

2064. Coleman, D. C. "Fun and Games: Two Pictures of Heart-
break House." Drama Survey, 5 (Winter 1966/67), 223-236.

2065. Coleman, John. "Ordinary Films: Paris." New Statesman,
72 (15 July 1966), 103. (FILM)

2066. Coleman, Robert. "The Play You'll Love to Loath." Daily
Mirror (New York), 15 October 1962, p. 20.
        Reprinted in New York Theatre Critics' Reviews, 23
(1962), 254.

2067. Connolly, Peter. "Chronicle: Stage and Screen." Furrow,
20 (June 1969), 306-309. (FILM)

2068. "Continuing Success Guaranteed." Times (London), 9 May
       1964, p. 5.

2069. "Controversial: Code Seal for Woolf Is Now Under Study;
       Warners, MPA Silent; Catholic Rating Is A-4." Motion Pic-
       ture Daily, 99 (1 June 1966), 1, 4. (FILM)

2070. Cooke, Richard P. "The Theater: Games for a Dark Hour."
       Wall Street Journal, 15 October 1962, p. 12.

2071. Corrigan, Robert W. "The American Theatre: 1960-1965."
       Arts and Sciences (New York University), 66 (13 June 1966),
       10-15.

2072. _____. The Theatre in Search of a Fix, pp. 277-282. New
       York: Delacorte Press, 1973.

2073. Cotter, Jerry. "The New Plays: Who's Afraid of Virginia
       Woolf?" Sign, 42 (December 1962), 54.

2074. _____. "Sleazy Semantics." Sign, 43 (November 1963),
       50.

2075. Coudert, Jo. [Letter] New York Times, 2 December 1962,
       Sec. 2, p. 5.

2076. "Court Permits Woolf? to Resume in Nashville." Motion Pic-
       ture Daily, 100 (21 July 1966), 1, 8. (FILM)

2077. Covington, William R. "One-Man Oversteps All." [Letter]
       Nashville (Tenn.) Tennessean, 23 July 1966, p. 4. (FILM)

2078. Crist, Judith. "Sins of Omission, If Such They Are."
       World-Journal-Tribune (New York), 29 January 1967, p. 31.
       (FILM)
            Reprinted in her The Private Eye, the Cowboy and the
       Very Naked Girl; Movies from Cleo to Clyde, pp. 217-219.
       New York: Holt, Rinehart and Winston, 1968.

2079. Croce, Arlene. "Staying Up Late, Talking Dirty, and All
       That." National Review, 18 (20 September 1966), 943-946.
       (FILM)

2080. Crowther, Bosley. "Who's Afraid of Audacity?" New York
       Times, 10 July 1966, Sec. 2, pp. 10, 20. (FILM)

2081. "DA Won't Bar Door on Woolf." Nashville (Tenn.) Tennessean,
       20 July 1966, pp. 1, 13. (FILM)

2082. Dafoe, Christopher. "A Moment of Truth." Winnipeg Free
       Press, 8 April 1965, p. 13.

2083. Dash, Irene G. "Virginia Woolf: Fact and Fiction, an Onomastic Study." Literary Onomastic Studies, 5 (1978), 172-
191.

2084. David, Gunter. "Virginia Woolf Opens." Newark Evening
News, 18 February 1970, p. 67.

2085. Davis, George. "Existing Condition." [Letter] Telegraph-
Herald (Dubuque, Iowa), 6 September 1966, p. 4. (FILM)

2086. Dawson, Ralph. "Who's Afraid of Virginia Woolf?; Officer
Cobb Clubs Big, Bad Film." Nashville (Tenn.) Tennessean,
18 July 1966, pp. 1, 4. (FILM)

2087. Day, Richard. "A Humorous Virginia Woolf." Bridgeport
(Conn.) Post, 19 April 1980, p. 18.

2088. "De Klerk Bans Controversial Hit Play." Eastern Province
Herald (Port Elizabeth, South Africa), 3 October 1963, p. 1.

2089. "De Klerk Bans Hit Play Who's Afraid...?" Cape Times
(Cape Town), 3 October 1963, pp. 1, 3.

2090. "Deacon-Turned-Cop Draws Rap for Unilateral Censoring of
Virg. Woolf." Variety, 27 July 1966, p. 23. (FILM)

2091. Dehlinger, Dawn. "Meaning of Virginia Wolf [sic] Lost in
Clutter, Search for Message." Perspective (Medaille College,
Buffalo, N.Y.), 1 May 1978, p. 11.

2092. Dent, Alan. "Walpurgisnacht." Illustrated London News,
249 (23 July 1966), 28. (FILM)

2093. Denton, Clive. "On Film." Take One, 1 (June 1967), 38.
(FILM)

2094. Dettmer, Roger. "Ivanhoe's Woolf the Greatest." Chicago
Today, 23 September 1970, p. 43.

2095. "Dewhurst, Gazzara in Woolf." New York Post, 27 January
1976, p. 21.

2096. "Dialogue That Is a Sheer Joy for Film Actors." Times
(London), 7 July 1966, p. 17. (FILM)

2097. [Digest of New York newspaper reviews of Who's Afraid of
Virginia Woolf?"] Critical Digest, 14 (22 October 1962), p.
[2].

2098. Disney, Dorothy Cameron. "Can This Marriage Be Saved?"
Ladies' Home Journal, 83 (February 1966), 59, 109-111.
(FILM)

2099. Dollard, John. "The Hidden Meaning of Who's Afraid ...?"
       Connecticut Review, 7 (October 1973), 24-48.

2100. Dooley, John. "Nichols 'Was Not Concerned' Whether Woolf
       Got a Seal." Daily Variety, 132 (22 June 1966), 4. (FILM)

2101. Dorin, Rube. "Stage Review: McCambridge, Davis in
       Virginia Woolf." Morning Telegraph (New York), 15 January
       1964.

2102. Dozier, Richard J. "Adultery and Disappointment in Who's
       Afraid of Virginia Woolf?" Modern Drama, 11 (February 1969),
       432-436.

2103. Dreele, W. H. von. "The 20th Century and All That...."
       National Review, 14 (15 January 1963), 35-36.

2104. Drew, Bernard L. "Cheers and Catcalls." Hartford (Conn.)
       Times, 7 May 1966, p. 10.

2105. "Drunken Party Play Is Brilliant." Sunday Times (Johannes-
       burg), 8 September 1963, p. 24.

2106. "Dubuque County Atty. Refuses to Cry 'Woolf' vs. Local
       Exhibitor." Variety, 7 September 1966, p. 5. (FILM)

2107. "Dubuque, Ia., Prosecutor Refuses Councilman's Request for
       Court Action vs. Virginia Woolf?" Motion Picture Daily, 100
       (1 September 1966), 1. (FILM)

2108. Ducker, Dan. "'Pow!' 'Snap!' 'Pouf!': The Modes of Commu-
       nication in Who's Afraid of Virginia Woolf?" CLA Journal
       (College Language Association), 26 (June 1983), 465-477.

2109. Dukore, Bernard F. "A Warp in Albee's Woolf." Southern
       Speech Journal, 30 (Spring 1965), 261-268.

2110. Duplessis, Rachel Blau. "In the Bosom of the Family: Eva-
       sions in Edward Albee." Recherches anglaises et américaines,
       5 (1972), 85-96.

2111. Duprey, Richard A. "Play of the Month: Who's Afraid of
       Virginia Woolf?" Catholic World, 196 (January 1963), 263-
       264.

2112. Dwyer, John. "Studio Arena Theater: Excellent Cast
       Balances Acid Woolf Production." Buffalo Evening News, 8
       April 1978, Sec. C, p. 2.

2113. Eckman, Fern Marja. "A Split Vote Cost Albee That Pulit-
       zer." New York Post, 7 May 1963, pp. 3, 23.

2114. "Edward Albee on a Love-Hate Marriage." Times (London),
5 November 1962, p. 14.

2115. Elder, Rob. "Cobb Woolf Tactics Wrong: Kemp; Doyle Drops
Case, Blames Metro Error." Nashville (Tenn.) Tennessean,
21 July 1966, pp. 1-2. (FILM)

2116. _____. "Woolf Film Returned to Theater." Nashville
(Tenn.) Tennessean, 19 July 1966, pp. 1, 6. (FILM)

2117. Engstrom, John. "Who's Afraid of Elaine May?; Albee Re-
furbished." Boston Phoenix, 22 April 1980, Sec. 3, pp. 5,
13.

2118. Esterow, Milton. "Albee Drama Rejected." New York Times,
7 May 1963, pp. 1, 35.

2119. Evans, Arthur. "Love, History and Edward Albee."
Renascence, 19 (Spring 1967), 115-118, 131.

2120. Evans, Gareth Lloyd. "American Connections: O'Neill,
Miller, Williams and Albee." In his The Language of Modern
Drama, pp. 177-204. London: Dent; Totowa, N.J.: Rowman
and Littlefield, 1977.

2121. E[vica], G[eorge] M[ichael]. "Fun and Games." West Hartford (Conn.) News, 12 May 1966, p. 6.

2122. Falk, Eugene H. "No Exit and Who's Afraid of Virginia
Woolf: A Thematic Comparison." Studies in Philology, 67
(July 1970), 406-417.

2123. Farber, Manny. "Rain in the Face, Dry Gulch and Squalling
Mouth." In his Negative Space; Manny Farber on the Movies,
pp. 175-179. New York: Praeger, 1971. (FILM)

2124. Feldman, David. "Stage: American Classic Goes the
Distance." Syracuse (N.Y.) New Times, 19 March 1980,
p. 19.

2125. Ferguson, (Mrs.) Elliot. "She's Afraid." [Letter] New
York Herald Tribune, 18 November 1962, Sec. 4, p. 7.

2126. Ferguson, Francis R. "A Conversation with Digby R. Diehl."
Transatlantic Review, No. 18 (Spring 1965), 115-121.

2127. Feynman, Alberta E. "The Fetal Quality of 'Character' in
the Plays of the Absurd." Modern Drama, 9 (May 1966),
18-25.

2128. Fiedler, Leslie A. "The New Mutants." Partisan Review, 32
(Fall 1965), 505-525.

2129. Filandro, Anthony, and Dolores Filandro. "Albee vs.
       Chester." [Letter] Commentary, 36 (October 1963), 272,
       274.

2130. "Finale: Trail's End for Virginia Woolf." Newark Evening
       News, 16 May 1964, p. 8.

2131. Finkelstein, Sidney. "The Existentialist Trap: Norman
       Mailer and Edward Albee." American Dialog, 2 (February/
       March 1965), 23-28.

2132. "First Woolf Grosses." Variety, 29 June 1966, p. 7. (FILM)

2133. Fischer, Gretl Kraus. "Edward Albee and Virginia Woolf."
       Dalhousie Review, 49 (Summer 1969), 196-207.

2134. [Flanner, Janet] "Letter from Paris." New Yorker, 40
       (26 December 1964), 67-68. (signed "Genêt")

2135. Flasch, Joy. "Games People Play in Who's Afraid of Virginia
       Woolf?" Modern Drama, 10 (December 1967), 280-288.

2136. Fletcher, John. "'A Psychology Based on Antagonism:'
       Ionesco, Pinter, Albee and Others." In The Two Faces of
       Ionesco, ed. by Rosette C. Lamont and Melvin J. Friedman,
       pp. 175-195. Troy, N.Y.: Whitston, 1978.

2137. Foran, Jack. "Who's Afraid of Virginia Woolf? an Illuminating
       Play." Niagara Gazette (Niagara Falls, N.Y.), 22 October
       1977, p. 5A.

2138. Funke, Lewis. "News of the Rialto." New York Times, 21
       October 1962, Sec. 2, p. 1.

2139. Gagnard, Frank. "Albee Play." Times-Picayune (New
       Orleans), 17 November 1969, Sec. 4, p. 10.

2140. _____. "At Home with George, Martha." Times-Picayune
       (New Orleans), 17 January 1975, Sec. 2, p. 2.

2141. _____. "Le Petit's Virginia Woolf Follows Text Verbatim;
       Maturity and Stamina Are Established." Times-Picayune (New
       Orleans), 27 January 1968, Sec. 2, p. 5.

2142. _____. "A Male Martha in Albee Play." Times-Picayune
       (New Orleans), 29 January 1975, Sec. 2, p. 6.

2143. Galbraith, John Kenneth. "The Mystique of Failure: A
       Latter-Day Reflection on Who's Afraid of Virginia Woolf?"
       Show, 4 (May 1964), 112.

2144. Gale, William K. "Trinity's Virginia Woolf Just About a Per-
fect Play." Providence (R.I.) Journal, 2 May 1979, p. A12.

2145. "Game of Truth." Newsweek, 60 (29 October 1962), 52-53.

2146. Gardner, Paul. "Backers of Play by Albee in Doubt." New
York Times, 4 July 1962, p. 11.

2147. _____. "Director Meshes 4 Virginia Woolf Casts." New
York Times, 3 July 1963, p. 17.

2148. _____. "Matinee Troupe Gives Albee Play." New York
Times, 1 November 1962, p. 34.

2149. _____. "Troupe May Omit Matinees." New York Times,
23 July 1962, p. 17.

2150. Gardner, R. H. The Splintered Stage; the Decline of the
American Theater, pp. 147-153. New York: Macmillan,
1965.

2151. Gascoigne, Bamber. "Theatre: Four Domestic Savages."
Observer (London), 9 February 1964, p. 25.

2152. Gassner, John. "Broadway in Review." Educational Theatre
Journal, 15 (March 1963), 75-84.
Reprinted partially in his Dramatic Soundings; Evaluations
and Retractions Culled from 30 Years of Dramatic Criticism,
pp. 592-595. New York: Crown, 1968.

2153. _____. [Introduction] In 50 Best Plays of the American
Theatre, comp. by Clive Barnes, vol. 4, pp. 364-366. New
York: Crown, 1969.

2154. _____. "Who's Afraid of Virginia Woolf on LP." Saturday
Review, 46 (29 June 1963), 39-40, 55.
Reprinted in his Dramatic Soundings; Evaluations and Retractions Culled from 30 Years of Dramatic Criticism, pp.
595-599. New York: Crown, 1968.

2155. Gellert, Roger. "Sex-War Spectacular." New Statesman, 67
(14 February 1964), 262.

2156. Gelmis, Joseph. "Mike Nichols." In his The Film Director
as Superstar, pp. 265-292. Garden City, N.Y.: Doubleday,
1970. (FILM)

2157. Gilbert, E. J. "Record Notes." Impresario, Fall 1963, p. 25.

2158. Gilder, Rosamond. "World Reviews: U.S.A." World Theatre,
12 (Spring 1963), 76.

2159. Gill, Brendan. "The Theatre: In Vino Veritas." New
       Yorker, 52 (12 April 1976), 101.

2160. Gillenwater, Kelso. "Barter's Virginia Woolf Said Exciting,
       Shocking." Virginia-Tennessean (Bristol, Va.), 28 June
       1967, p. 7.

2161. Gilman, Richard. "Here We Go Round the Albee Bush."
       Commonweal, 77 (9 November 1962), 175-176.
       Reprinted in his Common and Uncommon Masks; Writings
       on Theatre 1961-1970, pp. 133-136. New York: Random
       House, 1971.

2162. _____. "Nobody Here But Us Weeklies." Commonweal, 77
       (4 January 1963), 391.

2163. Gottfried, Martin. "Woolf Returns with Same Bite." New
       York Post, 2 April 1976, p. 29.
       Reprinted in New York Theatre Critics' Reviews, 37
       (1976), 311.

2164. Gow, Gordon. "Who's Afraid of Virginia Woolf?" Films and
       Filming, 12 (September 1966), 6. (FILM)

2165. Griffin, William. "Stage: Who's Afraid of Virginia Woolf?"
       Sign, 55 (June 1976), 40.

2166. Groves, Bob. "Studio Arena Review: Virginia Woolf a Tasty
       Topping." Buffalo Courier-Express, 8 April 1978, p. 12.

2167. Guidry, Frederick H. "Albee Drama Brought to Screen."
       Christian Science Monitor, 2 July 1966, p. 6. (FILM)

2168. Haas, Barbara. "Virginia Woolf Masterful Production."
       Post-Standard (Syracuse, N.Y.), 15 March 1980, p. A8.

2169. Hadley, Ted R. "Review: Studio Arena's Virginia Woolf
       Likened to 'Boozed Up LaVerne [sic] and Shirley.'"
       Lockport (N.Y.) Union-Sun and Journal, 13 April 1978, p. 18.

2170. Hale, Wanda. "Hollywood Visitor: After Baby Jane What?"
       Daily News (New York), 20 April 1964, p. 31. (FILM)

2171. Hall, Vernon. "Albee's Who's Afraid of Virginia Woolf?"
       Explicator, 37 (Winter 1979), 32.

2172. Halperen, Max. "What Happens in Who's Afraid ...?" In
       Modern American Drama: Essays in Criticism, ed. by William
       E. Taylor, pp. 129-143. Deland, Fla.: Everett/Edwards,
       1968.

2173. Hamblen, Abigail Ann. "Edward Albee ... and the Fear of
      Virginia Woolf." Trace, No. 68 (1968), 198-203.

2174. Hankiss, Elemér. "Who's Afraid of Edward Albee?" New
      Hungarian Quarterly, 5 (Autumn 1964), 168-174.

2175. Harkins, William E. "Albee Analyzed." [Letter] New York
      Times, 4 November 1962, Sec. 2, p. 3.

2176. Harper, James. "Be Grateful for This Man." [Letter]
      Nashville (Tenn.) Tennessean, 21 July 1966, p. 16. (FILM)

2177. _____. [Letter] Nashville (Tenn.) Banner, 23 July 1966,
      p. 4. (FILM)

2178. Hart, Henry. "1966's Ten Best." Films in Review, 18 (Feb-
      ruary 1967), 65-70. (FILM)

2179. H[art], H[enry]. "Who's Afraid of Virginia Woolf?" Films in
      Review, 17 (August/September 1966), 448-450. (FILM)

2180. Hartung, Philip T. "The Screen: Long Night's Journey."
      Commonweal, 84 (22 July 1966), 474-475. (FILM)

2181. Haun, Harry. "Sgt. Cobb Dealt the City a Civil Black Mark."
      Nashville (Tenn.) Tennessean, 20 July 1966, p. 10. (FILM)

2182. Hayes, Joseph. "Distorted Views: Theater Misrepresents
      Life in America." New York Times, 11 August 1963, Sec. 2,
      p. 1.

2183. Hazard, Forrest E. "The Major Theme in Who's Afraid of
      Virginia Woolf?" CEA Critic, 31 (December 1968), 10-11.

2184. Hemeter, Mark. "Theater Review: Gallery Cast Saves
      Beginning-to-Age Virginia Woolf." New Orleans States-Item,
      17 January 1975, p. B-4.

2185. Hentoff, Nat. "Second Chorus: Invitations to an Argument."
      Village Voice, 15 November 1962, p. 7.

2186. Herron, Ima Honaker. "Albee's New Carthage: The Decay
      of an American House of Intellect." In her The Small Town
      in American Drama, pp. 467-474. Dallas: Southern Metho-
      dist University Press, 1969.

2187. Hewes, Henry. "At Home with the Burtons." Saturday
      Review, 49 (9 July 1966), 40. (FILM)

2188. _____. "Broadway Postscript: Who's Afraid of Big Bad
      Broadway?" Saturday Review, 45 (27 October 1962), 29.

2189. _____. "The Season in New York." In his The Best Plays
       of 1962-1963, pp. 3-24. New York: Dodd, Mead, 1963.

2190. _____. "The Theater: Bravo Belgrade." Saturday Re-
       view, 51 (20 July 1968), 35.

2191. Hilfer, Anthony C. "George and Martha: Sad, Sad, Sad."
       In Seven Contemporary Authors; Essays on Cozzens, Miller,
       West, Golding, Heller, Albee, and Powers, ed. by Thomas B.
       Whitbread, pp. 119-139. Austin, Tex.: University of Texas
       Press, 1966.

2192. Hill, Carol D. "Edward Albee." [Letter] Massachusetts Re-
       view, 6 (Summer 1965), 649-650.

2193. Hipp, Edward Sothern. "Surprise Package: Who's Afraid
       of Virginia Woolf? Stirring." Newark Evening News, 15
       October 1962, p. 38.

2194. Hirschhorn, Clive. The Warner Bros. Story: The Complete
       History of Hollywood's Great Studio, pp. 369-370. New York:
       Crown, 1979. (FILM)

2195. Hobson, Harold. "Bacchae in London." Christian Science
       Monitor, 10 February 1964, p. 4.

2196. Holtan, Orley I. "Who's Afraid of Virginia Woolf? and the
       Patterns of History." Educational Theatre Journal, 25 (March
       1973), 46-52.

2197. Hope-Wallace, Philip. "Review: Who's Afraid of Virginia
       Woolf?" Guardian (Manchester), 7 February 1964, p. 11.

2198. Hopwood, Alison. "'Hey, What's That From/'--Edward Albee's
       Who's Afraid of Virginia Woolf?" Atlantis; A Woman's Studies
       Journal/Revue des études sur la femme, 3 (Spring 1978), 101-
       111.

2199. Houglan, Marylyn. "Many Allies." [Letter] New York
       Times, 1 September 1963, Sec. 2, p. 1.

2200. Howell, (Mrs.) Ray T. [Letter] Nashville (Tenn.) Banner,
       23 July 1966, p. 4. (FILM)

2201. Hughes, Catharine. "Edward Albee: Who's Afraid of What?"
       Critic, 21 (February/March 1963), 16-19.

2202. _____. "Theatre: Truth, Illusion and Virginia Woolf."
       America, 134 (24 April 1976), 362-363.

2203. "If Albee OKs Cuts, Woolf Can Tour S. Africa Again."
       Variety, 18 December 1963, pp. 53, 56.

2204. "If Woolf Is Only a 'Oncer'!" Variety, 29 June 1966, p. 7.
(FILM)

2205. Inge, M. Thomas. "Edward Albee's Love Story of the Age of
the Absurd." Notes on Contemporary Literature, 8 (November 1978), 4-9.

2206. Irwin, Ray. "Who's Afraid of Virginia Woolf, Hunh?" Atlantic, 213 (April 1964), 122-124.

2207. "Jack Warner Remarks Re Woolf." Variety, 1 June 1966, p. 7. (FILM)

2208. Jacobi, Peter P. "Chicago's Homegrown Theater Hits."
Christian Science Monitor, 2 November 1970, p. 4.

2209. Jennings, C. Robert. "All for the Love of Mike." Saturday
Evening Post, 238 (9 October 1965), 83-87. (FILM)

2210. _____. "Playboy Interview: Mike Nichols." Playboy, 13
(June 1966), 63-64, 66, 68, 70, 72-74. (FILM)

2211. Johnson, Malcolm L. "Stage: Albee Directs Woolf Revival."
Hartford (Conn.) Courant, 3 March 1976, p. 59.

2212. _____. "Stage: New Life for Albee Play." Hartford
(Conn.) Courant, 11 April 1980, p. 73.

2213. _____. "Stage Co. Gets Right to Edward Albee Play."
Hartford (Conn.) Courant, 7 April 1965, p. 29.

2214. Johnson, Martha J. "Note on a Possible Source for Who's
Afraid of Virginia Woolf?" Radford Review, 21 (1967), 231-233.

2215. Jones, (Mrs.) Paul E. "Now, Nashville Has a Protector."
[Letter] Nashville (Tenn.) Tennessean, 22 July 1966, p. 12.
(FILM)

2216. "June Dates for Woolf Set in 42 Situations." Motion Picture
Daily, 99 (17 June 1966), 1, 2. (FILM)

2217. K., L. "Theatre Uptown." Village Voice, 8 November 1962,
p. 12.

2218. K[alem], T. E. "Till Death Do Us Part." Time, 107 (12
April 1976), 82-83.
Reprinted in New York Theatre Critics' Reviews, 37
(1976), 313.

2219. Kansa, Edward. "An Overgrown Country Village." [Letter]

Nashville (Tenn.) Tennessean, 21 July 1966, p. 16.
(FILM)

2220. Kaplan, Donald H. "Homosexuality and American Theatre:
A Psychoanalytic Comment." Tulane Drama Review, 9
(Spring 1965), 25-55.

2221. Kaplan, Lisa Faye. "New Virginia Woolf Lacks Vigor, Passion." Fairpress (Norwalk, Conn.), 23 April 1980, pp. F1,
F6.

2222. Kauffmann, Stanley. "Screen: Funless Games at George
and Martha's." New York Times, 24 June 1966, p. 28.
(FILM)
Reprinted in his Figures of Light; Film Criticism and
Comment, pp. 1-4. New York: Harper & Row, 1971.

2223. Keiningham, Jean. "Who's Afraid of Virginia Woolf?"
Henrico Herald (Richmond, Va.), 10 March 1966, p. 1.

2224. Kelley, Kitty. Elizabeth Taylor, the Last Star, pp. 244-251,
257-261. New York: Simon and Schuster, 1981. (FILM)

2225. Kelly, Kevin. "Straightforward Virginia Woolf." Boston
Globe, 19 January 1968, p. 29.

2226. _____. "Virginia Woolf Haunts Again at Trinity Sq."
Boston Globe, 25 May 1979, p. 28.

2227. _____. "Who's Afraid of Virginia Woolf: Blistering, Brilliant Drama by Edward Albee." Boston Globe, 3 September
1963, p. 26.

2228. Kemper, Robert Graham. "Allegory of the American Dream:
Another View of Virginia Woolf." [Letter] Christian Century,
83 (5 October 1966), 1214, 1216.

2229. Kenn. "Who's Afraid of Virginia Woolf?" Variety, 7 November
1962, p. 56.

2230. _____. "Who's Afraid of Virginia Woolf?" Variety, 7
August 1963, p. 64.

2231. K[ennedy], J[ohn] S. "Tricks, Not Drama." Catholic
Transcript (Hartford, Conn.), 17 January 1963, p. 5.

2232. Kerr, Walter. "Albee's Inferno: All Is Malice." New York
Herald Tribune, 21 October 1962, Sec. 4, pp. 1, 3.

2233. _____. "Along Nightmare Alley." Vogue, 141 (1 April
1963), 119.

Reprinted in his Thirty Plays Hath November; Pain and
Pleasure in the Contemporary Theater, pp. 55-58. New
York: Simon and Schuster, 1969.

2234.   _____. "First Night Report: Who's Afraid of Virginia
Woolf?" New York Herald Tribune, 15 October 1962, p. 12.
Reprinted in New York Theatre Critics' Reviews, 23
(1962), 252.
Reprinted with revisions in his The Theatre in Spite of
Itself, pp. 122-126. New York: Simon and Schuster, 1963.

2235.   _____. Tragedy and Comedy, pp. 325-327. New York:
Simon and Schuster, 1967.

2236.   _____. "Virginia Woolf--Sparks Still Fly." New York
Times, 11 April 1976, Sec. 2, pp. 1, 7.

2237. Kilgallen, Dorothy. "The Voice of Broadway: New Play Is
a Stunner." New York Journal-American, 15 October 1962,
p. 13.

2238. "Kilty Believes Albee Stand on Integration Causes Ban."
New York Times, 4 October 1963, p. 29.

2239. "Kilty Blames Mrs. Kushlick for Stopping Woolf Play." Sunday
Express (Johannesburg), 6 October 1963, p. 11.

2240. Kissell, Howard. "Who's Afraid of Virginia Woolf?" Women's
Wear Daily, 2 April 1976, p. 51.
Reprinted in New York Theatre Critics' Reviews, 37
(1976), 312.
Reprinted in Contemporary American Theater Critics:
A Directory and Anthology of Their Works, comp. by M. E.
Comtois and Lynn F. Miller, p. 432. Metuchen, N.J.:
Scarecrow Press, 1977.

2241. Kloten, Edgar. "Theater: Nichols and May Bring Depth to
Virginia Woolf." Hamden (Conn.) Chronicle, 23 April 1980,
p. 5.

2242. Knickerbocker, Paine. "Gay Approach to Edward Albee's
Play." San Francisco Chronicle, 5 April 1972, p. 48.

2243.   _____. "The Weird Ancestry of Who's Afraid of Virginia
Woolf?" San Francisco Examiner & Chronicle, 12 March 1967,
Date Book sec., p. 13.

2244. Koch, John F. "Who's Afraid? They Aren't." [Letter]
Telegraph Herald (Dubuque, Iowa), 6 September 1966, p. 4.
(FILM)

2245. Koch, Marvin B. "Bravo for Cobb--However Wrong."
       [Letter] Nashville (Tenn.) Tennessean, 22 July 1966, p. 12.
       (FILM)

2246. Kosman, Joshua. "Nichols & May Flounder in LWT's Limp
       Virginia Woolf." Yale Daily News (New Haven, Conn.), 17
       April 1980, p. 5.

2247. Koven, Stan. "The Playwright Rides Out a Stormy Opening
       Night." New York Post, 15 October 1962, p. 5.

2248. Kretzmer, Herbert. "Cannibalism--or What's Eating Albee."
       Daily Express (London), 7 February 1964, p. 15.

2249. Krim, Seymour. "The Press of Freedom: Who's Afraid of
       the New Yorker Now?" Village Voice, 8 November 1962, pp.
       16-17.

2250. Kroll, Jack. "Albee's Blackjack." Newsweek, 87 (12 April
       1976), 109, 111.
          Reprinted in New York Theatre Critics' Reviews, 37
       (1976), 314.

2251. La Belle, Jenijoy. "Albee's Who's Afraid of Virginia Woolf?"
       Explicator, 35 (Fall 1976), 8-9.

2252. Lamport, Harold. "Who's Afraid of Virginia Woolf?" In
       Best American Plays: Fifth Series, 1957-1963, ed. by John
       Gassner, pp. 146-148. New York: Crown, 1963.
          Reprinted in 50 Best Plays of the American Theatre,
       comp. by Clive Barnes, vol. 4, pp. 366-368. New York:
       Crown, 1969.

2253. Lask, Thomas. "Original Cast Records Albee Play." New
       York Times, 15 September 1963, Sec. 2, p. 13.

2254. Laufe, Abe. Anatomy of a Hit: Long Run Plays on Broad-
       way from 1900 to the Present Day, pp. 302-309. New York:
       Hawthorn, 1966.

2255. Lazarus, Arnold. "Playing the Piano with More Than One
       Finger." CEA Critic, 27 (February 1965), 2.

2256. Leff, Leonard J. "Albee's Who's Afraid of Virginia Woolf?"
       Explicator, 35 (Winter 1976), 8-10.

2257. _____. "Play into Film: Warner Brothers' Who's Afraid of
       Virginia Woolf?" Theatre Journal, 33 (December 1981), 453-
       466. (FILM)

2258. _____. "A Test of American Film Censorship: Who's

Afraid of Virginia Woolf? (1966)." In Hollywood as Historian;
American Film in a Cultural Context, ed. by Peter C.
Rollins, pp. 211-229. Lexington: University Press of Ken-
tucky, 1983. (FILM)

2259. Lehman, Ernest. Edward Albee's "Who's Afraid of Virginia
Woolf?": Screenplay. Burbank, Calif.: Warner Brothers;
distributed by Writers Guild of America, c1965. (FILM)

2260. Leonard, Hugh, and Charles Marowitz. "Who's Afraid of
Virginia Woolf/Two Views." Plays and Players, 11 (April
1964), 32-34.
Marowitz review reprinted with revisions in his Confes-
sions of a Counterfeit Critic; a London Theatre Notebook
1958-1971, pp. 85-87. London: Methuen, 1973.

2261. Leonard, William. "Albee in Revival Still a Thriller."
Chicago Tribune, 23 September 1970, Sec. 2, p. 6.

2262. Lerman, Leo. "Catch Up With." Mademoiselle, 63 (September
1966), 100. (FILM)

2263. Lerner, Max. "Pulitzer Lost." New York Post, 7 May 1963,
p. 49.

2264. _____. "Who's Afraid?" New York Post, 17 October 1962,
p. 53.

2265. Lewis, Allan. "Theater: Albee's George, Martha Still
Worthy Combatants." New Haven (Conn.) Register, 20 April
1980, Sec. D, pp. 3-4.

2266. Lewis, Emory. "The Theatre: Some Heavy Drinking on
Campus." Cue, 31 (27 October 1962), 13.

2267. Lewis, Peter. "They're All Afraid of Virginia Woolf." Daily
Mail (London), 7 February 1964, p. 14.

2268. Lewis, Theophilus. "Theatre: Reviewer's Notebook."
America, 111 (3 October 1964), 391-392.

2269. _____. "Theatre: Who's Afraid of Virginia Woolf?"
America, 107 (17 November 1962), 1105-1106.

2270. "Life's Exhaustive Pictorial-Critical Slant on Afraid of Virginia
Woolf?" Variety, 15 June 1966, p. 20. (FILM)

2271. Lightman, Herb A. "The Dramatic Photography of Who's
Afraid of Virginia Woolf?" American Cinematographer, 47
(August 1966), 530-533, 558-559. (FILM)

2272. Lineberger, James. "Albee Damned." [Letter] Reporter,
       30 (30 January 1964), 10.

2273. Little, Stuart W. "At the Virginia Woolf Box Office: Who
       Needs the Pulitzer Prize?" New York Herald Tribune, 8
       May 1968, p. 19.

2274. _____. "Drama Critics Vote Virginia Woolf Best Play."
       New York Herald Tribune, 26 April 1963, p. 17.

2275. _____. "Theater News: A Director's Double Trouble--Re-
       hearsing 2 Casts for 1 Show." New York Herald Tribune, 11
       October 1962, p. 19.

2276. _____. "Theater News: Cuts for Boston." New York
       Herald Tribune, 6 September 1963, p. 11.

2277. _____. "Theater News: Full-Length Albee." New York
       Herald Tribune, 14 September 1962, p. 12.

2278. _____. "Theater News: Matinee Cast of Virginia Woolf
       May Accept Out-of-Town Dates." New York Herald Tribune,
       1 November 1962, p. 13.

2279. _____. "Theater News: Moby Dick Is Closing; Virginia
       Woolf in Black." New York Herald Tribune, 5 December 1962,
       p. 17.

2280. _____. "Theater News: No One's Afraid of Virginia
       Woolf." New York Herald Tribune, 16 October 1962, p. 18.

2281. _____. "Theater News: Virginia Woolf Signs Elaine
       Stritch." New York Herald Tribune, 5 April 1963, p. 17.

2282. _____. "Virginia Woolf Hits Road; 500% Profit on Home
       Stand." New York Herald Tribune, 2 September 1963, p. 10.

2283. _____. "Woolf's Hagen & Hill Named Best by Critics."
       New York Herald Tribune, 25 July 1963, p. 11.

2284. "London Acclaims Virginia Woolf." New York Times, 8 Feb-
       ruary 1964, p. 15.

2285. "A Long Wait Pays Off." New York Herald Tribune, 18 No-
       vember 1962, Sec. 4, p. 3.

2286. "Longer Rand Run for Play That Shocked Durban Critics."
       Sunday Express (Johannesburg), 29 September 1963, p. 10.

2287. Loughery, Patricia. "Virginia Woolf at Long Wharf."
       Evening Sentinel (Ansonia, Conn.), 28 April 1980, p. 5.

2288. Lyons, Charles R. "Some Variations of 'Kindermord' as Dramatic Archetype." Comparative Drama, 1 (Spring 1967), 56-71.

2289. Lyons, Leonard. "The Lyons Den." New York Post, 25 June 1966, p. 35. (FILM)

2290. Maddocks, Melvin. "Albee's Happy Family; Author and Producers Dottily Genial." Christian Science Monitor, 12 December 1962, p. 13.

2291. _____. "Who's Afraid of Virginia Woolf? Edward Albee: Highly Gifted and Very Angry." Christian Science Monitor, 20 October 1962, p. 4.

2292. Maddox, Brenda. Who's Afraid of Elizabeth Taylor?, pp. 191-197. New York: M. Evans, 1977. (FILM)

2293. Mah, Kai-Ho. "Albee's Who's Afraid of Virginia Woolf?" Explicator, 35 (Summer 1977), 10-11.

2294. Mahoney, John C. "Stage Review: Albee Play in San Diego." Los Angeles Times, 10 February 1972, Sec. 4, p. 18.

2295. _____. "Stage Review: Virginia Woolf at Met Theater." Los Angeles Times, 18 February 1976, Sec. 4, p. 15.

2296. _____. "Virginia Woolf at ICCC." Los Angeles Times, 28 January 1977, Sec. 4, p. 19.

2297. Mallett, Richard. "Cinema." Punch, 251 (13 July 1966), 87-88. (FILM)

2298. Mannes, Marya. "The Half-World of American Drama." Reporter, 28 (25 April 1963), 48-50.

2299. Manvell, Roger. "Who's Afraid of Virginia Woolf? (1966)." In his Theater and Film: A Comparative Study of the Two Forms of Dramatic Art, and of the Problems of Adaptation of Stage Plays into Films, pp. 228-237. Rutherford, N.J.: Fairleigh Dickinson University, c1979. (FILM)

2300. "Many Are Angry with De Klerk Decision." Sunday Times (Johannesburg), 6 October 1963, p. 15.

2301. "Marital Armageddon." Time, 88 (1 July 1966), 78. (FILM)

2302. Marowitz, Charles. "Theatre Abroad: Albee in England." Village Voice, 2 April 1964, pp. 16, 18.

2303. _____. "Who's Afraid of Virginia Woolf?" Encore, 11 (March-April 1964), 51-52.

2304. M[arriott], R. B. "Alan Schneider Says Who's Afraid of
      Virginia Woolf? Cannot Be Ignored Whether You Like It or
      Not." Stage and Television Today, No. 4321 (6 February
      1964), 15.

2305. Martin, Richard. "One v. One, or Two Against All? A Note
      on Edward Albee's Who's Afraid of Virginia Woolf?" Die
      Neueren Sprachen, 72 (N.S. 22) (October 1973), 535-538.

2306. Maskoulis, Julia. "Woolf Loses Bite in Translation."
      Gazette (Montreal), 19 March 1977, p. 40.

2307. "May Bowdlerize Virginia Woolf to Lift South Africa Censor
      Ban; To Submit Cuts to Edward Albee." Variety, 23 October
      1963, pp. 63-64.

2308. Mazzanti, Vincent. "The Editor's Analyst." Psychology
      Today, 2 (July 1968), 12. (FILM)

2309. McCarten, John. "The Theatre: Long Night's Journey into
      Daze." New Yorker, 38 (20 October 1962), 85-86.

2310. McClain, John. "He's Ready!" New York Journal-American,
      7 October 1962, p. 19-L.

2311. _____. "A Real Big One Has Arrived." New York Journal-
      American, 15 October 1962, p. 14.
      Reprinted in New York Theatre Critics' Reviews, 23
      (1962), 252-253.

2312. _____. "Two Faces of Mr. Albee." New York Journal-
      American, 21 October 1962, p. 36.

2313. McDonald, Daniel. "Truth and Illusion in Who's Afraid of
      Virginia Woolf?" Renascence, 17 (Winter 1964), 63-69.

2314. McElfresh, Tom. "Playhouse Rightly Shows No Fear of
      Albee's Virginia Woolf." Cincinnati Enquirer, 22 November
      1974, p. 18.
      Reprinted in Contemporary American Theater Critics: A
      Directory and Anthology of Their Works, comp. by M. E.
      Comtois and Lynn F. Miller, pp. 512-514. Metuchen, N.J.:
      Scarecrow Press, 1977.

2315. McGrady, Mike. "On the Isle: Virginia Woolf Captivates
      Another Critic." Newsday (Garden City, N.Y.), 26 August
      1963, p. 3C.

2316. McManus, Otile. "Colleen Dewhurst: That Kind of Lady."
      Boston Globe, 7 March 1976, Sec. A, pp. 9, 14.

2317. _____. "Colleen Dewhurst and the Woolf at the Door."
After Dark, 9 (June 1976), 67-71.

2318. McVay, Douglas. "Now About These Women." Film (London),
No. 46 (Summer 1966), 18. (FILM)

2319. Meadows, (Mrs.) Edna. "She Sends Thanks to Sgt. Cobb."
[Letter] Nashville (Tenn.) Tennessean, 21 July 1966, p. 16.
(FILM)

2320. Meyer, Ruth. "Language, Truth, and Illusion in Who's Afraid
of Virginia Woolf?" Educational Theatre Journal, 20 (March
1968), 60-69.

2321. Michener, John A. "A Film Critic Out of Place." [Letter]
Nashville (Tenn.) Tennessean, 22 July 1966, p. 12. (FILM)

2322. "Mike Nichols Homers as 'Director of Yr.'" Variety, 28
September 1966, p. 16. (FILM)

2323. Milstein, Fredric. "Fun and Games at Dominguez Hills."
Los Angeles Times, 18 January 1973, Sec. 4, p. 10.

2324. Mitchell, Gee. "Virginia Woolf Unexpurgated." Dayton
(Ohio) Daily News, 9 July 1966, p. 5A. (FILM)

2325. "Mixed Emotions Voiced on Movie Censorship." Nashville
(Tenn.) Tennessean, 21 July 1966, p. 2. (FILM)

2326. "Moira Walsh Re Woolf: A Sample of Latterday Catholic
Reassessment." Variety, 10 August 1966, pp. 2, 70.
(FILM)

2327. Montgomery, Roger. "Long Wharf's Woolf Has Arrived."
Day (New London, Conn.), 12 April 1980, p. 14.

2328. _____. "Trinity Offering Quality Albee." Day (New London, Conn.), 4 May 1979, p. 13.

2329. Moore, (Mrs.) Lyla. "Clean Influences Badly Needed."
[Letter] Nashville (Tenn.) Tennessean, 23 July 1966, p. 4.
(FILM)

2330. Morehouse, Ward. "First Nighter: Virginia Woolf Powerful."
Long Island Press (Jamaica, N.Y.), 15 October 1962, p. 10.

2331. Morris, Kay. "Virginia Woolf Hearing Postponement Granted."
Nashville (Tenn.) Banner, 18 July 1966, p. 2. (FILM)

2332. [Morrison], Hobe. "Who's Afraid of Virginia Woolf?" Variety,
17 October 1962, p. 54.

2333. _____. "Who's Afraid of Virginia Woolf?" Variety, 7
April 1976, p. 80.

2334. Morsberger, Robert E. "The Movie Game in Who's Afraid of
Virginia Woolf? and The Boys in the Band." Costerus: Essays in English Language and Literature, 8 (1973), 89-99.

2335. "Movie Rights to Virginia Woolf Sold to Warners for
$500,000." New York Times, 5 March 1964, p. 37. (FILM)

2336. "MPAA Nixes Its Seal for Woolf; Puts WB, sans 'Art' Sub-
sidiary, in Possibly Awkward Position." Variety, 8 June
1966, p. 4. (FILM)

2337. Murf. "Who's Afraid of Virginia Woolf?" Variety, 22 June
1966, p. 6. (FILM)

2338. [Myers, Harold]. "Who's Afraid of Virginia Woolf?" Variety,
12 February 1964, p. 78. (signed "Myro")

2339. "N.Y. Premiere Plans for Virginia Woolf Set." Motion Picture
Daily, 99 (20 April 1966), 1, 12. (FILM)

2340. Nadel, Norman. "Cast Change Gives Woolf New Tone."
New York World-Telegram and Sun, 14 January 1964, p. 10.

2341. _____. "Rose Theater Gives Two Virginia Woolfs." New
York World-Telegram and Sun, 1 November 1962, p. 19.

2342. _____. "Theater: Virginia Woolf Revisited at Billy Rose
Theater." New York World-Telegram and Sun, 3 November
1962, magazine, p. 5.

2343. _____. "Theater: Who's Afraid at Billy Rose." New
York World-Telegram and Sun, 15 October 1962, p. 14.
Reprinted in New York Theatre Critics' Reviews, 23
(1962), 254.

2344- "Nancy Wilson, Basie's Beatle Bag, Arabesque, Virg. Woolf
45.   Tracks, The Cyrkle, Medallions Top LPs." Variety, 20 July
1966, p. 50. (FILM)

2346. "Nashville Judge Dismisses Virginia Woolf Charges." New
York Times, 21 July 1966, p. 23. (FILM)

2347. "Nashville Police Sergeant, Acting Under Local Anti-Obscenity
Ordinance, Halts Virginia Woolf." Motion Picture Daily, 100
(19 July 1966), 1. (FILM)

2348. "Nashville Shutdown of Virg. Woolf." Variety, 20 July 1966,
p. 22. (FILM)

2349. Nathan, David. "Savage and Superb." Daily Herald (Lon-
       don), 7 February 1964, p. 5.

2350. "National Boxoffice Survey: Biz Holding Well; Woolf Again
       Champ...." Variety, 24 August 1966, p. 7. (FILM)

2351. "National Boxoffice Survey: Biz Still Sock, Woolf No. 1...."
       Variety, 27 July 1966, p. 5. (FILM)

2352. "National Boxoffice Survey: Heat No B.O. Handicap; Woolf
       Again Champ...." Variety, 20 July 1966, p. 5. (FILM)

2353. "National Boxoffice Survey; July Week Booms Biz; Woolf New
       Champ...." Variety, 6 July 1966, p. 7. (FILM)

2354. Neill, Robert. "Edward Albee's Not the Enemy." [Letter]
       Nashville (Tenn.) Tennessean, 20 July 1966, p. 10. (FILM)

2355. Newquist, Roy. "Behind the Scenes of a Shocking Movie."
       McCall's, 93 (June 1966), 86-89, 138-145. (FILM)

2356. Nichols, Mike. "The Woolf Duds." [Letter] New York
       Times, 10 July 1966, Sec. 2, p. 19. (FILM)

2357. "No Censor Board Is Needed Here." [Editorial] Nashville
       (Tenn.) Tennessean, 21 July 1966, p. 16. (FILM)

2358. Norton, Elliot. "Woolf Lovingly, Hatefully Superb." Boston
       Herald-American, 26 May 1979, p. 10.

2359. Norton, Rictor. "Folklore and Myth in Who's Afraid of
       Virginia Woolf?" Renascence, 23 (Spring 1971), 159-167.

2360. "Notables Will Attend New York Woolf Bow." Motion Picture
       Daily, 99 (20 June 1966), 2. (FILM)

2361. Novick, Julius. "It's Still the Best Play Since 1962."
       Village Voice, 12 April 1976, pp. 121-122.

2362. "'Nuts in May.'" Times (London), 7 March 1967, p. 10.

2363. O'Connor, Patrick. "Chronicle: Theatre." Furrow, 18
       (January 1967), 37-40.

2364. "... of Jack Valenti?" Newsweek, 68 (4 July 1966), 84-85.
       (FILM)

2365. Oliver, Edith. "The Current Cinema: Yes, Yes." New
       Yorker, 42 (2 July 1966), 64-65. (FILM)

2366. "Openings/New York: Who's Afraid of Virginia Woolf?"
       Theatre Arts, 46 (November 1962), 10-11.

2367. Oppenheimer, [George]. "Albee Directs a Powerful Woolf."
       Newsday (Garden City, N.Y.), 11 April 1976, Sec. 2, p. 11.

2368. Otten, Terry. After Innocence; Visions of the Fall in Modern
       Literature, pp. 174-191. Pittsburgh: University of Pitts-
       burgh Press, 1982.

2369. _____. "Ibsen and Albee's Spurious Children." Compara-
       tive Drama, 2 (Summer 1968), 83-93.

2370. _____. "'Played to the Finish': Coward and Albee."
       Studies in the Humanities (Indiana, Pa.), 6 (June 1977),
       31-36.

2371. "P.E. [Port Elizabeth] Is Disgusted by 'Crude' American
       Play." Cape Argus (Cape Town, South Africa), 16 September
       1963, p. 13.

2372. Pacheco, Patrick. "Reviews; Theater on Broadway and Off."
       After Dark, 9 (June 1976), 83-84.

2373. P[arker], T[heodore] H. "Stage Co. Presents Albee Play."
       Hartford (Conn.) Courant, 7 May 1966, p. 15.

2374. Patrick, Corbin. "The Lively Arts: IRT Opens Albee Play
       on 2d Stage." Indianapolis Star, 16 December 1976, p. 58.

2375. Paul, Lewis. "A Game Analysis of Albee's Who's Afraid of
       Virginia Woolf?: The Core of Grief." Literature and
       Psychology, 17 (1967), 47-51.

2376. "Peanut Butter." Newsweek, 60 (5 November 1962), 74-75.

2377. Petrie, (Mrs.) Claude. "Some Questions." [Letter] New
       York Times, 2 December 1962, Sec. 2, p. 5.

2378. Pickar, Gertrud Bauer. "The Drama of Marital Conflict."
       USF Language Quarterly (University of South Florida, Tampa),
       14 (Fall/Winter 1975), 39-44.

2379. "Pinkertons Enforce Juvenile Shutdown at Virg Woolf Show-
       ings." Variety, 29 June 1966, p. 7. (FILM)

2380. Platt, Brainard. "Virginia Woolf Lives Up to Its Advance
       Publicity; 'Slightly Less Foul' than Play." Journal Herald
       (Dayton, Ohio), 9 July 1966, p. 11. (FILM)

2381. "Playboy After Hours: Theater." Playboy, 10 (January
       1963), 30.

2382. "Players in Duplicate." Stage and Television Today, No.
       4321 (6 February 1964), 8.

2383. Pond, Elizabeth. "Albee Under Polish Lens." Christian Science Monitor, 24 April 1965, p. 4.

2384. Porter, Thomas E. "Fun and Games in Suburbia: Who's Afraid of Virginia Woolf?" In his Myth and Modern American Drama, pp. 225-247. Detroit: Wayne State University Press, 1969.

2385. Potter, Stephen. Who's Afraid of Virginia Woolf? Not Columbia...." American Record Guide, 29 (August 1963, 924-927.

2386. Powers, James. "Play Reviews: Who's Afraid of Virginia Woolf?" Hollywood Reporter, 191 (2 June 1966), 3.

2387. _____. "Who's Afraid of Virginia Woolf? Is a Motion Picture Masterpiece; Production Triumph for Lehman, Nichols; Taylor, Burton Give Top Performances." Hollywood Reporter, 191 (22 June 1966), 3. (FILM)

2388. Price, James. "Who's Afraid of Virginia Woolf?" Sight and Sound, 35 (Autumn 1966), 198-199. (FILM)

2389. Prideaux, Tom. "'Coward, Flop, Pig,' Marital Sweet Talk on Broadway." Life, 53 (14 December 1962), 107-108.

2390. Pryce-Jones, David. "The Rules of the Game." Spectator, 212 (14 February 1964), 213-214.

2391. "Pulitzer Prizes, Minus One." [Editorial] New York Times, 7 May 1963, p. 42.

2392. Quigley, Isabel. "Cinema: Fly's Eye View." Spectator, 217 (15 July 1966), 84. (FILM)

2393. Quigley, Martin. "The Code Is Dead." [Editorial] Motion Picture Daily, 99 (27 June 1966), 1-2. (FILM)

2394. _____. "Virginia Woolf and the Code." [Editorial] Motion Picture Daily, 99 (15 June 1966), 1, 3. (FILM)

2395. _____, and Richard Gertner. Films in America 1929-1969, p. 319. New York: Golden Press, 1970. (FILM)

2396. Quinn, James P. "Myth and Romance in Albee's Who's Afraid of Virginia Woolf?" Arizona Quarterly, 30 (Autumn 1974), 197-204.

2397. Radcliffe, E. B. "Taylor Great; Woolf's a Smasher Movie!" Cincinnati Enquirer, 29 June 1966, p. 12. (FILM)

2398. Read, David H. C. "Virginia Woolf Meets Charlie Brown."

In his <u>Virginia Woolf Meets Charlie Brown</u>, pp. 88–94. Grand
Rapids, Mich.: Eerdmans, 1968.

2399. Reinert, Otto. <u>Classic Through Modern Drama; an Introductory Anthology</u>, pp. 819–828. Boston: Little, Brown, 1970.

2400. Reinhart, Molly. "With Love and Hisses: Play That Shows
Us a Hideous Flash of Ourselves." <u>Sunday Times</u> (Johannesburg), 29 September 1963, magazine sec., p. 3.

2401. [Review of <u>Who's Afraid of Virginia Woolf?</u>] <u>New Mexico</u>
<u>Quarterly</u>, 33 (Winter 1963–64), 465–466.

2402. "Revised Albee Play Approved." <u>New York Times</u>, 18 December 1963, p. 47.

2403. Rich. "<u>Who's Afraid of Virginia Woolf?</u>" <u>Variety</u>, 3 June
1964, p. 80.

2404. Rich, Alan. "Theater: The Survival of George and Martha."
<u>New York</u>, 9 (19 April 1976), 93.

2405. Rich, Frank. "Stage View: Who's Afraid of Nichols and
May?" <u>New York Times</u>, 4 May 1980, Sec. 2, pp. 1, 8.

2406. Richards, Stanley. "Theatre in New York." <u>Players Maga-</u>
<u>zine</u>, 39 (December 1962), 85.

2407. Richmond, Hugh M. "Shakespeare and Modern Sexuality:
Albee's <u>Virginia Woolf</u> and <u>Much Ado</u>." In his <u>Shakespeare's</u>
<u>Sexual Comedy; a Mirror for Lovers</u>, pp. 177–196.
Indianapolis: Bobbs-Merrill, 1971.

2408. Robbins, J. Albert. "Albee's <u>Who's Afraid of Virginia Woolf?</u>"
<u>Explicator</u>, 37 (Summer 1979), 17–18.

2409. Robertson, Heather. "Albee's Vicious Comedy Coming: MTC
Opens Door to <u>Woolf</u>." <u>Winnipeg Tribune</u>, 6 March 1965,
Showcase sec., p. 1.

2410. _____. "<u>Virginia</u> May Be Indecent But the Comedy Isn't
Dirty." <u>Winnipeg Tribune</u>, 8 April 1965, p. 5.

2411. Roddy, Joseph. "The Night of the Brawl." <u>Look</u>, 30 (8
February 1966), 42–48. (FILM)

2412. Rodriguez, Meriemil. "A U.S. Play in Spanish." <u>Daily News</u>
(New York), 16 October 1972, p. 54.

2413. "Rome Sees <u>Virginia Woolf</u> in an Italian Version." <u>New York</u>
<u>Post</u>, 10 November 1963, p. 16.

2414. Rosa, Steve. "One-Man Decision Was Unfortunate." [Letter]
       Nashville (Tenn.) Tennessean, 21 July 1966, p. 16. (FILM)

2415. Roy, Emil. "Who's Afraid of Virginia Woolf? and the Tradi-
       tion." Bucknell Review, 13 (March 1965), 27-36.

2416. Ruckman, Roger. "Woolf Leads Shine Above Set, Supporters."
       Daily Orange (Syracuse University, Syracuse, N.Y.), 27
       March 1980, p. 5.

2417. "Run in Tokyo Ends for Virginia Woolf." New York Times,
       26 November 1964, p. 52.

2418. Ryan, Roger. "A Glowing Hymn." [Letter] Telegraph
       Herald (Dubuque, Iowa), 6 September 1966, p. 4. (FILM)

2419. Sabbath, Lawrence. "Duceppe Woolf? Powerful Despite
       Problems; Duelling Couple's Ire Towers over Staging Flaws."
       Montreal Star, 18 March 1977, p. B17.

2420. Sainer, Arthur. "Sons Without Fathers." Village Voice, 25
       October 1962, p. 11.
          Reprinted in his The Sleepwalker and the Assassin; a
       View of the Contemporary Theatre, pp. 26-27. New York:
       Bridgehead Books, 1964.

2421. Sanders, Kevin. Review of Who's Afraid of Virginia Woolf?,
       WABC television, New York, 1 April 1976.
          Reprinted in New York Theatre Critics' Reviews, 37
       (1976), 314.

2422. Sarris, Andrew. "Films." Village Voice, 28 July 1966, p. 19.
       (FILM)
          Reprinted in his Confessions of a Cultist: On the Cinema,
       1955-1969, pp. 259-262. New York: Simon and Schuster,
       1970.

2423. Sauvage, Leo. "Parisian Theatrics." New Leader, 67 (6
       August 1984), 21.

2424. Sawyer, Paul. "Some Observations on the Character of
       George in Who's Afraid of Virginia Woolf?" CEA Critic, 42
       (May 1980), 15-19.

2425. Scanlan, Tom. Family, Drama, and American Dreams, pp.
       189-194. Westport, Conn.: Greenwood Press, 1978. (Con-
       tributions in American Studies; no. 35)

2426. Schechner, Richard. "Reality Is Not Enough: An Interview
       with Alan Schneider." Tulane Drama Review, 9 (Spring 1965),
       118-152.

Reprinted partially in Edward Albee: A Collection of
Critical Essays, ed. by C. W. E. Bigsby, pp. 69-75.
Englewood Cliffs, N.J.: Prentice-Hall, 1975.

2427. _____. "Who's Afraid of Edward Albee?" Tulane Drama
Review, 7 (Spring 1963), 7-10.
Reprinted in Edward Albee: A Collection of Critical
Essays, ed. by C. W. E. Bigsby, pp. 62-65. Englewood
Cliffs, N.J.: Prentice-Hall, 1975.

2428. Schickel, Richard. "What Film Has Done for Virginia."
Life, 61 (22 July 1966), 8. (FILM)

2429. Schier, Donald. "Who Cares Who's Afraid of Virginia Woolf?"
Carleton Miscellany, 5 (Spring 1964), 121-124.

2430. Schimel, John L. "Love and Games." Contemporary Psy-
choanalysis, 1 (1965), 99-109.

2431. Schlesinger, Arthur, Jr. "Movies: Who's Not Afraid of
Virginia Woolf?: History Is Surely the Key." Vogue, 148
(1 August 1966), 59. (FILM)

2432. Schlueter, June. "Albee's Martha and George." In her
Metafictional Characters in Modern Drama, pp. 79-87. New
York: Columbia University Press, 1979.

2433. Schmidt, Sandra. "Theatre Uptown." Village Voice, 21 November 1963, p. 18.

2434. Schneider, Alan. "Why So Afraid?" Tulane Drama Review,
7 (Spring 1963), 10-13.
Reprinted in Edward Albee: A Collection of Critical Essays, ed by C. W. E. Bigsby, pp. 66-68. Englewood Cliffs,
N.J.: Prentice-Hall, 1975.

2435. Schnettler, Bob. "Virginia Woolfe [sic] through April 29;
Studio Arena Ends Season with Top-Rate Selection." Olean
(N.Y.) Times Herald, 21 April 1978, p. 2.

2436. "Sergeant Cobb Is a Real Go-Getter." [Editorial] Nashville
(Tenn.) Tennessean, 19 July 1966, p. 8. (FILM)

2437. "Sets Precedent: Woolf Pacts Will Include 'Adults Only;'
Warner Sees Responsibility to Children, to Subject." Motion
Picture Daily, 99 (26 May 1966), 1, 4. (FILM)

2438. Sheed, Wilfrid. "A Bunch of Drunks." Jubilee, 10 (February 1963), 55-56.

2439. Showell, Philip S. "More Woolf; Second Cast of Play Not Up

to Night Quartet." Newark Evening News, 8 November 1962,
p. 50.

2440. Shulman, Milton. "No Exits in Albee's Madhouse." Evening
Standard (London), 7 February 1964, p. 4.

2441. Siegel, Larry [text], and Drucker, Mort [drawings]. "Who
in Heck Is Virginia Woolfe [sic]?" Mad, No. 109 (March 1967),
4-10. (FILM)

2442. Silver, Margery. "Albee vs. Chester." [Letter] Commentary, 36 (October 1963), 272.

2443. Simon, John. "On Broadway and Off: A Midseason View of
the Current Plays." Harper's Magazine, 226 (March 1963),
98-104.

2444. _____. "On Screen: Woolf Dog." New Leader, 49 (18
July 1966), 21-22. (FILM)
Reprinted in his Private Screenings, pp. 235-239. New
York: Macmillan, 1967.

2445. _____. "On Stage: Torture Chamber Music." New
Leader, 45 (29 October 1962), 31-32.

2446. _____. "Theatre Chronicle." Hudson Review, 15 (Winter
1962/63), 565-573.

2447. Sincock, Stuart. "The Godless Industry." [Letter]
Telegraph-Herald (Dubuque, Iowa), 17 September 1966, p. 4.
(FILM)

2448. Skolsky, Sidney. "Hollywood Is My Beat." New York Post,
4 October 1965, p. 69. (FILM)

2449. Smith, (Mrs.) A. C. "Profanity and Sex Not Cultural Up-
lift." [Letter] Today (Cocoa, Fla.), 16 August 1982, p. 8A.

2450. Smith, Ardis. "At the Century: Playwright Albee Is Asking
a Very Powerful Question: Who's Afraid of Virginia Woolf?"
Puts a Blinding Spotlight on Contemporary Life." Buffalo
Evening News, 22 October 1963, Sec. 2, p. 14.

2451. Smith, Herbert R., Jr. "Woolf Parable and a Shepherd."
[Letter] Nashville (Tenn.) Tennessean, 21 July 1966, p. 16.
(FILM)

2452. Smith, Margaret. "Woolf Ban Lifted; Control Board Approves
Script Censors Rejected." Sunday Times (Johannesburg), 15
December 1963, p. 9.

2453. Smith, Milton. "Moral Decadence." [Letter] Telegraph-
      Herald (Dubuque, Iowa), 10 September 1966, p. 4. (FILM)

2454. "South Africa Managers Condemn Woolf Closing; Request Re-
      instatement." Variety, 16 October 1963, pp. 55, 60.

2455. Staff, Charles. "Small Theater Transforms Edward Albee's
      Classic." Indianapolis News, 16 December 1976, p. 40.

2456. "Stage Fright: Who's Afraid of Virginia Woolf?" Newsweek,
      62 (16 September 1963), 52.

2457. Standish, Myles. "The New Films: Brilliant and Shattering
      Drama." St. Louis Post-Dispatch, 22 July 1966, p. 3D.
      (FILM)

2458. Stasio, Marilyn. "Scenes: The Revival Bonanza." Pent-
      house, 7 (August 1976), 44-45.

2459. Stein, Jerry. "Theater: Living Room Battles." Cincinnati
      Post, 22 November 1974, p. 44.

2460. Stein, Ruthe. "Who's Afraid of a Gay Virginia Woolf?" San
      Francisco Chronicle, 5 April 1972, p. 23.

2461. "Stick to the Script." New York Times, 5 August 1984, Sec.
      4, p. 7.

2462. Straub, John. "High Caliber." Telegraph Herald (Dubuque,
      Iowa), 6 September 1966, p. 4. (FILM)

2463. Sturgin, Michael. Edward Albee's "Who's Afraid of Virginia
      Woolf?" and Other Works; a Critical Commentary. New York:
      Monarch Press, c1972. (Monarch Notes; 00907)

2464. Sullivan, Dan. "Stage Review: Virginia Woolf Now 10."
      Los Angeles Times, 22 June 1972, Sec. 4, p. 20.

2465. _____. "Theater: Albee in Croatian." New York Times,
      4 July 1968, p. 13.

2466. Summers, Carmine. "Virginia Woolf View Shocked." [Letter]
      Nashville (Tenn.) Tennessean, 22 July 1966, p. 12. (FILM)

2467. "A Surprising Liz in a Film Shocker." Life, 60 (10 June
      1966), 87-91. (FILM)

2468. Syna, Sy. "The Old Prof Takes the Stage." Players Maga-
      zine, 46 (1971), 76-79.

2469. Syse, Glenna. "Virginia Woolf Is More Than It Used to Be."
      Chicago Sun-Times, 23 September 1970, pp. 71, 82.

2470. Tallmer, Jerry. "Virginia Woolf Is Revived at Paramus."
      New York Post, 16 June 1965, p. 66.

2471. Tannenbaum, Paul H. "Smashing the Drama." [Letter] New
      York Times, 24 July 1966, Sec. 2, p. 18. (FILM)

2472. Tanner, Mabel DeVries. "Six Broadway Plays Are Reviewed
      by Local Critic." Times-West Virginian (Fairmont, W. Va.),
      23 June 1963, p. 24.

2473. "Taubie Kushlick's Who's Afraid...? Has Whiplash of Truth."
      Sunday Express (Johannesburg), 8 September 1963, p. 16.

2474. Taubman, Howard. "Cure for Blues; an Exciting Play Is
      Good Antidote for What Ails Broadway Theater." New York
      Times, 28 October 1962, Sec. 2, p. 1.

2475. _____. "The Theater: Albee's Who's Afraid." New York
      Times, 15 October 1962, p. 33.
      Reprinted in New York Theatre Critics' Reviews, 23
      (1962), 253.

2476. Taylor, Charlene M. "Coming of Age in New Carthage:
      Albee's Grown-Up Children." Educational Theatre Journal,
      25 (March 1973), 53-65.

2477. Taylor, Marion A. "Edward Albee and August Strindberg:
      Some Parallels Between The Dance of Death and Who's Afraid
      of Virginia Woolf?" Papers on English Language and Liter-
      ature, 1 (Winter 1965), 59-71.

2478. _____. "A Note on Strindberg's The Dance of Death and
      Edward Albee's Who's Afraid of Virginia Woolf?" Papers on
      Language and Literature, 2 (Spring 1966), 187-188.

2479. Terrien, Samuel. "Demons Also Believe." Christian Century,
      87 (9 December 1970), 1481-1483, 1485-1486.

2480. "That Gabby Albee Tom 'n' Tabby a Squeak-In for MPAA
      Code Seal; 'Adults Only' Tag as Motive." Variety, 15 June
      1966, pp. 4, 24. (FILM)

2481. Thomas, Charles H. "Adults Can Decide for Themselves."
      [Letter] Nashville (Tenn.) Tennessean, 20 July 1966, p. 10.
      (FILM)
      Reprinted with minor revisions in Nashville (Tenn.)
      Banner, 23 July 1966, p. 4.

2482. Thomas, Diane. "Movies in Review: Who's Afraid of Virginia
      Woolf?" Lives Up to Every Expectation." Atlanta Constitution,
      1 July 1966, p. 30. (FILM)

2483. Thompson, Howard. "Making of Virginia Woolf Film Enlivens
       Smith College Campus." New York Times, 28 August 1965,
       p. 12. (FILM)

2484. _____. "Theater: Virginia Woolf en Espanol." New York
       Times, 15 October 1972, p. 71.

2485. _____. "Unafraid of Virginia Woolf." New York Times, 5
       September 1965, Sec. 2, pp. 7, 10. (FILM)

2486. Thompson, Thomas. "Raw Dialogue Challenges All the Cen-
       sors." Life, 60 (10 June 1966), 92, 96, 98.

2487. Timmons, Leon. "How Did He Sit Through Movie?" [Letter]
       Nashville (Tenn.) Tennessean, 23 July 1966, p. 4. (FILM)

2488. "Title of Albee's Work Sung to Different Tune." New York
       Times, 15 October 1962, p. 33.

2489. "Towards a Theatre of Cruelty?" Times Literary Supplement,
       No. 3235 (27 February 1964), 166.

2490. Trevisan, A. F. [Letter] Reporter, 30 (30 January 1964),
       10, 12.

2491. Trewin, J. C. "Nights with the Ripsaw." Illustrated Lon-
       don News, 244 (22 February 1964), 288.

2492. Trilling, Diana. "The Riddle of Albee's Who's Afraid of
       Virginia Woolf?" In her Claremont Essays, pp. 203-207.
       New York: Harcourt, Brace and World, 1964.
           Reprinted partially in Edward Albee: A Collection of
       Critical Essays, ed. by C. W. E. Bigsby, pp. 80-88.
       Englewood Cliffs, N.J.: Prentice-Hall, 1975.

2493. _____. "Who's Afraid of the Culture Elite?" Esquire, 60
       (December 1963), 69, 72, 74, 76, 78, 80, 82-84, 86, 88.

2494. "Two Phrases Cut from Soundtrack of Who's Afraid of Virg
       Woolf?" Variety, 13 July 1966, p. 1. (FILM)

2495. Tynan, Kenneth. "Signs of Fear on Broadway." Observer
       (London), 31 March 1963, p. 29.
           Reprinted in his Tynan Right and Left; Plays, Films,
       People, Places and Events, pp. 135-136. New York:
       Atheneum, 1967.

2496. [Untitled news item reporting the closing of play by South
       African board of censors.] Times (London), 11 October
       1963, p. 10.

2497. "Uproar at Cape, Too." Sunday Times (Johannesburg), 6
October 1963, p. 15.

2498. "Valenti Backs Code on Woolf; But Holds MPAA Reivew Board
Has Final Say, as WB Appeals Denial of Seal." Daily Variety,
132 (6 June 1966), 1, 18. (FILM)

2499. Valentine, Ed. "Theater: Edward Albee the Feminist."
Christopher Street, 1 (July 1976), 48-49.

2500. "View from the Penthouse." Newsweek, 65 (5 April 1965),
89. (FILM)

2501. "Virginia Cut Again." Star (Johannesburg), 29 October 1963,
p. 3.

2502. "Virginia Producer Is Still Hopeful." Star (Johannesburg),
24 October 1963, p. 9.

2503. "Virginia Reaches Her First Year on Broadway." Sunday
Times (Johannesburg), 6 October 1963, p. 15.

2504. "Virginia Woolf Actors Doubling in Other Shows." Variety,
6 May 1964, p. 79.

2505. "Virginia Woolf? Adults-Only Policy Complete Success, Jack
Warner Says." Motion Picture Daily, 100 (20 September 1966),
1, 5. (FILM)

2506. "Virginia Woolf at American." St. Louis Post-Dispatch, 2
February 1964, p. 4I.

2507. "Virginia Woolf at Pitlochry Festival." Stage and Television
Today, No. 4806 (24 May 1973), 19.

2508. "Virginia Woolf Honored." New York Times, 8 July 1963,
p. 24.

2509. "Virginia Woolf in Rome." New York Times, 9 November
1963, p. 15.

2510. "Virginia Woolf Is Banned from Nova Scotia Screens." New
York Times, 9 August 1966, p. 29. (FILM)

2511. "Virginia Woolf Is Halted." New York Times, 19 July 1966,
p. 34. (FILM)

2512. "Virginia Woolf Is Named Best Play of Year." New York
Times, 29 April 1963, p. 25.

2513. "Virginia Woolf Okayed to Play So. Africa Only in Integrated
Houses." Variety, 11 September 1963, pp. 1, 81.

2514. "Virginia Woolf Opens Here June 29." Columbus (Ohio) Citizen-Journal, 27 June 1966, p. 13. (FILM)

2515. "Virginia Woolf Opens Tonight in New York." Motion Picture Daily, 99 (23 June 1966), 1, 4. (FILM)

2516. "Virginia Woolf Probably Year's Best Film." Columbus (Ohio) Citizen-Journal, 1 July 1966, p. 15. (FILM)

2517. "Virginia Woolf to Be Shown as a 'For Adults Only' Film." New York Times, 26 May 1966, p. 57. (FILM)

2518. "Virginia Woolf's 42 Starts in June." Variety, 22 June 1966, p. 26. (FILM)

2519. "W.B. Asks Review of Woolf? Ban in Canada." Motion Picture Daily, 100 (10 August 1966), 1, 6. (FILM)

2520. Walker, Alexander. "Invaded." Evening Standard (London), 8 April 1976, p. 26.

2521. _____. "The Triumph of the Shrew." Evening Standard (London), 7 July 1966, p. 7. (FILM)

2522. Wallach, Allan. "On the Isle: Virginia Woolf Is Still Worth Talking About." Newsday (Garden City, N.Y.), 9 September 1964, p. 3-C.

2523. Walsh, Moira. "Who's Afraid?" America, 115 (30 July 1966), 121-122. (FILM)

2524. _____. "Who's Afraid of Virginia Woolf?" America, 115 (6 August 1966), 141-143. (FILM)

2525. "Warner Sees '18' Rule a Success on Virg. Woolf." Variety, 21 September 1966, pp. 11, 19. (FILM)

2526. Watt, Douglas. "Albee & Virginia: Passion Spent." Daily News (New York), 15 April 1978, p. 91.

2527. _____. "Long Night's Journey into Day." Daily News (New York), 2 April 1976, p. 64.
        Reprinted in New York Theatre Critics' Reviews, 37 (1976), 310-311.

2528. Watts, Richard. "Two on the Aisle: A Notable Event in the Theater." New York Post, 28 October 1962, p. 13.

2529. _____. "Two on the Aisle: Shattering Play by Edward Albee." New York Post, 15 October 1962, p. 14.
        Reprinted in New York Theatre Critics' Reviews, 23 (1962), 251.

2530. _____. "Two on the Aisle: The Yugoslav Virginia Woolf."
New York Post, 5 July 1968, p. 52.

2531. Watzlawick, Paul; Janet Helmick Beavin; and Don D. Jackson.
"A Communicational Approach to the Play Who's Afraid of
Virginia Woolf?" In their Pragmatics of Human Communication;
a Study of Interactional Patterns, Pathologies, and Paradoxes,
pp. 149-186. New York: Norton, 1967.

2532. "WB Exacting Exhib Pledge Not to Show Minors Woolf, Valenti's
1st Hot Potato?" Daily Variety, 131 (26 May 1966), 1, 4.
(FILM)

2533. Weales, Gerald. "Theatre Survey; New York, Spring, 1963."
Drama Survey, 3 (October 1963), 276-279.

2534. Wear, Mike. "Woolf Tops Aug. in Variety B.O...." Variety,
31 August 1966, p. 4. (FILM)

2535. _____. "Woolf Tops July in Variety B.O...." Variety, 10
August 1966, p. 17. (FILM)

2536. Weatherby, W. J. "Albee on Broadway." Guardian (Manchester), 15 October 1962, p. 7.

2537. Weaver, William B. "Review: Who's Afraid of Virginia Woolf?"
Motion Picture Daily, 99 (22 June 1966), 1, 4. (FILM)

2538. Weiner, Leslie. "Dissent on Virginia Woolf." [Letter] New
York Times, 3 July 1966, Sec. 2, p. 5. (FILM)

2539. Weitz, A. L. "Bad, Bad Woolf." [Letter] Telegraph-Herald
(Dubuque, Iowa), 1 September 1966, p. 4. (FILM)

2540. Wells, Palmer. "Don't Miss Virginia Woolf." Kingsport (Tenn.)
Times-News, 11 July 1965, Sec. B, p. 5.

2541. _____. "Virginia Woolf: A 'Dismal Image' or Does It Mean
Something More?" Kingsport (Tenn.) Times-News, 15 August
1965, Sec. B, p. 7.

2542. White, Robert J. "Albee's Who's Afraid of Virginia Woolf?"
Explicator, 43 (Winter 1985), 52-53.

2543. White, Sam. "Who's Afraid of Mlle. Robinson? Nearly Every-
one." Evening Standard (London), 3 December 1965, p. 7.
(FILM)

2544. "Who's?" New Yorker, 39 (26 October 1963), 41-43.

2545. "Who's Afraid...." Newsweek, 68 (4 July 1966), 84. (FILM)

2546. "Who's Afraid and Why?" [audiotape] Los Angeles: Pacifica
       Tape Library, 1963. (72 min.) (INTERVIEW)
       Discussion of the play by Albee and critics John Simon and
       Lionel Abel.

2547. "Who's Afraid of Virginia Woolf?" Filmfacts, 9 (15 August
       1966), 149-152. (FILM)

2548. "Who's Afraid of Virginia Woolf?" Listener and BBC Television
       Review, 71 (20 February 1964), 313.

2549. "Who's Afraid of Virginia Woolf?" Show, 2 (October 1962),
       33-34.

2550. "Who's Afraid of Virginia Woolf?; Albee Play, with Nancy Kelly,
       to Open Here Thursday." Courier-Journal (Louisville, Ky.),
       26 January 1964, Sec. 6, p. 1.

2551. "Who's Afraid of What?" Newsweek, 61 (20 May 1963), 67.

2552. "Why Is Virginia Woolf Classified A-4?" Witness (Dubuque,
       Iowa), 28 July 1966, p. 3. (FILM)

2553. Willoughby, Bob, and Richard Schickel. The Platinum Years,
       pp. 37-39, 146-161. New York: Random House, 1974.
       (FILM)

2554. Wilson, Edwin. "Sound and Fury in a Living Room." Wall
       Street Journal, 7 April 1976, p. 20.
       Reprinted in New York Theatre Critics' Reviews, 37
       (1976), 312-313.

2555. Wilson, Raymond J. "The Dynamics of Who's Afraid of
       Virginia Woolf?" In Edward Albee: Planned Wilderness;
       Interview, Essays, and Bibliography, ed. by Patricia De La
       Fuente, pp. 58-69. Edinburg, Tex.: School of Humanities,
       Pan American University, 1980. (Living Author Series;
       no. 3)

2556. Wilson, Sam. "On the Rialto: So 'Who's Afraid of Etc' Has
       Now Become a Movie." Columbus (Ohio) Dispatch, 30 June
       1966, p. 40A. (FILM)

2557. Winsten, Archer. "Virginia Woolf Bows at 2 Theaters."
       New York Post, 24 June 1966, p. 38. (FILM)

2558. Wishengrad, H. R. "'Vulgarities.'" [Letter] New York
       Times, 4 November 1962, Sec. 2, p. 3.

2559. Wolfson, Martin. "Emancipated People." [Letter] New York
       Times, 1 September 1963, Sec. 2, pp. 1, 3.

2560. "Woolf Benefit Bow Committee Is Named." Motion Picture
Daily, 99 (13 May 1966), 2. (FILM)

2561. "Woolf Breaks Record in Nearly All Openings." Hollywood
Reporter, 191 (1 July 1966), 3. (FILM)

2562. "Woolf Gets Code Exemption; Review Board Grants Seal to
Warners Film in View of Its Quality." Hollywood Reporter,
191 (13 June 1966), 1, 4. (FILM)

2563. "Woolf Gets Vast Magazine Coverage." Hollywood Reporter,
191 (24 June 1966), 9. (FILM)

2564. "The Woolf Goes on Trial Again." Sunday Times (Johannesburg), 20 October 1963, p. 3.

2565. "Woolf Has Earned $750,000 Profit; Includes Coin from 500G
Pic Sale." Variety, 18 March 1964, p. 60.

2566. "Woolf N.Y. Opens for Dick Burton's Charity But Actor
Stuck O'Seas." Variety, 29 June 1966, p. 7. (FILM)

2567. "Woolf Premiere Tonite at Hollywood's Pantages." Motion
Picture Daily, 99 (21 June 1966), 2. (FILM)

2568. "Woolf Sets B'way Record." Daily Variety, 132 (27 June
1966), 3. (FILM)

2569. "Woolf Sets Records in Its Opening Week." Motion Picture
Daily, 100 (5 July 1966), 2. (FILM)

2570. "Woolf Smashes Marks in National Openings." Motion Picture Daily, 100 (1 July 1966), 2. (FILM)

2571. "Woolf Sold Out in NY Premiere." Hollywood Reporter, 191
(23 June 1966), 2. (FILM)

2572. "Woolf SRO $22,500 Sparks London...." Variety, 20 July
1966, p. 29. (FILM)

2573. "Woolf Too Hot for Nashville Cop; Grabs Reel." Daily
Variety, 132 (19 July 1966), 1, 10. (FILM)

2574. "Woolf Wham in Canada." Variety, 13 July 1966, p. 9.
(FILM)

2575. Wooten, Dick. "Euclid Players Brilliant in Virginia Woolf."
Cleveland (Ohio) Press, 25 April 1968, p. B-5.

2576. "WOR Dubious as to Woolf Tease Copy." Variety, 29 June
1966, p. 7. (FILM)

2577.   "Worries Allayed; Woolf Will Play at Clowes Hall." Variety,
        1 January 1964, p. 49.

2578.   Wortman, Alan J. "Virginia Woolf Debate Continues."
        [Letter] New York Times, 24 July 1966, Sec. 2, p. 18.
        (FILM)

2579.   Wurster, Grace Stewart. "Albee's Festival Chant: Who's
        Afraid of Virginia Woolf?" Michigan Academician, 9 (Summer
        1976), 61-67.

2580.   "Yank Leads Approved; Work Out Woolf Cuts." Variety, 15
        January 1964, p. 68.

2581.   "Yes, Virginia, Philly Is Afraid of Woolf." Variety, 17 Feb-
        ruary 1965, p. 1.

2582.   "Yes, Virginia....: Woolf Wins Code Approval After Review;
        Appeals Board Grants an Exemption; Cites Merit." Motion
        Picture Daily, 99 (13 June 1966), 1, 7. (FILM)

2583.   Young, B. A. "At the Play." Punch, 246 (12 February
        1964), 245-246.

2584.   _____. "Who's Afraid of Virginia Woolf?" Financial Times
        (London), 7 February 1964, p. 24.

2585.   Zeff, Dan. "Foursome at Ivanhoe Performs Brilliantly in
        Virginia Woolf." Waukegan (Ill.) News-Sun, 3 October 1970,
        p. 10.

2586.   Zolotow, Sam. "Albee to Unveil First Full Play." New York
        Times, 27 November 1961, p. 35.

                            THE ZOO STORY

2587.   "Albee Double Bill Is Praised in Paris." New York Times,
        13 February 1965, p. 10.

2588.   Anderson, Mary Castiglie. "Ritual and Initiation in The Zoo
        Story." In Edward Albee: An Interview and Essays, pp.
        93-108. Houston: University of St. Thomas, 1983.

2589.   Aston, Frank. "Theater: Avant-Garde's Double Scores."
        New York World-Telegram and Sun, 15 January 1960, p. 18.

2590.   Atkinson, Brooks. "Theatre: A Double Bill Off Broadway."
        New York Times, 15 January 1960, p. 37.

2591.   _____. "Village Vagrants." New York Times, 31 January
        1960, Sec. 2, p. 1.

2592. Barker, Felix. "Molière with Parasol and Braces." Evening News (London), 9 February 1965, p. 5.

2593. _____. "This Is the Age of the Lonely Playwright." Evening News (London), 26 August 1960, p. 8.

2594. Barnes, Clive. "The Theater: Krapp's Last Tape and Zoo Story; Plays by Beckett and Albee Are Revived." New York Times, 11 October 1968, p. 41.

2595. Beaufort, John. "Beckett Takes Another Look at Human Folly." Christian Science Monitor, 23 January 1960, p. 6.

2596. Bennett, Robert B. "Tragic Vision in The Zoo Story." Modern Drama, 20 (March 1977), 55-66.

2597. Bolton, Whitney. "Exceptional Albee, Beckett Duo." Morning Telegraph (New York), 10 June 1965.

2598. _____. "New Beckett Play Is Fascinating." Morning Telegraph (New York), 16 January 1960.

2599. _____. "Theater: Of Albee, Brecht and Dogs." Morning Telegraph (New York), 20 August 1969, p. 3.

2600. Branche, Bill. "Kenan Center Theater Offers Twin Hit Plays." Niagara Gazette (Niagara Falls, N.Y.), 7 June 1974, p. 5B.

2601. Brien, Alan. "Theatre: They Asked for It." Sunday Telegraph (London), 14 February 1965, p. 12.

2602. Brody, Jane E. "The Case Is Familiar, But the Theater Is Absurd." New York Times, 15 July 1967, p. 15.

2603. Brooks, Jeremy. "Flowering Bolt." New Statesman, 60 (3 September 1960), 304-305.

2604. Brustein, Robert. "Krapp and a Little Claptrap." New Republic, 142 (22 February 1960), 21-22.
       Reprinted in his Seasons of Discontent; Dramatic Opinions 1959-1965, pp. 26-29. New York: Simon and Schuster, 1965.

2605. Burm. "Beckett-Albree [sic] Dual-Bill." Variety, 27 January 1960, p. 56.

2606. Cain, Alex Matheson. "Class Rears Its Ugly Head." Tablet, 219 (20 February 1965), 214.

2607. Calta, Louis. "Beckett and Albee Back in Double Bill." New York Times, 9 June 1965, p. 42.

2608.   Candide. "The Theatre: Albee at the Cherry Lane."
        Villager (New York), 13 September 1962, p. 11.

2609.   Clurman, Harold. "Theatre." Nation, 190 (13 February 1960),
        153-154.
        Reprinted in his The Naked Image; Observations on the
        Modern Theatre, pp. 13-15. New York: Macmillan, 1966.
        Reprinted in his The Divine Pastime; Theatre Essays, pp.
        107-109. New York: Macmillan, 1974.

2610.   Coe, Richard L. "Theater: Linking Millay and Albee."
        Washington Post, 30 June 1973, Sec. C, p. 9.

2611.   Cohn, Ruby, and Bernard F. Dukore, eds. Twentieth Cen-
        tury Drama: England, Ireland, the United States, pp. 605-
        652. New York: Random House, 1966.

2612.   Cooper, Michael. "Edward Albee's 'Zoo World.'" Great
        Speckled Bird (Atlanta), 7 (30 September 1974), 9.

2613.   Craig, Russell. "Plays in Performance: Experimental."
        Drama; the Quarterly Theatre Review, No. 111 (Winter 1973),
        52-53.

2614.   Cramer, Garth. "Sexual Comedy Is Overshadowed."
        Winnipeg Tribune, 1 March 1979, p. 24.

2615.   Deutsch, Robert H. "Writers Maturing in the Theater of the
        Absurd." Discourse, 7 (Spring 1964), 181-187.

2616.   Dietrich, Richard F. "Jesus as Narrator: Albee's Case for
        Fiction in The Zoo Story." Theatre Annual, 33 (1977), 57-69.

2617.   Doran, Terry. "Studio Arena: Davis, Piazza Brilliant in
        Repertory Series." Buffalo Evening News, 18 September
        1968, Sec. 3, p. 48.

2618.   Downer, Alan S. "Love in Several Masques: Notes on the
        New York Theatre 1959-1960." Quarterly Journal of Speech,
        46 (October 1960), 253-261.

2619.   Driver, Tom F. "Drama: Bucketful of Dregs." Christian
        Century, 77 (17 February 1960), 193-194.

2620.   Eichelbaum, Stanley. "Two Piercing Glimpses at Loneliness
        of Man." San Francisco Examiner, 10 June 1967, p. 10.

2621.   Elem. "Zoo Story--Miss Julie." Variety, 12 July 1961, p. 64.

2622.   Findlater, Richard. "This Property Is Condemned; The Zoo
        Story." Financial Times (London), 26 August 1960, p. 19.

2623. Force, William M. "The What Story? or Who's Who at the
       Zoo?" Studies in the Humanities (Indiana, Pa.), 1 (Winter
       1969/70), 47-53.
       Reprinted in Costerus: Essays in English Language and
       Literature, 2 (1972), 71-82.

2624. Frank, Elizabeth. "Touching, Terrifying and Brilliant."
       News Chronicle (London), 26 August 1960, p. 3.

2625. Frank, Leah D. "Tiger, Zoo Story Share Double Bill."
       New York Times, 8 July 1984, Sec. 21, p. 15.

2626. [Frederick], Robe[rt B.] "Zoo Story and Krapp's Last Tape."
       Variety, 16 June 1965, p. 56.

2627. Gabbard, Lucina P. "At the Zoo: From O'Neill to Albee."
       Modern Drama, 19 (December 1976), 365-374.

2628. Gilliatt, Penelope. "The Outclassed Husband." Observer
       (London), 14 February 1965, p. 25.
       Reprinted in her Unholy Fools; Wits, Comics, Disturbers
       of the Peace: Film and Theater, pp. 236-238. New York:
       Viking, 1973.

2629. Gottfried, Martin. "Theatre: Albee-Beckett Revival."
       Women's Wear Daily, 9 June 1965, p. 67.

2630. Grande, (Brother) Luke. "Existentialism in Modern Drama."
       Critic, 21 (April/May 1963), 33-38.

2631. Hadley, Ted R. "Review: Two Good Plays Ending at
       Kenan." Lockport (N.Y.) Union-Sun and Journal, 19 June
       1974, p. 12.

2632. Hastings, Ronald. "Ophelia-Type Strangers; a Brief Sketch
       on Adolescence." Daily Telegraph and Morning Post (London),
       26 August 1960, p. 14.

2633. Hewes, Henry. "Broadway Postscript: Benchmanship."
       Saturday Review, 43 (6 February 1960), 32.

2634. _____. "Broadway Postscript: It's Not All Bananas."
       Saturday Review, 43 (30 January 1960), 28.

2635. _____. "Off Broadway." In The Best Plays of 1959-1960,
       ed. by Louis Kronenberger, pp. 38-50. New York: Dodd,
       Mead, 1960.

2636. Hobson, Harold. "The Gentlemanly Thing." Sunday Times
       (London), 14 February 1965, p. 45.

190   Edward Albee

2637. _____. "London Theater: Gallant, Undemanding."
Christian Science Monitor, 16 February 1965, p. 10.

2638. Hope-Wallace, Philip. "Albee and Molière at the Theatre
Royal, Stratford, E.15." Guardian (Manchester), 9 February
1965, p. 9.

2639. Irwin, Robert. "The 'Teaching Emotion' in the Ending of the
Zoo Story." Notes on Contemporary Literature, 6 (September
1976), 6-8.

2640. Kennedy, Andrew K. "The Confessional Duologue from Ibsen
to Albee." In his Dramatic Dialogue; the Duologue of Personal
Encounter, pp. 167-197. Cambridge: Cambridge University
Press, 1983.

2641. Kerr, Walter. "Off Broadway: Two One-Act Plays Given at
Provincetown Playhouse." New York Herald Tribune, 15
January 1960, p. 8.

2642. Keys, Janice. "Two Versions, One Theme, at Warehouse;
Actors Leap from Albee to Mamet." Winnipeg Free Press, 28
February 1979, p. 55.

2643. Kingston, Jeremy. "Theatre." Punch, 248 (17 February
1965), 253.

2644. Knickerbocker, Paine. "An Audacious Pair of One-Act Plays."
San Francisco Chronicle, 12 June 1967, p. 43.

2645. Kostelanetz, Richard. "Albee Edward." In his Recyclings,
a Literary Autobiography, Volume One: 1959-67, p. 25.
Brooklyn, N.Y.: Assembling Press, 1974.

2646. Lambert, J. W. "Theatre: A Man Apart." Sunday Times
(London), 28 August 1960, p. 33.

2647. Lask, Thomas. "Grooved Theatre." New York Times, 4
February 1962, Sec. 2, p. 19.

2648. Lazier, Gil; Douglas Zahn; and Joseph Bellinghiere. "Em-
pirical Analysis of Dramatic Structure." Speech Monographs,
41 (November 1974), 381-390.

2649. Lenoir, Jean-Pierre. "2 Plays by Albee Offered in Paris."
New York Times, 11 June 1963, p. 29.

2650. Lester, Bill. "This Property Is Condemned and The Zoo
Story." Plays and Players, 7 (October 1960), 13.

2651. Levin, Bernard. "A Talk at the Zoo ... Too Late." Daily
Express (London), 26 August 1960, p. 7.

2652. Levine, Mordecai H. "Albee's Liebestod." CLA Journal
(College Language Association), 10 (March 1967), 252-255.

2653. Lewis, Theophilus. "Theatre: The Zoo Story and The
American Dream." America, 108 (22 June 1963), 891-892.

2654. Litowitz, Norman S., and Kenneth M. Newman. "Borderline
Personality and the Theatre of the Absurd." Archives of
General Psychiatry, 16 (March 1967), 268-280.

2655. Lowell, Sondra. "Zoo Story, Lemonade." Los Angeles
Times, 9 March 1979, Sec. 4, pp. 15, 18.

2656. Lyons, Charles R. "Two Projections of the Isolation of the
Human Soul: Brecht's Im Dickicht der Staedte and Albee's
The Zoo Story." Drama Survey, 4 (Summer 1965), 121-138.

2657. Macklin, Anthony. "The Flagrant Albatross." College
English, 28 (October 1966), 58-59.

2658. Malcolm, Donald. "Off Broadway: And Moreover...." New
Yorker, 35 (23 January 1960), 72, 74-76.

2659. Matthews, Honor. The Primal Curse; the Myth of Cain and
Abel in the Theatre, pp. 201-205. London: Chatto and
Windus, 1967.

2660. McClain, John. "Krapp's Last Tape; Only a One-Acter But
a Superb One." New York Journal-American, 15 January
1960, p. 15.

2661. McHarry, Charles. "Beckett, Albee Make Absorbing Double
Bill." Daily News (New York), 15 January 1960, p. 44.

2662. Miller, Margo. "Double Bill: Madness Near Allied in Genet,
Albee Plays." Boston Globe, 23 August 1963, p. 11.

2663. Missey, James. "A McCullers Influence on Albee's The Zoo
Story." American Notes & Queries, 13 (April 1975), 121-
123.

2664. "Molière's Dandin with Scots Accent and Deerstalker." Times
(London), 9 February 1965, p. 8.

2665. [Morrison], Hobe. "Krapp's Last Tape and The Zoo Story."
Variety, 16 October 1968, p. 70.

2666. Muller, Robert. "That's What I Don't Like About the South."
Daily Mail (London), 26 August 1960, p. 3.

2667. Nathan, David. "Theatre: What a Strange Couple." Sun
(London), 9 February 1965, p. 5.

2668. "New Yorkers Crowd to New American Satire." Times (London), 10 April 1961, p. 3.

2669. Nilan, Mary M. "Albee's The Zoo Story: Alienated Man and the Nature of Love." Modern Drama, 16 (June 1973), 55-59.

2670. O'Connor, Patrick. "Chronicle: Theatre." Furrow, 14 (August 1963), 524-525.

2671. "Off-Broadway Closings." New York Times, 10 May 1961, p. 54.

2672. "Off-Broadway: The Lights Are Just as Bright." Newsweek, 57 (13 March 1961), 91.

2673. Oppenheimer, George. "Light in the Gloom." Newsday (Garden City, N.Y.), 5 June 1963, p. 3-C.

2674. _____. "On Stage: It's Alive!" Newsday (Garden City, N.Y.), 3 February 1960, p. 9-C.

2675. Ramsey, Roger. "Jerry's Northerly Madness." Notes on Contemporary Literature, 1 (September 1971), 7-8.

2676. Reinert, Otto. Modern Drama, pp. 610-613. Alternate edition. Boston: Little, Brown, 1966.

2677. Richards, Stanley. "On and Off Broadway." Players Magazine, 37 (October 1960), 9-10.

2678. Rivers, Bryan. "Plays Investigate Human Interaction." Winnipeg Free Press, 1 March 1979, p. 32.

2679. "Rockport, Mass., Bans Two Plays." New York Times, 14 July 1962, p. 11.

2680. Rosselli, John. "At the Theatre: This Property Is Condemned; The Zoo Story." Guardian (Manchester), 27 August 1960, p. 3.

2681. Rutherford, Malcolm. "The Case for Theatre." Spectator, 214 (12 February 1965), 200.

2682. Sato, Susumu. "The Fourth Wall in an Age of Alienation: The Zoo Story and The Connection." In American Literature in the 1950's: Annual Report, 1976, pp. 161-166. Tokyo: American Literature Society of Japan, Tokyo Chapter, c1977.

2683. Schechner, Richard. "Exploding Time and Space; an Interview with Milton Katselas," ed. by Robert Merritt. Tulane Drama Review, 9 (Winter 1964), 182-190.

2684. Share, Peter. "Theatre Revival: Krapp's Last Tape and
       The Zoo Story." Village Voice, 17 June 1965, p. 12.

2685. Sharma, R. C. "Edward Albee: The Zoo Story." Banasthali
       Patrika (Rajasthan), 3 (January 1968), 27-34.

2686. Sheed, Wilfrid. "Back to the Zoo." Commonweal, 82 (9 July
       1965), 501-502.

2687. Shulman, Milton. "Exercise for Two Vacuum Pumps."
       Evening Standard (London), 26 August 1960, p. 4.

2688. Smith, Andrew. "Showpiece: Three Men and a Girl Just
       Fail." Daily Herald (London), 26 August 1960, p. 3.

2689. Spielberg, Peter. "The Albatross in Albee's Zoo." College
       English, 27 (April 1966), 562-565.

2690. _____. "Reply: The Albatross Strikes Again!" College
       English, 28 (October 1966), 59.

2691. Swan, Jon. "The Zoo Story." Villager (New York), 21
       January 1960, p. 16.

2692. Sykes, Carol A. "Albee's Beast Fables: The Zoo Story and
       A Delicate Balance." Educational Theatre Journal, 25 (Decem-
       ber 1973), 448-455.

2693. Tallmer, Jerry. "Edw. Albee's Zoo Story, American Dream
       Reopen." New York Post, 5 September 1962, p. 81.

2694. _____. "Hold That Tiger." Evergreen Review, 5 (May/
       June 1961), 109-113.

2695. _____. "Theatre: The Tape & the Zoo." Village Voice,
       20 January 1960, pp. 9, 10.

2696. Thomizer, Cynthia. "Child's Play: Games in The Zoo Story."
       College Literature, 9 (Winter 1982), 54-63.

2697. Thompson, Jack. "Off-Broadway: A Fascinating Double
       Bill." New York Journal-American, 9 June 1965, p. 21.

2698. "Twin Bill to Reopen." New York Times, 24 May 1961, p. 46.

2699. "Two Duologues from U.S." Times (London), 26 August 1960,
       p. 5.

2700. "U.S. Play Bows at Berlin Fete." New York Times, 29 Sep-
       tember 1959, p. 45.

2701. Waith, Eugene M. "Understanding and Suggestion." In his
       The Dramatic Moment, pp. 76-77. Englewood Cliffs, N.J.:
       Prentice-Hall, 1967.

2702. Wallace, Robert S. "The Zoo Story: Albee's Attack on Fic-
       tion." Modern Drama, 16 (June 1973), 49-54.

2703. W[ardle], I[rving]. "New Plays in London." Observer
       (London), 28 August 1960, p. 24.

2704. Watts, Richard. "Two on the Aisle: An Absorbing Off-
       Broadway Evening." New York Post, 15 January 1960, p.
       52.

2705. Weales, Gerald. "The Small White Way." Reporter, 24 (16
       February 1961), 46-47.

2706. White, Fred D. "Albee's Hunger Artist: The Zoo Story as
       a Parable of the Writer vs. Society." Arizona Quarterly, 39
       (Spring 1983), 15-22.

2707. Woods, Linda. "Isolation and the Barrier of Language in
       The Zoo Story." Research Studies (Washington State Univer-
       sity), 36 (September 1968), 224-231.

2708. Young, B. A. "At the Play." Punch, 239 (31 August 1960),
       318.

2709. _____. "The Zoo Story and George Dandin." Financial
       Times (London), 9 February 1965, p. 22.

2710. Zimbardo, Rose A. "Symbolism and Naturalism in Edward
       Albee's The Zoo Story." Twentieth Century Literature, 8
       (April 1962), 10-17.
          Reprinted in Edward Albee: A Collection of Critical Essays,
       ed. by. C. W. E. Bigsby, pp. 45-53. Englewood Cliffs, N.J.:
       Prentice-Hall, 1975.

2711. "Zoo Story in London." New York Times, 26 August 1960,
       p. 13.

Abel, Lionel 1376, 2546
Acharya, Shanta 1937
Adams, Herbert R. 86
Adelugba, Dapo 857
Adler, Thomas P. 87, 137, 1104,
    1426, 1562, 1592, 1941
Agel, Julie 1943
Agnihotri, Satish Mohan 594,
    1944
Agueros, Jack 1945
Aguglia, John 1946
All Over 272, 332, 461, 549,
    600, 751-856
Allen, E. 1959
Allen, Morse 107
Allen, Rex Eugene 595
Alpert, Arthur 1575
Amacher, Richard E. 108-10
Amata, Carmie 1024
Amaya, Mario 111
The American Dream 79, 189,
    228, 271-72, 393, 529, 637,
    640, 645, 649, 660-61, 674,
    690, 709, 738, 857-959, 1053,
    1159, 1170, 1177, 1181, 1183-
    84, 1761, 2587, 2608, 2653,
    2693-94
Amory, Cleveland 113
Anastas'ev, N. 114
Anderson, Jack 1577
Anderson, Mary Castiglie 116,
    596, 1681, 2588
Anderson, Robert 1682
Anderson, Stan 961
Andreucci, Costanza 117
Angell, Richard C. 1960
Anzalone, Frank Michael 597
Argenio, Joseph 598
Armstrong, Madeleine 118
Arnold, Christine 119, 1563
Arnold, Gary 1197
Arnould, E. R. 120

Arpe, Verner 121
Ashford, Gerald 1683
Ashley, Leonard R. N. 122
Aston, Frank 859, 1160, 1419,
    2589
Atkinson, Brooks 123, 1961,
    2590-91
Atlee, Howard 860
Auchincloss, Louis S. 1025
Auld, Hugh 752
Avery, Nicholas C. 1965
Axel, Marian 1967

B., C. 1968
Bachman, Ch. R. 1198
Bail 1684
Baker, Burton 599
Baker, Robb 1969
The Ballad of the Sad Café 612,
    615, 622, 648-49, 706, 960-
    1021
Ballew, Leighton M. 1685
Balliett, Whitney 861, 1161
Balmer, John 753
Bane, Michael 1199
Bannon, Anthony 1686
Bannon, Barbara A. 1972
Barber, John 754, 1106, 1200,
    1687-88
Bardacke, Frances 1201, 1593-
    94
Barker, Felix 744, 862, 1202,
    1689, 1973, 2592-93
Barnes, Clive 756-57, 1026-27,
    1107, 1377, 1428, 1595, 1690,
    1974, 2252, 2594
Barr, Richard 125-26, 1429,
    1975
Barron, Karl 1203, 1691
Barrows, Marjorie Wescott 1578
Bart, Peter 1976-77

Barter, Christie 963
Bartleby 872, 874-75, 890-91,
    897, 900, 908, 946, 953
Bates, John 1978
Battelle, Phyllis 1514
Baumhover, Betty 1979
Bauzyte, Galina 127
Baxandall, Lee 128, 1980
Bayer, Jerome 1204
Beatty, Dale T. 600
Beaufort, John 758-59, 1430,
    1487, 1564, 1596, 1981, 2595
Beavin, Janet Helmick 2531
Bell, Eleanor 1982
Bell, Muriel 863
Bellamy, Peter 964, 1983
Bellinghiere, Joseph 2648
Belsnick, Morris 1692
Bender, Marilyn 1693
Benedictus, David 1694
Benmussa, Simone 285
Bennett, Robert B. 2596
Bennetts, Leslie 129
Ben-Zvi, Linda 1424
Berger, Jere Schindel 601
Berger, Joseph 130
Berkvist, Robert 131, 1488
Bermel, Albert 1205, 1378,
    1695
Bernard, Sidney 132
Bernstein, Samuel J. 1597
Bierhaus, E. G. 1206
Bigsby, C. W. E. 134-136, 137,
    138, 241, 517, 555, 602, 760,
    794, 955, 965, 1006, 1028,
    1168, 1207, 1212, 1313, 1696-
    97, 1751, 1772, 1869, 1985,
    2055, 2426, 2427, 2434, 1492,
    2710
Bilbatua, Miguel 139
Billington, Michael 761, 966,
    1108
Billman, Carol 140
Binder, Wolfgang 141
Björkstén, Ingmar 143-44
'Bladen, Barbara 1698-99
Blades, Larry Thomas 603
Blaha, Franz 604
Blake, Jeanie 145
Blank, Edward L. 1986
Blankenship, Jayne 605

Blau, Eleanor 1489
Blau, Herbert 1987
Blevins, Phebe 1988
Blinken, Donald M. 1989
Blum 1490
Blum, Harold P. 1991
Boardman, Kathryn 1208
Bobker, Lee R. 1992
Bock, Hedwig 146, 580
Bogard, Travis 147
Boge, Elaine 1993
Bolton, Whitney 148, 864-66,
    967, 1029, 1163, 1209, 1379,
    1515-16, 1700-01, 1994-99,
    2597-99
Bone 2000
Bonin, Jane F. 1210, 2001-02
Booth, John E. 149
Booth, Wayne C. 1702
Boros, Donald 606
Bosworth, Patricia 150
Bourdonnay, Katherine 607
Bourne, James Thomas 608
Bowers, Faubion 151
Box and Quotations from Chair-
    man Mao Tse-tung 77, 392,
    659, 684, 839, 1022-93
Boyd, Malcolm 2005
Boyer, Mark 1109-10
Brackett, Samuel J. 152
Braem, Helmut M. 153
Branche, Bill 2006, 2600
Brand, Patricia Ann 609
Branigan, Alan 2007
Braun, Pinkas 141
Breakfast at Tiffany's (Holly
    Golightly) 1094-1103
Brede, Regine 154, 610
Brendle, Mary 1598
Brennan, James 1030
Brennan, Thomas 1703
Brenner, Marie 155
Brien, Alan 1517, 1704, 2601
Bristow, Donald Gene 611
Britton, Burt 69
Brockett, Oscar G. 158
Brody, Benjamin 2009
Brody, Jane E. 2602
Brooks, Jeremy 2603
Brown, Daniel R. 159
Brown, Dennis 160

Brown, James 1473
Brown, John Lindsay 2010
Brown, John Mason 161
Brown, John R. 230, 955
Brown, Terence 1211
Bruer, Thomas 2011
Brunel, Pierre 165
Brüning, Eberhard 162, 350,
    479
Brunkhorst, Martin 163
Brustein, Robert 164, 867, 968,
    1212-13, 1380, 1431, 1491,
    1518, 1705, 2012-13, 2604
Bryant, Hallman R. 2014
Bryden, Ronald 1214, 1706
Bryson, Rhett B. 612
Buchanan, D. E. 2015
Bucher, Bernadette 165
Buck, Louise 166
Buck, Richard M. 762, 1599
Buckley, Tom 2016
Bunce, Alan 167, 1031, 1215,
    1381, 1707, 2017
Burchard, Hank 868
Burdison, Neva Evonne 613
Burgess, Martha K. P. 2018
Burm 2605
Burnett, Whit 77
Burns, Carol Ann 614
Burns, Carolyn Dolinich 615
Burns, Cherie 168
Byars, John A. 2020

Cahill, Kathleen 169
Cahn, Judah 1708
Cain, Alex Matheson 2021, 2606
Calhoun, Charles 170-71
Callaghan, Barry 1032
Callahan, J. Stephen 616
Callenbach, Ernest 2023
Callow, James T. 172
Calta, Louis 173-75, 763-64,
    1519-20, 1709, 2025, 2607
Caltabiano, Frank P. 1432
Cameron, Ben 1492
Cameron, Kate 2026
Campbell, Mary Elizabeth 1710-
    11
Canady, Nicholas 869
Canby, Vincent 2027-29

Candide 2030, 2608
Capéllan Gonzalo, Angel 176
Cappalletti, John 177
Cardullo, Bert 1216
Carey, Verna 178
Carmines, Al 765
Carnes, Del 2031
Carney, Brian R. 2032
Carr, Duane R. 2033
Carr, Jay 179, 1033-34, 1433
Carragher, Bernard 180
Carruth, Grant F. 2034
Carver, Mabel MacDonald 181
Casper, Leonard 1712
Cassidy, Claudia 2035
Cavan, Romilly 766, 1713
Cavanaugh, Arthur 767, 1382,
    1714
Cavarozzi, Joyce Pennington 617
Chabrowe, L. E. 182
Chadbourne, Malcolm K. 1434
Champlin, Charles 1217
Champlis, Charles 2040
Chapin, Louis 183, 1521, 1715-
    16
Chapman, John 184, 969-70,
    1035-36, 1218-19, 1522, 1717-
    18, 2041-43
Chernowitz, Rose M. 1220
Cherrin, David 185
Chester, Alfred 2045
Chiaromonte, Nicolo 2047
Chodorov, Edward 186
Choudhuri, A. D. 2048
Christadler, Martin 456
Christiansen, Richard 1600,
    1719, 2049
Christie, Roy 2050
Christon, Lawrence 870, 1601
Chubb, Kenneth Richard 618
Clark, Glenn 2051
Clark, Margy 2052
Clarke, Gerald 1435
Clarkson, Adrienne 187
Clay, Carolyn 2054
Clay, Jack 188
Cleaves, Henderson 189
Clergé, Claude 250
Clum, John M. 1720
Clurman, Harold 190-91, 768-69,
    871, 971, 1037, 1164, 1221,

1383, 1436, 1602, 1721-22,
2055-56, 2609
Cocks, Jay 1222, 1372
Coe, Richard L. 192, 770,
1111, 1603, 2058-62, 2610
Coe, Richard M. 1723
Cognard, Roger A. 619
Cohen, Marshall 1223
Cohen, Nathan 1038, 1224
Cohn, Ruby 193-97, 1039, 2611
Cole, Douglas 2063
Coleman, A. D. 1040
Coleman, D. C. 2064
Coleman, John 1225, 2065
Coleman, Robert 2066
Collins, William B. 1604-06
Collis, John 1474
Coltrera, Joseph T. 1761, 1991
Comtois, M. E. 1614, 1623,
1632, 1647, 1668, 2240, 2314
Connolly, Patrick 199
Connolly, Peter 2067
Cook, Bruce 1041
Cook, Joy 1725
Cooke, Richard P. 872, 972,
1042, 1226, 1384, 1523, 1726-
27, 2070
Cooper, Michael 2612
Copeland, Roger 201
Corona, Mario 202
Corrigan, Robert W. 203, 1524,
2071-72
Corry, John 204, 1493-95
Cotter, Jerry 973, 2073-74
Coudert, Jo 2075
Counting the Ways 113, 254,
271, 276, 323, 424, 545,
1104-57, 1476
Covington, William R. 2077
Coward, Noel 62
Cowie, Denise 771
Coy, Javier 205, 208
Coy, Juan José 205-08, 620
Cragin, Donald H. 873
Craig, Russell 2613
Cramer, Garth 2614
Crinkley, Richmond 772, 1728
Crist, Judith 1165, 2078
Croce, Arlene 1227, 2079
Cross, Mary Ellen 1228
Crowther, Bosley 2080

Cubeta, Paul M. 1579
Cunliffe, Marcus 552
Cunningham, Dennis 1437, 1565
Curley, Dorothy Nyren 209
Currie, Glenne 1438
Curry, Ryder H. 1730
Curtis, Anthony 1475
Cuthbert, David 773-74, 1731

Dafoe, Christopher 2082
Daley, Ronald E. 621
Dalgard, Olav 211
Daniel, Walter C. 1166
Dannenberg, William J. 622
Darlington, W. A. 1732
Dash, Irene G. 2083
Dash, Tom 1525
Dassylva, Martial 212
David, Gunter 2084
Davis, George 2085
Davis, James 874, 1607
Davison, Richard A. 1733
Dawson, Helen 775
Dawson, Ralph 2086
Day, Richard 1112, 1734, 2087
De Jongh, Nicholas 213
De La Fuente, Patricia 87, 231,
260, 326, 460, 806, 1066,
1465, 1659, 2555
De Lappe, Pele 1167
De Meo, Raymond 1439
The Death of Bessie Smith 46,
65, 107, 188, 479, 554, 858,
862, 867, 879, 882-84, 888,
891, 894, 899, 903, 905-06,
913-16, 918, 931, 937-38,
948-50, 958-59, 1053, 1158-
90, 1576, 1584, 2649, 2668
Debusscher, Gilbert 214, 1168
Dehlinger, Dawn 2091
Delatiner, Barbara 215
Delatte, Ann Perkins 623
A Delicate Balance 44, 65, 184,
212, 228, 265, 501, 595, 598,
630, 654, 713, 736, 1195-1372,
1538, 2110, 2692
A Delicate Balance (FILM) 65,
1197, 1222, 1225, 1232, 1244,
1247-49, 1254, 1256, 1282,
1289, 1292-93, 1304, 1321,

1325-26, 1336, 1340, 1343,
  1348, 1355, 1361, 1372
Denby, David   1372
Dent, Alan   2092
Denton, Clive   2093
Derrickson, Howard   1476
Dessau, Frederik   216
Dettmer, Roger   2094
Deuel, Pauline B.   1526
Deutsch, Robert H.   2615
Dias, Earl J.   217
Dieb, Ronald   624
Diehl, Digby   218
Diesel, Leota   1385
Dietrich, Richard F.   2616
Dillon, Perry C.   625
Disney, Dorothy Cameron   2098
Doerry, Karl Wilhelm   626
Dollard, John   2099
Dommergues, Pierre   219-223
Donnelly, Tom   1232-33, 1608
Donovan, Mark   1496
Donovan, Phyllis S.   776, 1234
Dooley, John   2100
Doran, Terry   1045, 1170,
  1737, 2617
Dorin, Rube   876, 1738, 2101
Downer, Alan S.   126, 224,
  1235, 2618
Dozier, Richard J.   2102
Drake, Sylvie   225, 777
Dreele, W. H. von   975, 2103
Drew, Bernard L.   2104
Driver, Tom F.   226-27, 877,
  2619
Drucker, Mort   2441
Drugge, Herman   627
Drutman, Irving   1236
Dubler, Walter   628
Ducker, Dan   629, 2108
Dukore, Bernard F.   267, 1740,
  2109, 2611
Duncan, Nancy K.   630
Dundy, Elaine   1741
Duplessis, Rachel Blau   228,
  2110
Duprey, Richard A.   229-30,
  2111
Dusay, John M.   1742
Dwyer, John   2112

Eck   1113
Eckman, Fern Marja   2113
Edmonson, Doris Elaine   631
Edwards, Jeanne L.   778
Edwards, Sydney   236
Eichelbaum, Stanley   237, 878,
  1237, 1580, 1609, 1743-45,
  2620
Elder, Rob   2115-16
Elem.   2621
Elias, Michael   632
Elliott, George P.   1746
Ellis, Donald   633
Ellison, [Earl] Jerome   634, 1747
Elsom, John   238, 1114
Emerson, Paul   1748
Engle, William Francis   635
English, Emma Jean Martin   636
Engstrom, John   2117
Envy (in The Show of the Seven
  Deadly Sins/Faustus in Hell)
  1373-75
Esslin, Martin   240-41, 779, 1115
Esterow, Milton   242-43, 2118
Evans, Arthur   2119
Evans, Gareth Lloyd   2120
Everything in the Garden   65,
  160, 649, 743, 989, 1376-1418
Evica, George Michael   2121

Falb, Lewis W.   244
Falk, Eugene H.   2122
Fam & Yam   392, 1419-23
Fanning, Garth   1749
Farber, Manny   2123
Farinacci, John   637
Farra, Harry E.   1581
Farrell, William E.   245
Faustus in Hell   see Envy
Fayed, Haney S.   638
Fearnley, John   780
Fedor, Joan Roberta   639
Feingold, Michael   1116, 1497
Feldman, David   2124
Fender, Stephen   214
Ferguson, (Mrs.) Elliot   2125
Feynman, Alberta E.   2127
Fiedler, Leslie A.   2128
Fields, Sidney   246

Filandro, Anthony 2129
Filandro, Dolores 2129
Finding the Sun 1424-25
Findlater, Richard 2622
Findlay, Robert R. 158
Finkelstein, Sidney 247, 2131
Finnigan, Jacqueline S. 640
Fischer, Gretl Kraus 2133
Fission, Pierre 248
Fitzgerald, John E. 1238
Flanagan, William 83, 249-51
Flanner, Janet 2134
Flasch, Joy 2135
Flatley, Guy 252
Fleckenstein, Joan 781, 1117-18
Fleischer, Leonard 1239
Fleischer, Leonore 1750
Fleming, William P. 641
Fletcher, Florence 1610
Fletcher, John 2136
Fletcher, William D. 642
Flynn, Betty 253
Foran, Jack 2137
Forbes, Anthony 1387
Force, William M. 2623
Forney, Deanna Sue 643
Frank, Elizabeth 2624
Frank, Leah D. 2625
Frankel, Haskel 254, 782, 1440
Franzblau, Abraham 1751
Frasconi, Antonio 255
Fraser, C. Gerald 1477
Frederick, Robert B. 2626
Freedley, George 1752
Freedman, Morris 256-57
Freemon, Bill 1611
Fremantle, Anne 879
Fremont-Smith, Eliot 1498
French, Paul Douglas 644
French, Philip 1240
Frenz, Horst 80
Friedli, Max 645
Friedman, Melvin J. 2136
Fritzler, James Robert 646
Fruchter, Norm 258
Fumerton, M. Patricia 1241
Funke, Lewis 259, 880, 1094-
    95, 1753, 2138

Gabbard, Lucina P. 260, 1171,

1612, 2627
Gagnard, Frank 2139-2142
Gaines, Robert A. 647
Galano, Robert 1172
Galbraith, John Kenneth 2143
Gale, William K. 2144
Galey, Matthieu 261-262
Gapsis 1388
Gardella, Kay 1242
Gardner, Paul 263-64, 881,
    1754, 2146-50
Garfield, David 265
Garrity, Pat 266, 1441
Garza, Esmeralda N. 648
Gascoigne, Bamber 882, 2151
Gassner, John 80, 267, 883,
    977, 1243, 1755, 2152-54,
    2252
Geagley, B. 1244
Geisinger, Marion 268
Gelb, Arthur 269, 1420, 1582
Gelber, Benjamin 270
Gellert, Roger 884, 2155
Gelmis, Joseph 2156
Genêt see Flanner, Janet
George, Kathleen 1245
Giankaris, C. J. 433
Gianotti, Peter M. 783
Gibson, Norman 271
Gielgud, John 1757
Giger, Romeo 272
Gilbert, E. J. 2157
Gilder, Rosamond 2158
Gill, Brendan 784, 1046, 1442,
    1499, 1566, 1613, 1758, 2159
Gillenwater, Kelso 2160
Gilliatt, Penelope 2628
Gilman, Richard 978, 1500,
    1759, 2161-62
Gilroy, Harry 273
Gingrich, Arnold 274
Glackin, William 1614, 1760
Glaister, Larry L. 649
Glenn, Jules 1761
Glover, William 275-76, 1119,
    1615
Goetsch, Paul 277
Goldfaden, Bruce 785
Goldstein, Richard 278
Goldstone, Richard 80
Golenpol'skii, T. G. 279

Gontarski, Stanley E. 650
Goodman, Henry 280
Goodman, Randolph 281
Gottfried, Martin 282-83, 786,
    979, 1047-48, 1173, 1246,
    1389, 1528, 1616, 1762-63,
    2163, 2629
Gough-Yates, Kevin 284
Gould, Jean 285
Gow, Gordon 1247, 2164
Gram, Peter B. 787
Grande, Luke 1174, 2630
Gray, Beverly 1617
Gray, Wallace 885
Grayson-Grossman, Elizabeth
    651
Green, Benny 1248
Green, Charles Lee 286, 652
Green, Harris 788
Greenberger, Howard 45, 933
Greenfield, Thomas Allen 287
Greiner, Patricia Ann 653
Griffin, William 1618, 2165
Griffiths, Stuart 1764
Gross, Theodore L. 347
Groves, Bob 2166
Guarino, Ann 1249
Guernsey, Otis L. 48, 288,
    1529, 1765
Guidry, Frederick H. 2167
Gussow, Mel 289-90, 789, 1049,
    1250, 1373, 1443, 1619, 1766
Guthke, Karl S. 1767
Gysin, Fritz R. 291

Haas, Barbara 886, 1120, 2168
Haas, Rudolf 292, 458, 487
Haberman, Clyde 193-94
Hadley, Ted R. 2169, 2631
Hagopian, John V. 1768
Hale, Wanda 2170
Hall, John 980
Hall, Roger Allan 654
Hall, Vernon 2171
Halperen, Max 2172
Hamblen, Abigail Ann 2173
Hamilton, Kenneth 887
Hammel, Lisa 295
Hammerich, Richard C. 790,
    1121

Hankiss, Elemér 2174
Hanmel, Faye 1175
Hardwick, Elizabeth 1251-52,
    1530
Hardy, Hathaway 296
Harkins, William E. 2175
Harper, James 2176-77
Harper, Jay 1253
Harpprecht, Klaus 297
Harris, Andrew Bennett 655
Harris, Bernard 230, 955
Harris, James Neil 791
Harris, Leonard 792, 1050,
    1769
Harris, Phyllis Katz 656
Harris, Radie 1096
Harris, Sydney J. 1770
Harris, Wendell V. 298
Hart, Henry 2178-79
Hart, Tom 793
Harte, Barbara 200
Hartman, Murray 472
Hartnoll, Phyllis 95
Hartung, Philip T. 2180
Haskell, Molly 1254
Hassan, Ihab 299
Hastings, Ronald 2632
Hatch, Robert 888
Haun, Harry 2181
Hawkins, Robert F. 1255
Hayes, Joseph 300, 2182
Hayes, Richard 301
Hayman, Ronald 302-03
Hazard, Forrest E. 2183
Hefling, Joel 657
Heilman, Robert B. 305, 889
Hemeter, Mark 2184
Hempel, Peter Andrew 658
Henderson, Alexander 339
Henderson, Elizabeth 339
Henry, William A. 1771
Hensel, Georg 306
Hentoff, Nat 2185
Herridge, Frances 307-08, 1256,
    1421
Herring, Paul D. 481
Herron, Ima Honaker 2186
Hewes, Henry 794-95, 890-91,
    981-82, 1051-52, 1257-58,
    1390, 1620, 1772-75, 2187-90,
    2633-35

Higgins, David M. 659
Higgins, John 1621
Hilary, Jerome C. 1053
Hilfer, Anthony 108, 472, 2191
Hill, Carol D. 2192
Hill, Linda M. 660-892
Hinchliffe, Arnold P. 196, 309
Hinds, Carolyn Myers 893
Hipp, Edward Sothern 796,
     983, 1259-60, 1391, 1531-32,
     1776-77, 2193
Hirsch, Foster 310
Hirschfeld, Albert 1961
Hirschhorn, Clive 2194
Hobe see Morrison, Hobe
Hobson, Harold 297-98, 894,
     1261-64, 1778-80, 2195, 2636-
     37
Hoffenberg, Joseph 895
Hoffman, Leonard 1533
Hoffmann, Jean K. 799
Högel, Rolf K. 311
Holland, Glenn 1622
Holland, Mary 1265, 1445
Holly Golightly see Breakfast
     at Tiffany's
Holmes, Ann 800
Holstrom, John 1781
Holtan, Orley I. 2196
Hope-Wallace, Philip 1266-67,
     1782, 2197, 2638
Hopkins, Anthony 1054
Hopper, Stanley Romaine 1783
Hopwood, Alison 2198
Houghton, Morris 312
Houghlan, Marylyn 2199
Howell, (Mrs.) Ray T. 2200
Huberth, Jonathan C. 661
Hughes, Catharine 313, 801-02,
     1567, 1623-24, 2201-02
Hull, Elizabeth Anne 662, 1268
Hunter, Evan 314
Hunter, Gregg 315
Hurley, Paul J. 896
Hurren, Kenneth 803

Inge, M. Thomas 2205
INTERVIEWS 97, 111, 113, 119,
     130-32, 145, 149, 155, 160,

168-70, 178, 180, 187, 199,
204, 212, 215, 218, 220, 222,
224, 231-34, 236, 248, 150,
154, 264, 266, 275-76, 278,
288, 294, 297, 307, 315, 317,
323-24, 332, 348, 354, 358,
365, 369, 377, 390, 406, 409,
411, 418-19, 424, 428, 431,
437, 439, 444, 464, 468-69,
473-74, 476, 483-84, 489,
498, 503-06, 508, 515, 517,
521-27, 533, 545, 551, 557,
560, 574-75, 577, 585, 593,
1109, 1654, 1663, 2546
Irwin, Ray 2206
Irwin, Robert 2639
Itschert, Hans 292, 475, 582

Jaal. 1176
Jackson, Don D. 318, 2531
Jackson, Esther M. 319
Jackson, Katherine Gauss 1784
Jackson, Nancy-Dabney Roosevelt
     663
Jacob, Bonnie 1269
Jacobi, Peter P. 2208
Jacquot, Jean 219
James. 1055
Jamieson, Daniel J. 320
Jánský, Ann Leah Lauf 664-65
Jefferys, Allan 1056
Jenkins, J. A. 666
Jennings, C. Robert 2209-10
Johnson, Carolyn E. 322
Johnson, Greer 1057
Johnson, Helen 1785
Johnson, Malcolm L. 323-24,
     804-05, 1122-24, 1446-47,
     2211-13
Johnson, Martha J. 2214
Johnston, Laurie 325
Jones, David Richard 806
Jones, Donna Mae 667
Jones, Jimmie 1786
Jones, (Mrs.) Paul E. 2215
Julier, Laura 326

K., J. 327

K., L. 2217
Kahn, Carole 1270
Kain, Laila 1125
Kakutani, Michiko 328
Kalem, T. E. 807, 1501, 1626,
    2218
Kali 897
Kane, Leslie 329
Kansa, Edward 2219
Kaplan, Donald M. 2220
Kaplan, Lisa Faye 2221
Kapur, Banarsi Lal 668
Kauffmann, Stanley 808, 1502,
    1534, 1627, 1787, 2222
Kaufman, Michael T. 1628
Kaul, R. K. 330
Keating, John 331
Keating, William P. 669
Keezing, Henry M. 1448
Keiningham, Jean 2223
Kelley, Edward G. 670
Kelley, Kitty 2224
Kelly, Herbert L. 1788
Kelly, Kevin 332, 1097, 1126,
    1584, 1789, 2225-27
Kemper, Robert Graham 1271,
    2228
Kemper, Steve 1449
Kenn 898, 2229-30
Kennedy, Andrew K. 2640
Kennedy, John S. 2231
Keown, Eric 899
Kerensky, Oleg 1058
Kerjan, Liliane 333-34
Kernan, Alvin B. 80, 128, 227
Kerr, Walter 335-36, 809, 900,
    984-85, 1059-60, 1271-74,
    1392, 1450, 1503-04, 1535,
    1568, 1585, 1629, 1790-94,
    2232-36, 2641
Keys, Janice 2642
Kidd, Robert 338
Kienzle, Siegfried 339
Kihss, Peter 1275, 1630
Kilgallen, Dorothy 2237
Kilker, Marie J. 340
Killinger, John 341
Killingsworth, Kay 1061
King, Alberta Demorest 671
King, Kimball 342
Kingsley, Lawrence 344

Kingston, Jeremy 810, 1276,
    1795, 2643
Kirkpatrick, D. L. 193
Kissel, Howard 1451, 1631,
    2240
Kitchin, Laurence 345
Kitching, Jessie 1277
Klein, Alvin 986, 1278, 1374,
    1452
Kleiner, Dick 346
Klemesrud, Judy 1505
Kloten, Edgar 1127, 1279-80,
    1796-97, 2241
Knepler, Henry 347
Knickerbocker, Paine 348, 901,
    1281, 1586, 2242-43, 2644
Koch, John F. 2244
Koch, Marvin B. 2245
Kohen, Helen L. 349
Köhler, Klaus 350
Kolin, Philip C. 351-53, 1128
Kosman, Joshua 2246
Kosner, Edward 354
Kostelanetz, Richard 355-56,
    987-88, 2645
Koven, Stan 2247
Kramer, Carol 1282
Kramer, Elaine Fialka 209
Kramer, Maurice 209
Kraus, Ted M. 1062, 1283,
    1393, 1536, 1632, 1798
Krebs, Albin 294, 357
Kretzmer, Herbert 811, 1799,
    2248
Krim, Seymour 2249
Krohn, Charles S. 358
Kroll, Jack 812, 1063-64, 1129,
    1394, 1453, 1506, 1569, 1633,
    1800, 2250
Kronenberger, Louis 891
Kuner, M. C. 359
Kyria, Pierre 360

La Belle, Jenijoy 2251
La Fontaine, Barbara 361
The Lady from Dubuque 119,
    131, 169, 204, 266, 324, 390,
    504, 522, 525, 1426-72
Lahr, John 362, 813, 989,
    1395, 1801

Lallamant, Robert J. 672
Lambert, J. W. 814, 1284,
    1802, 2646
Lamont, Rosette C. 2136
Lamport, Felicia 1803
Lamport, Harold 2252
Landon, Bert 363
Langdon, Harry 673
Lannon, William W. 902
Lapole, Nick 364
Larner, Daniel 674
Laschever, Barnett D. 1804
Lask, Thomas 365, 990, 2253,
    2647
Laufe, Abe 2254
Lauricella, James 675
Lawson, Carol 366, 1454-56
Lawson, John Howard 378
Lazarus, Arnold 2255
Lazier, Gil 2648
Lee, A. Robert 367
Lee, Brian 108, 196, 214
Lee, Robert C. 1285
Leff, Leonard J. 2256-58
Lehman, Ernest 2259
Lenoir, Jean-Pierre 2649
Lenz, Harold 815
Leonard, Hugh 2260
Leonard, William 2261
Leonard, William Torbert 1098
Lerman, Leo 368, 2262
Lerner, Max 1634, 1805, 2263-
    64
Lesser, Betty 1396
Lester, Bill 2650
Lester, Elenore 369-70
Levene, Victoria E. 676
Levin, Bernard 903, 1130,
    2651
Levine, Mordecai H. 2652
Levy, Alan 371
Levy, Maurice 372
Levy, Valerie Brussel 677
Lewis, Allan 373, 2265
Lewis, Emory 1806, 2266
Lewis, Peter 816, 1131, 1286-
    87, 1807, 2267
Lewis, Theophilus 991, 1288,
    1397, 1808-09, 2268-69,
    2653
Leyden, William Henry 678

L'Heureux, John C. 679
Lietzmann, Sabina 61
Lightman, Herb A. 2271
Limbacher, James L. 1289
Lineberger, James 2272
Lipton, Edmond 1810
Listening 113, 254, 271, 276,
    323, 464, 545, 1107, 1109-13,
    1116-27, 1129, 1132, 1136-40,
    1142-46, 1148-49, 1151-52,
    1154-55, 1473-85
Liston, William T. 1290
Litowitz, Norman S. 2654
Little, Stuart W. 374, 1537-38,
    1811-15, 2273-83
Livingston, Bill 904
Livingston, Howard 1816
Loggem, Manuel van 375
Lohner, Edgar 458
Lolita 119, 278, 504, 1486-1513
Loney, Glenn M. 376, 1818
Long, Mary 377
Loughery, Patricia 2287
Lourie, S. 381
Louson, Dzhon Govard 378
Lowell, Sondra 1291, 1819,
    2655
Lowenthal, Lawrence David 680
Loynd, Ray 1635
Lucchese, S. 1292
Luce 1636
Lucey, William F. 1820
Luft, Herbert G. 1637
Lukas, Mary 379, 1177
Lumley, Frederick 380
Luri, S. 381
Lyons, Charles R. 2288, 2656
Lyons, Leonard 382, 2289

MacBeath, Innis 384
MacFarland, David 681
Macklin, Anthony 2657
MacPherson, Myra 385
Maday, Greg 905
Madden, David 889
Madden, John 1638
Maddocks, Melvin 993, 2290,
    2291
Maddox, Brenda 2292
Mah, Kai-Ho 2293

Mahoney, John C. 2294-96
Malcolm, Donald 2658
Malcolm 42, 81, 989, 1514-61
Mallery, David 1293
Mallett, Richard 2297
The Man Who Had Three Arms
    1562-74
Mandandis, Alice 1821
Mannes, Marya 2298
Mantel, Myrna Grace 682
Manvell, Roger 2299
Maravel, Harry 1822
Marcus, Frank 817, 1294, 1823
Markson, John W. 1824
Markus, Thomas B. 1825
Marowitz, Charles 387, 906-07,
    2260, 2302-03
Marriott, R. B. 818, 1295-96,
    1826, 2304
Marsden, Michael T. 1268
Marshall, Thomas F. 388
Mart 1375
Martin, Emma Jean 683
Martin, Paulette 1827
Martin, Richard 2305
Maskoulis, Julia 2306
Matlaw, Myron 389
Matthews, Anne McIlhenney 1297
Matthews, Honor 2659
Mattimore, Daniel P. 1065, 1298
Matys, Linda 819
Maund, Rupert 994
Mayberry, Robert 684, 1066
Mays, James L. 685
Mazzanti, Vincent 2308
McAlester, Constance A. 686
McCants, Sarah Maxine 687
McCarten, John 995, 1299, 1539,
    1828, 2309
McCaslin, Walt 1639
McClain, John 908, 996-97,
    1178, 1540, 1829-31, 2310-12,
    1660
McCormick, John 390, 1457
McCrindle, Joseph 218, 387,
    451, 541
McCullers, Carson 391
McDonald, Daniel 2313
McDowall, Roddy 57
McElfresh, Tom 1300, 2314
McEnroe, Colin 1458

McGinn, Larry 392
McGrady, Mike 2315
McHarry, Charles 2661
McKinnon, George 1832
McManus, Otile 2316-17
McMorrow, Tom 1640
McMurrian, Jacqueline Y. 688
McVay, Douglas 2318
Meadows, Edna 2319
Meehan, Thomas 393, 909, 1833
Meserve, Walter 80, 108, 147,
    196, 394
Meyer, B. Ruth 689
Meyer, Eve R. 1301
Meyer, Ruth 2320
Michaljević, M. 395
Michelson, Herb 1834
Michener, John A. 2321
Micklin, Bob 1302
Miers, Virgil 1303
Mignon, Paul-Louis 396-98
Millar, S. 1304
Miller, James E. 481
Miller, Jeanne 1835
Miller, Jonathan 998
Miller, Jordan Y. 137, 910
Miller, Lynn F. 1614, 1623,
    1632, 1647, 1668, 2240, 2314
Miller, Margo 2662
Miller, Richard 477
Miller, Robert Royce 690
Miller, Terry 399
Milofsky, David 1478
Milstein, Fredric 2323
Minahen, Betty 1836
Minot, Stephen 1132
Mishkin, Leo 821, 1541, 1837
Missey, James 2663
Mitchell, Gee 2324
Mohanty, M. P. 400
Molli, Jeanne 401
Montgomery, Roger 1459, 2327-
    28
Moody, Richard 147
Moore, Don D. 911
Moore, Lyla 2329
Mootz, William 999
Mor 1570
Moran, Rita 1641
Morehouse, Ward 1000, 2330
Morgan, Al 1067

Morgan, Thomas B. 402
Morgenstern, Joseph 912
Morley, Sheridan 1133
Morris, Kay 2331
Morris, Penny W.   403
Morrison, Hobe 913, 1068, 1306,
    1460, 1542, 1642, 1838, 2332-
    33, 2665
Morrison, Kristin 404, 1839
Morriss, Frank 1307
Morse, Ben 1001
Morseberger, Robert E. 2334
Moses, Robbie 405, 691, 823
Moskow, Shirley 406
Mottram, Eric 407
Muggeridge, Malcolm 1840
Muller, Robert 914, 2666
Mullin, Donald 1069
Munk, Erika 408-09
Munroe, Richard C. 1422
Murf 2337
Murray, Michael 824
Mussoff, Lenore 410
Myers, Charles Robert 692
Myers, Harold 915, 2338
Myers, Joseph T. 693
Myro see Myers, Harold

Nadel, Norman 916-17, 1002,
    1308-09, 1544, 1841-42,
    2340-43
Natale, Richard 411
Nathan, David 918, 1310, 2349,
    2667
Neblett, Joseph M. 694
Neill, Robert 2354
Nelson, Gerald 413
Nemy, Enid 414
Neuweiler, Siegfried 277
Nevelson, Louise 59
Neville, John 1311, 1843
Newman, David 417
Newman, Edwin 825
Newman, Kenneth M. 2654
Newmark, Judy J. 418, 919
Newquist, Roy 419, 2355
Nichols, Mike 2356
Nicoll, Allardyce 420
Nightingale, Benedict 826, 1135,
    1312, 1844

Nilan, Mary M. 2669
Normand, J. 421
Norton, Elliot 827, 1136-37,
    2358
Norton, Rictor 695, 2359
Novick, Julius 828, 1138, 1461,
    1643, 1845, 2361
Nyren, Dorothy 209

Oakes, Philip 424, 920
Oberg, Arthur K. 425
O'Brian, Jack 1398
O'Connor, Garry 829
O'Connor, John J. 830
O'Connor, Patrick 2363, 2670
O'Doherty, Brian 426
O'Gorman, Ned 1003
Ōhashi, Kenzaburō 427
Ohringer, Frederic 51
Oi, Judith T. 696
Olin, Carol 697
Oliver, Edith 2365
Olles, Helmut 146
Ollington, Marcus H. 698
Oppenheim, Irene 1846
Oppenheimer, George 831, 921,
    1004, 1545, 1645, 1847-48,
    2673-74
Otten, Terry 514, 2368-70

Pacheco, Patrick 1462, 1646,
    2372
Paetel, Karl O. 429
Page, Michael 1139
Palazzo, Laura Maria 699
Pallavicini, Roberto 430
Panciera, H. Victor 1140
Pangalos, Mary 431
Paolucci, Anne 432-34, 1313
Papa, Sam 435
Parker, Theodore H. 1314,
    1849, 2373
Parthasarathy, R. 436
Patrick, Corbin 1315, 2374
Paul, Lewis 2375
Pearre, Howard 1316
Pease, Donald 1850
Peck, Joshua 437
Peck, Seymour 438

Pennington, Ron 1647
Pérez Rivas, Marcelo 547
Perlin, Judith Ann 1851
Perry, Virginia I. 1317
Petrie, (Mrs.) Claude 2377
Phillips, Elizabeth C. 441
Philp, Richard 833
Pickar, Gertrud Bauer 2378
Pietropolli, Cecilia 442
Pinkston, Claude A. 700
Pit 834, 1141
Platt, Brainard 2380
Plett, Heinrich F. 445
Plotinsky, Melvin L. 446
Plunka, Gene Alan 701
Pond, Elizabeth 2383
Popkin, Henry 447, 922, 1071, 1400, 1853-54
Popovici, Ruxandra 448
Porte, Michael 1730
Porter, Bob 1855
Porter, M. Gilbert 1319
Porter, Peter 1479
Porter, Thomas E. 2384
Post, Robert M. 449, 1320, 1856
Potter, Christopher 923
Potter, Stephen 2385
Powell, Dilys 1321
Powers, Dennis 924
Powers, James 1857, 2386-87
Pradhan, Narindar S. 450, 702
Pree, Barry 451
Preuss, Renate 703
Price, James 2388
Prideaux, Tom 452, 1322, 1401, 1858
Probst, Leonard 1072, 1649, 1859
Pryce-Jones, Alan 453, 925, 1179
Pryce-Jones, David 2390
Przybylska, Krystyna 454
Pumphrey, Bryon 1860
Purdon, Liam O. 1650
Purdy, James 52, 81

Quetz, Jürgen 704
Quigley, Isabel 2392
Quigley, Martin 2393-95
Quinn, James P. 2396

Quotations from Chairman Mao Tse-tung see Box and ....

Rachow, Louis A. 1323
Radcliffe, E. B. 926, 2397
Rahv, Philip 164
Raidy, William A. 835, 1073, 1324, 1402, 1546, 1651, 1862
Ramsey, Roger 2675
Rand, Calvin 1074
Rauter, Herbert 456
Raymont, Henry 457
Razum, Hannes 458
Read, David H. C. 2398
Redmon, Elizabeth Daron 705
Reed, Michael D. 460
Reed, Rex 1325
Reilly, Charles Phillips 1326
Reilly, Robert S. 172
Reinert, Otto 927, 2399, 2676
Reinhart, Molly 2400
Reuben, Elaine 928
Rewald, Alice 462
Ribner, Clayre 463
Rich 2403
Rich, Alan 464, 2404
Rich, Frank 1507-08, 1571, 2405
Richards, Leila 1865
Richards, Stanley 2406, 2677
Richardson, James G. 706
Richardson, Kenneth R. 284
Richmond, Hugh M. 2407
Richter, Judy 1866
Ridley, Clifford A. 1144, 1652
Riley, Carolyn 200
Riley, Clayton 1867
Rios, Charlotte Rose 707
Rissover, Fredric 930
Ritcher, Geraldine 708
Rivers, Bryan 2678
Robb, Pat 1587
Robbins, J. Albert 2408
Robe see Frederick, Robert B.
Roberts, Peter 931
Robertson, Heather 2409-10
Robertson, Roderick 465
Robinson, James A. 466
Rocha Filho, Rubem 467
Roddy, Joseph 2411
Rodriguez, Meriemil 2412

Roe, G. F. 1480
Rogoff, Gordon 1145, 1868
Rohleder, Patricia J. 709
Roht, Helen G. 837
Rolfe, Lee 838
Rollins, Peter C. 2258
Rosa, Steve 2414
Rosador, Kurt Tetzeli von 153
Rosenfeld, Megan 1180
Rosenthal, David 1509
Rosselli, John 2680
Roth, Emalou 710
Roth, Philip 1869-70
Rothstein, Irma 1329-30
Roud, Richard 1331
Roudané, Matthew C. 468, 1464
Roush, Matt 469
Roy, Emil 2415
Ruben, Paul A. 712
Rubin, Don 932
Ruckman, Roger 2416
Rudin, Seymour 839
Rudisill, Cecil Wayne 713
Rule, Margaret W. 108, 110, 470, 714
Rusinko, Susan 471
Russ, Carla E. 715
Rutenberg, Michael 472, 716, 1006, 1332
Rutherford, Malcolm 2681
Ryan, Roger 2418
Ryan, Terry 1333

S., E. 1007
Sabbath, Lawrence 2419
Sachs, Lloyd 1871
Sainer, Arthur 1334, 2420
Sales, Grover 1872
Salmaggi, Robert 473, 1099, 1335
Salvesen, Veronica 474
Samuels, Charles Thomas 475
The Sandbox 107, 188, 392, 554, 640, 932, 954, 1171, 1575-91
Sanders, Kevin 1653, 2421
Sanders, Rebecca Gayle 717
Sanders, Walter E. 718
Sandoe, James 1077, 1404
Saporta, Marc 476

Sapoznik, Ran 719
Sarotte, Georges-Michel 477
Sarris, Andrew 2422
Sato, Susumu 2682
Sauvage, Leo 2423
Sawyer, Paul 2424
Sayre, Nora 1336
Scanlan, Tom 2425
Schaap, Dick 1337, 1550-51
Schaffer, Quentin 1654
Schechner, Richard 2426-27, 2683
Scheller, Bernhard 478-79, 720
Schickel, Richard 2428, 2553
Schieber, Larry 1338
Schier, Donald 2429
Schier, Ernest 1655
Schiff, Chester 480
Schimel, John L. 2430
Schlesinger, Arthur 2431
Schlueter, June 1465, 2432
Schmalz, Wayne E. 721
Schmidt, Sandra 1423, 2433
Schneider, Alan 481-82, 933, 2434
Schneider, Howard 483-84
Schneider, Paul 485
Schneider, Ruth Morris 722
Schnettler, Bob 2435
Schöne, Annemarie 486
Schubeck, John 840
Schultze, Edward W. 1874
Schulz-Seitz, Ruth Eva 487
Schupbach, Deanne Justina 723
Schvey, Henry L. 488
Schwartz, Jerry 489
Scutt, Ed 1181
Seascape 130, 199, 315, 474, 646, 658, 1592-1674
Serreau, Geneviève 490
Share, Peter 2684
Sharma, R. C. 2685
Sharp, Anne 1146
Sharpe, Jacqueline 492
Shaw, Howard N. 1875
Shearhouse, Chris 934
Sheed, Wilfrid 1339, 1552, 1876, 2438, 2686
Shelton, Frank W. 493
Shelton, Lewis Edward 724
Shepard, Richard F. 494-95

Shepard, Sam 73
Sheppard, Eugenia 496, 1877
Shere, Charles 935
Sherman, Howard 497
Sherman, Thomas B. 1878
Shirley, Don 498
Shorey, Kennth Paul 1340
Short, Kathryn 1405
Shorter, Eric 841, 1008-1010
The Show of the Seven Deadly
    Sins see Envy
Showell, Philip S. 936, 2439
Shrapnel, Norman 937
Shuh, Susan Elizabeth 725
Shulman, Milton 842, 938, 1147,
    2440, 2687
Shuster, Alvin 1341
Siegel, Jack 1342
Siegel, Joel 1466, 1510, 1572
Siegel, Larry 2441
Siegel, Paul N. 939
Silver, Lily Jay 499
Silver, Margery 2442
Silverman, Stephen M. 1467
Simard, Rodney 500
Simon, John 501, 843, 1011,
    1078-79, 1343-44, 1406, 1468,
    1511, 1573, 1657, 1879-80,
    2443-46, 2546
Simpson, Herbert M. 1881
Sincock, Stuart 2447
Siskind, Jacob 1182
Skal, David J. 444
Skir, Leo 1882
Skloot, Robert 1883
Skolsky, Sidney 2448
Skow, John 503
Sloan, Robin Adams 1658
Smilgis, Martha 504
Smith, (Mrs.) A. C. 2449
Smith, Andrew 2688
Smith, Ardis 505, 1080-81,
    1346, 2450
Smith, Bruce Marc 726
Smith, Cecil 844, 940, 1347
Smith, Donna 1884
Smith, (Sister) Gertrude 727
Smith, Herbert R. 2451
Smith, Liz 1348
Smith, Margaret 2452
Smith, Michael 506, 941-42, 1012,

1349, 1407, 1553, 1588, 1885-
    86
Smith, Milton 2453
Smith, Rebecca Louise 728
Smither, Kitty Harris 1659
Sokolsky, Bob 1082-83, 1183,
    1350, 1887
Solomon, Jerry 507
Somoza, Joseph M. 729
Sontag, Susan 1013
Spencer, Sharon D. 509
Spielberg, Peter 2689-90
Spurling, Hilary 1351, 1888
Stace, Ann Carolyn 730
Staff, Charles 1352, 2455
Stagg, Anne 510
Standish, Myles 2457
Stark, John 1889
Starr, John 511
Stasio, Marilyn 2458
Stavrou, C. N. 512
Steadman, Dan 731
Steele, Mike 1481
Stein, Jerry 1354, 2459
Stein, Ruthe 2460
Steiner, Donald Lee 732
Steinfirst, Donald 1084
Stenz, Anita Maria 514
Stephens, Suzanne Schaddelee
    733
Stern, Daniel 515
Sterritt, David 1355
Stevens, Dale 943
Stewart, Phyllis 516
Stewart, R. S. 517
Stone, Judy 1890
Storrer, William A. 734, 845
Straub, John 2462
Stugrin, Michael 1891, 2463
Stutzin, Leo 1892
Styan, J. L. 518-19
Sullivan, Dan 520-21, 1100,
    1148, 1184, 1408, 1425, 1482,
    1660, 1893, 1931, 2464-65
Sullivan, (Rev.) Patrick Sullivan,
    S.J. 1894
Summers, Carmine 2466
Swan, Jon 2691
Swan, Mary B. 735
Sykes, Carol A. 2692
Syna, Sy 2468

Syse, Glenna 522, 1356, 1661,
    1895, 2469
Szeliski, John J. von 1357

Tallmer, Jerry 528-29, 846,
    945, 1185, 1589, 1897-98,
    2470, 2693-95
Tanner, Henry 530
Tanner, Mabel DeVries 2472
Taubman, Howard 531-32, 946,
    1014-15, 1186, 1899-1901,
    2474-75
Taylor, Charlene M. 2476
Taylor, Joseph 947
Taylor, Marion A. 2477-78
Taylor, Markland 847, 1149
Taylor, Robert 533, 1150, 1902
Taylor, William E. 2172
Tempkin, Romola 736
Terrien, Samuel 1903, 2479
Thies, Henning 534
Thomas, Bethe 1151
Thomas, Charles H. 2481
Thomas, Diane 2462
Thomizer, Cynthia 2696
Thompson, David 1590
Thompson, Howard 1358, 1662,
    2483-85
Thompson, Jack 2697
Thompson, Thomas 2486
Timmons, Leon 2487
Tiny Alice 393, 517, 534, 596,
    606, 619, 643, 658, 673, 704,
    713, 746, 1676-1930
Todd, Thomas 848
Tolpegin, Dorothy Dunlap 1908
Tompkins, June 849
Toohey, John L. 1359
Topor, Tom 535
Townley, Raymond D. 737
Treib, Manfred 536
Trevisan, A. F. 2490
Trewin, Ion 537
Trewin, J. C. 850, 948, 1360,
    1909, 2491
Trilling, Diana 2492-93
Trotta, Geri 538
Tucker, John Bartholomew 1910
Turcotte, Dick 1152
Turner, W. L. 539

Tynan, Kenneth 950, 2495

Ulanov, Barry 1017, 1911
Umberger, Norman C. 738
Unger, Leonard 196
Unger, Michael D. 1912

Valentine, Ed 2499
Valgemae, Mardi 1913
Vallano, Louis 1085
Vallbona, Rima de 540
Van Itallie, Jean-Claude 541
Vaughan, S. B. 1361
Vickery, John B. 109
Villa, Jacquie 1410
Villard, Leonie 543
Vinson, James 193
von Ranson, Brooks 545, 851
Vos, Nelvin 546-49

Wade, David 1484-85
Wager, Walter 317
Wager, Willis 550
Wagner, Marlene Strome 739
Waith, Eugene M. 2701
Wakeman, John 579
Walker, Alexander 1362, 2520-21
Walking 1931
Wallace, Robert S. 740, 2702
Wallach, Allan 1555, 2522
Walsh, Moira 2523-24
Wardle, Irving 551-52, 1153,
    1363, 1411, 1914-16, 2703
Ware, Robert Gorton 741
Warfield, Polly 1663-64
Washburn, Martin 1087
Washer, Ben 1917
Wasserman, Debbi 1154
Wasserman, Julian N. 358, 553
Watt, Douglas 852-53, 1155,
    1412, 1470, 1665-66, 2526-27
Watts, Richard 854-55, 953,
    1018, 1088-89, 1188-89, 1364-
    65, 1413-14, 1556-58, 1667-
    68, 1918-22, 2528-30, 2704
Watzlawick, Paul 2531
Wax, Mel 954
Way, Brian 955

Weales, Gerald 554-56, 1090,
 1366, 1415, 1574, 2533, 2705
Wear, Mike 2534-35
Weatherby, W. J. 557, 1471,
 2536
Weaver, Neal 1091
Weaver, William B. 2537
Weber, Alfred 277
Weil, Herbert S. 956
Weiler, A. H. 558-59
Weiner, Bernard 560-61, 957,
 1669, 1923
Weiner, Leslie 2538
Weintraub, Stanley 1367, 1924
Weitz, A. L. 2539
Welch, David A. 742
Welland, Dennis 562
Wells, Palmer 2540-41
Wellwarth, George E. 563
Wertheim, Albert 580
West, Anthony 1092, 1368,
 1416, 1591
Westerfield, William 743
Westermann, Susanne 744
Wetzsteon, Ross 564
White, Fred D. 2706
White, James E. 108, 566,
 1925-26
White, James T. 422
White, Robert J. 2542
White, Sam 2543
Whitman, Alden 567
Whittaker, Herbert 1093
Who's Afraid of Virginia Woolf?
 46, 63, 113, 160, 228, 265,
 332, 360, 381, 393, 515, 529,
 534, 596, 629, 651, 654, 657-
 58, 682, 689, 693-95, 704-05,
 712, 718, 734, 739, 747,
 1932-2586, 2659
Who's Afraid of Virginia Woolf?
 (FILM) 694, 734, 1933, 1935-
 36, 1956, 1959, 1962, 1970,
 1976-77, 1979, 1982, 1993,
 2005, 2008, 2010-11, 2014-15,
 2019, 2022-24, 2026-29, 2031-
 32, 2034, 2036-37, 2057, 2065,
 2067, 2069, 2076-81, 2085-86,
 2090, 2092-93, 2096, 2098,
 2100, 2106-07, 2115-16, 2123,
 2132, 2156, 2164, 2167, 2170,
 2176-81, 2187, 2194, 2200,

2204, 2207, 2209-20, 2215-16,
 2219, 2222, 2224, 2244-45,
 2257-59, 2262, 2270-71, 2289,
 2292, 2297, 2299, 2301, 2308,
 2318, 2319, 2321-22, 2324-26,
 2329, 2331, 2335-37, 2339,
 2345-48, 2350-57, 2360, 2364-
 65, 2379-80, 2387-88, 2392-95,
 2397, 2411, 2414, 2418, 2422,
 2428, 2431, 2436-37, 2441,
 2444, 2447-48, 2451, 2453,
 2457, 2462, 2466-67, 2471,
 2480-83, 2485, 2487, 2494,
 2498, 2500, 2505, 2510-11,
 2514-19, 2521, 2523-25, 2532,
 2534-35, 2537-39, 2543, 2545,
 2547, 2552-53, 2556-57, 2560-
 63, 2566-74, 2576, 2578, 2582
Wilder, Clinton 1975
Wilderman, Marie R. 745
Willeford, William 108, 196, 472,
 1927
Williams, Marcellette Gay 746
Williams, Nick B. 1670
Williams, Tennessee 438, 570
Willoughby, Bob 2553
Wilson, Earl 1671-72
Wilson, Edwin 1472, 1512, 1673,
 2554
Wilson, Garff B. 571
Wilson, Raymond J. 747, 2555
Wilson, Robert A. 572
Wilson, Sam 2556
Wimble, Barton L. 856
Winchell, Cedric R. 748
Winchell, Walter 1019
Winer, Linda 1674
Wines, Mildred Halo 749
Winsten, Archer 2557
Wishengrad, H. R. 2558
Witherington, Paul 573, 1190
Witt, Erwin A. 1370
Woggon, Paul 574-75
Wolf, Reinhart 61
Wolfe, Peter 576
Wolff, Millie 577
Wolfson, Martin 2559
Woods, Linda 2707
Woolsey, F. W. 1020
Wooten, Dick 2575
Worsley, Thomas C. 959
Worth, Katharine 580

Wortis, Irving   1559
Wortman, Alan J.   2578
Wunderlich, Lawrence   581
Wurster, Grace Stewart   2579
Wyatt, Euphemia Van Rensselaer
    1021
Wyler, Siegfried   582

Yakir, Dan   1513
Yates, M. S.   583
Yerby, Loree   585
Young, B. A.   1156-57, 1371,
    1928, 2583-84, 2708-09
Yugendranath, Birakayala   750

Zahn, Douglas   2648
Zasurskii, Ia   584
Zeff, Dan   2585
Zeiger, Henry A.   1929
Zimbardo, Rose A.   2710
Zimmerman, Paul D.   1372
Zindel, Paul   585
Zolotow, Sam   586-592, 1101-03,
    1417-18, 1560-61, 1930, 2586
The Zoo Story   107, 188, 265,
    271-72, 529, 554, 675, 692,
    704, 713, 718, 722, 863, 865-
    66, 868, 876, 878-80, 886,
    895, 907, 917, 919, 923, 928,
    933, 935, 941, 942, 952, 955,
    957, 1171, 1576, 1581, 1937,
    2120, 2127, 2587-2711